water
in a
broken
pot

Celebrating 35 Years of
Penguin Random House India

water
in a
broken
pot

a memoir

YOGESH MAITREYA

PENGUIN
VIKING
An imprint of Penguin Random House

VIKING

USA | Canada | UK | Ireland | Australia
New Zealand | India | South Africa | China

Viking is part of the Penguin Random House group of companies
whose addresses can be found at global.penguinrandomhouse.com

Published by Penguin Random House India Pvt. Ltd
4th Floor, Capital Tower 1, MG Road,
Gurugram 122 002, Haryana, India

Penguin
Random House
India

First published in Viking by Penguin Random House India 2023

Copyright © Yogesh Suresh Wanjari 2023

All rights reserved

10 9 8 7 6 5 4 3 2 1

This is a work of fiction. Names, characters, places and incidents are either the
product of the author's imagination or are used fictitiously, and any resemblance
to any actual person, living or dead, events or locales is entirely coincidental.

ISBN 9780670095186

Typeset in Adobe Caslon Pro by Manipal Technologies Limited, Manipal
Printed at Thomson Press India Ltd, New Delhi

www.penguin.co.in

Contents

To
My father, Suresh Gariba Wanjari, whose sweat,
My mother, Baby Suresh Wanjari, whose blood,
have become the foundation
of my words

Learning to See

the world I inherited
erased by the world I longed for,
nothing remains, but the evidence of me:
a soldier, a battlefield, a war.

For a Dalit person, his identity is always in transition as soon as he steps out of his home. Just as a black person is not black within their own community but just another fellow human being, a Dalit too is just another fellow human being as long as they breathe, only among Dalits. To be a Dalit is to be in the constant process of discovering the self. Who is a Dalit? To me, a Dalit is a person whose identity is shaped by untouchability, practised against him by society. He is *untouched* in all spheres of life in India. He is *untouched* in imagination as well. And when you don't exist for the society, except when serving it as its 'slave' because you need to survive, you become a repository of colossal dilemmas, inferiorities, paradoxes and volcanic substances in their embryonic state. A Dalit person's liberation lies in overcoming these dilemmas, inferiorities, paradoxes and eventually erupts like

1

a volcano, careless and free. For a Dalit person, breaking free is an act of challenging the casteist conscience of this nation which has hitherto shaped them. Their arrival at themselves is ruthlessly met with the scorn of this society. Only a few among us become capable enough to acquire this state of liberation. Most of us, before reaching the state of liberation, are consumed by the consumption of commodities produced by a Brahminical-capitalist system. But these 'most' too have a story. This may not be the story of victory, but a story of their struggle. So let me tell you this: This story isn't about a dream, but its murder. This story isn't about a hope, but its mutilation. This story isn't about assertion, but its suppression. This story is not about liberation. It is about conditions that make liberation impossible. If you read it carefully, you will find that this is the story of silence and the violence it carries.

*

I grew up in a Dalit basti in Nagpur called Takli Sim. Like all Dalits (Mahar–Buddhists), we too have come from some village to the city. But I do not know from which village my grandfather came to Nagpur. The land on which our basti stands today was 'settlement land'. That's what the elders say. My father was born here. The birth year of my father is 1953, at least as per his school leaving certificate. Three years after his birth, in 1956, Dr Babasaheb Ambedkar publicly embraced Buddhism in Nagpur. The place where his conversion took place is not more than five kilometres away from my home. Today, this place is called Deekshabhoomi. In this mesmerising conversion ceremony, nearly half a million Mahars converted to Buddhism, following the path which their guide and liberator, Dr Ambedkar, had shown them. Did my grandparents too participate in that historical event? I do not know. I was never told a story by them or any anecdote about it. But in my home, there was always a small statue of the Buddha and a couple of photos of Babasaheb, placed *at* and *as* a shrine. In front of this shrine, every morning and evening by eight o'clock, my grandmother (who is now dead) used to light up candles and incense sticks, followed by reciting a Buddhist prayer and the Panchsheel.

But conversion to Buddhism in Maharashtra did not affect everyone on the same scale. Many among those who became Buddhists in 1956 had readily and aptly taken Babasaheb's call for education seriously and invested their time, energy and emotions into the education of their children. But some of them did not do it, or were perhaps incapable of so doing as they were subjected to dire social and economic circumstances. My grandparents were part of those 'some' who did not invest in the education of their children.

*

The more I try to know, the more I am convinced that the story of my family is like that of a broken pot—some pieces of it have inevitably gone missing, and without them this story will never be whole again. This is the story of a broken pot. A story of some of its pieces. I know nothing about my grandfather's family, except his father's name: Baliram. My grandfather's name was Gariba (literally, 'poor'). My grandmother was Muktabai. The first child born to them was a boy, Ramchandra. He was tall and dark and muscular. Followed by him, my grandparents bore six children: one boy, five girls. As far as my observations are concerned, in our lives, stories and facts were not told—they were learnt, often painfully. The only way to know them now is to get some clues from certificates, government papers, in which nothing is mentioned about us except a year, caste or name of a person and the institutions from which these papers were acquired. In addition, at times, these certificates are painful manifestations of our failures.

But these certificates are also proof of us being a part of this country and what this country owes to us. How can they then be capable of telling me a story? They cannot. Making this worse, I have no record of my family, whether oral or textual or even pictorial. So I know nothing about my father's elder brother, whom I saw until I was about twenty-one years old. He was a truck driver, met with an accident and later died as an alcoholic. Suresh, my father, survived. He survived the scorn, humiliation, rejection and pain that I cannot comprehend because it has not been passed onto me as stories.

As I was growing up, we never had anything between us that could be called a dialogue or a conversation. But this was not the case when I was a child. I feel that when you are deprived of stories, your imagination makes up for it and helps you, though painfully, to overcome this deprivation. So I have my own memories—with my father—my only clue and bridge to *my* story. In my imagination, my memories work as a guide in creating my history of being and becoming. Memory is the only possession that no one can take away from a Dalit; otherwise caste-society has this heinous power to make a Dalit forget who they are because they are made to hate themselves. On top of this, caste is a multilayer skin to the body of the mind. And that is why, in this story—in my story—caste is like a snake skin: The old one gets faded so that a new one can appear.

*

It was 1970 or 1971. My father studied till eighth standard and then he left the school. Or rather, as he blabbers in a drunken state often, he had lost interest in school. Why? Was he too discriminated against in school like all Dalit students from his time? He told me nothing about his school days, except that he used to walk seven kilometres everyday to go to school and walk back the same distance. One fact he confirmed, however—by this time, he was addicted to Bollywood movies. But he didn't know that this addiction was the cunning, cold-blooded murder of his dreams, of his aspirations. And the worst is, he never got to know this.

My father drank throughout his life. Today, he is sixty-six years old,[1] and when he is drunk, he often behaves insanely. But alcoholism and insanity in the life of a Dalit person like him do not stand for their moral corruption. It stands for failures of us as a society. You may find it strange. It may sound out of the context, and it is. The life of a Dalit person is always *out of the context* of this casteist society. And since we, as a society, do not possess the moral stamina and perceptive capacity to understand the lives of people like him—who are the lumpenproletariat in the truest sense and on whose labour the comfort of this society is built—we also lack an ethical eye to see their emotional world. This emotional world is the only source to learn about their existence, since the 'literate' society has rarely provided a space to their stories in their imagination. Caste-society, in their imagination, has restricted the entry of the emotional world of a person like my father.

My father drove a trailer-truck (a long goods carrier with fourteen wheels) for nearly fifty years. He was a hard worker, and he has always been. The labour, the sweat, diesel smoke, irritating engine-heat and some injuries have been an integral part of his daily life. I have never seen him complaining about this. What he did for a living was not what he always wanted to do. Like all, he too had some aspirations, perhaps some dreams. Somewhere around the 1970s, when he was in eighth standard, he appeared for some clerical examination conducted by the Indian Navy. He was good at mathematics. He cleared the examination. Elated, he told my grandmother. She refused to let him go and take up this job. She insisted on keeping him close to her, since he was the only other son of hers. 'What will I do if you die in the sea?' It was her reaction as well as explanation.

My grandmother was a weird and selfish woman. Seeing her emotions, and unable to argue against her nonsensical values, my father abandoned his decision. My grandfather was a very different person than her. He was tall, of ebony complexion and very handsome. I remember, as a child, when I used to poke his six-pack abs while he was sleeping on the *khat* (or cot), he brandished his lathi to scare me. He was harmless, but his physical appearance was muscular, that of a beast, shaped by his toil. All throughout his life, his occupation was to crush stones with a sledgehammer. He must have crushed millions of stones, which were used to build roads, buildings, canals across the city. As far as I remember, his sledgehammer was his only possession in life.

It was the mid-1990s. On Tuesdays, when he was paid wages, he used to bring *namkeen-khara* (fried snacks) for me and my sisters. The next day, on Wednesday, he insisted on eating mutton and resting for the day. But most of the time, my grandmother accused my grandfather of being lazy, especially on Wednesday. Her words were an assault on the mind.

I would like to think that when my grandmother refused to allow my father to go for a job in the Indian Navy, it was the first wound to his emotional world. Besides, he was not a particularly social being. He was never attracted to politics or a cultural movement within the Dalit community in Nagpur, which was, during this time, still at its peak; in fact, it was the time of the beginning of the Dalit Panthers in Maharashtra. Although he was a ferocious youth, he preferred solitude. And the first wound in the emotional world of a lonely person proves very septic, throughout his life. As an introvert, he must have imagined exploring different lands, breaking free from family ties, who knows . . . But his ties turned into shackles. No one could see this wound, and he lacked the language and ability to make it visible to the world.

Much later in life, I heard a story about an eagle. The eagle, when it teaches its eaglet to fly, takes it high in the sky and then drops it. The eaglet swiftly falls, dangerously approaching the ground; this moment is the most courageous and emotionally tough moment for an eagle. But it knows that being the child of an eagle, it has to learn to fly against all risks, all odds, all dangers. When an eaglet is very close to the ground, it opens up its wings and flaps them. It flies. And it flies high.

This story is engraved in my mind as a symbol of courage and sensibility that animals often possess, which are lacking in us humans. A bird takes all the risks to teach its child to fly in the world. It could have been possible that my father too wanted to fly, away from family ties, but my grandmother's emotions tricked him. That is when I realized, if not used wisely, emotions are also capable of destroying our dreams.

So, he started working in a cycle-repair shop, partly to support the family of nine people, and to buy tickets to watch movies in the theatre. His fascination with movies developed into an addiction with the rise of the figure of the 'Angry Young Man'. It was 1973. He was nineteen years old, when Amitabh Bachchan's *Zanjeer* was released. This film was instrumental in the lives of many youths of this time, making them think that rage was necessary to fight injustice. Not many realized that the idea of this anger against injustice was essentially shaped by the Dalit Panthers and their ideological positions, in the city of Bombay (now Mumbai). *Zanjeer*'s Amitabh reflected the anger of many Dalit youths, though as a part of state's mechanism. My father was no exception to this. This was the reason why Amitabh became a phenomenal image of the anger of this generation on-screen. Yet, what this generation of Dalit youths did not know was that it was not the uninformed anger of any random person in India. They did not know that it was the anger shaped by their misery, exploitation and social life, being used by Bollywood through upper-caste characters, only to create an idea that the *end* would be happy and justice would be served. As a consumer of these movies, many Dalit youths were deceived. People like my father were prohibited from reaching this truth, their truth.

Zanjeer instilled the image of a justice-loving, angry policeman in the minds of this generation. But the reality of Dalits and their lives was paradoxical to this cinematic depiction. In 1974, two years after the Dalit Panthers came into existence and were disrupting the ever-increasing silence against waves of atrocities against Dalits across the nation, Bhagwat Jadhav, a young leader and promising playwright, was killed as the Shiv Sena launched the attack on their rally.[2] When I met his brother, Sumedh Jadhav, in 2014 in Mumbai, he confirmed this incident and told me that rallies of the Dalit Panthers were regularly attacked by the police and the Shiv Sena. So in reality, the police were seemingly angry *about* Dalits who were demanding their rights and seeking justice.

But this paradox had never been exposed to people like my father. It was largely because they were disconnected from education and the Dalit movement. It was also because their life demanded too much labour to survive. And after toiling so hard, their bodies and minds needed rest. No art could soothe them; they had no access to any. Only one or other kind of instant intoxication was capable of giving them solace. My father sought this *rest* in alcohol, and found in movies a nonchalant space to *live* his aspiration. Alcohol made it easy for my father to endure the harsh reality; movies put colours in it. But both have contributed to his life an illusion in which the world was either cinematic or full of vileness. He remained aloof from the anti-caste movement, which was tirelessly working to create an egalitarian, liberal society.

We have to risk all in this society which, in the process of identifying people to know their caste location, hurts them constantly. In fact, lately, I have begun to sense that our lives are nothing but a *risk* against society's fear of us being alive and assertive of our rights. I think every Dalit grows up with this instinct, carrying it in their gut. My father was no exception. Because, although he had led a fractured life, he survived. Among us, not all fight; some just survive. But both survivors and fighters are inseparably interconnected and complete the whole of resistance.

*

In my life, my memories, unspoken and protected from the world, are the only source to see myself in history; or, to put it simply, my memories are my *only* history. Since history in this country is not written to explore the meanings of the life of a Dalit person, what they are taught as history is for them nothing more than a lesson in self-deception. If they accept what they are taught as *history*, then they are likely to alienate themselves, not only from their conscience, but also from their memories.

Whatever books I had read about the history and culture of my community written by *Savarna* (upper-caste) writers, I found them incapable of understanding the essence of our lives in caste-society. In their books, not only is our ability to love undermined, but our anger is misunderstood too. This is one more reason why I rely on my memories to understand my history and also the history of others. My memories grow under my skin and they float in my blood cells. Protecting my history means protecting

my memories. Protecting my memories means protecting my
father in history. In the books I read, he was erased from them.

*

1988. I was three years old. The television was a rare device in
Indian households. On my third birthday, my father brought
one home. An AT&T, it was a small black-and-white TV, with
two antennae fixed on a small plastic pyramid-shaped cubicle,
separated from the TV but attached to it with a wire. It was the
second TV in my Dalit basti. To me, a three-year-old, that TV
was a life-changing experience. It was my first point of access to
the other world, the world which has always been different from
mine, which was always indifferent to mine. But that was no age
when one could think or could learn to judge. That was the age
when one felt, floated with feelings and let life open many avenues
of fascinating bewilderment.

A day after my third birthday, on 2 October 1988, the Ravi
Chopra-directed *Mahabharat* was first aired on the Doordarshan
channel. It completely changed the experience of watching
television and films in India. On Sundays, when it was telecast
on TV, roads were deserted, public activities came to a standstill,
and people were completely immersed in watching this epic
mythological drama. My home, which was then made up of mud
walls and with a roof of English tiles, used to be full with people
who came to watch *Mahabharat*. For an hour, among them, there
grew a curious anxiety to know what is what, to see the *end of evil*
and *victory of truth*. This was the public who did not know that what
they were watching was the reason for their *fall* in history. This
was the public who did not know that the history of this country
is a constructed one, and not an organic one. This was the public
who had their own stories that had never reached the national

imagination. This was the public whose stories and histories were erased by those who now made for them mythological dramas. The majority of the public, its consumers, who erstwhile did not even know whether the story existed, were absorbed fully in this make-believe propaganda of mythology. The majority of them started believing it as *history*. With Dalits as the audience of this mythological drama, it was altogether a different case.

A year prior to this, in 1987, the Government of Maharashtra had published the fourth volume of Babasaheb Ambedkar's writing and speeches. This volume contained his most critical, dialectical and controversial interpretation of the Hindu–Brahminical religion, titled *Riddles in Hinduism*. Babasaheb has ruthlessly laid bare the intentions behind the creation of gods and goddesses by Brahmins, paradoxes in Hinduism, how Brahmins could not help but be hypocritical in their own creation of myths and how Brahmins alone benefited from these stories, making all other castes mentally servile to these *holy scriptures*. In this volume, he exercised impeachment against the Vedas, Upanishads and shastras and concluded how they impaired the growth of rationality among the Indian people, convincingly arguing that these *holy scriptures* too were fallible. His biggest contribution was to explain the need of rationality and logic for Indian society, if it has to survive the test of time. Its biggest blow was first felt by the Brahmins.

After the publication of *Riddles in Hinduism*, Madhav Gadkari, then the editor of the Marathi daily *Loksatta*, wrote in it a vitriolic piece, arguing that *Riddles in Hinduism* would hurt the feelings of Hindu people.[3] This piece was written with a purely emotive tone. There was nothing intellectual in it. But this was enough to provoke caste-Hindus, especially from Mumbai and the rest of Maharashtra. By this time, the political influence of the Shiv Sena was at its peak in Mumbai. Bal Thackeray's outlook as an Ambedkar-hater[4] fuelled this provocation further. Thousands of caste-Hindus agitated against the publication of this fourth volume, mostly without reading it or having any original criticism against it.

To give a fitting answer to this unmindful agitation of caste-Hindus, lakhs of Dalits, majorly Mahar–Buddhists across Maharashtra and from other parts of India, led a historic march in Mumbai[5] to support the publication of *Riddles in Hinduism*, to stand behind the anti-caste culture, to inculcate democratic values, risking everything to establish the culture of reason and logic in society. These were conscious Dalits, who were more or less part of the anti-caste movement. The morcha they led came to be known, later on, as *Riddles Cha Morcha* (Riddles' March). As far as I know, my basti was hardly aware of or affected by this. At this point, they were consumers of *counter-revolution* in the form of the audience of *Mahabharat* on TV. There was a reason for this.

Half of the families in my basti were in government services, either in Ordnance Factories or the Railways. And the other half were daily wage earners, mostly drivers, and some were factory workers. My entire family—my father, his elder brother, my cousin uncles—all were drivers. Those in our basti who had secure jobs cared little for social activism or the Dalit movement. While growing up, I got to observe this. The lives of those who did not have any proper or secure jobs demanded rigorous labour. Most of their day was spent in working on the streets. Those who had secure jobs did not have to face the question of hunger and survival. But those who did not have a proper income were troubled by the question of hunger and survival. Both these conditions were very fertile for Brahminical—capitalist commodities to enter and affect their lives, to make them aspire for Brahminical values.

With the introduction of TV, the poor among us felt fascination in finding escape in the Brahminical imagination of life; the newly prosperous among us strangely started to emulate them. Neither the rich nor the poor realized our subtle alienation from Babasaheb's movement. And the strangest thing about my basti was that neither rich nor poor seemed to possess any substantial vision, when it came to investing in the education of their children. The majority of girls and boys from my basti of my generation did not study further after school. A few of them graduated, but either got married or continued to work for survival, and only for survival. I too was a victim of this *survival trap* for a while after my school, away from education, away from the life Babasaheb envisioned for us. But with my father, I grew up differently. I was introduced to the world of cinema, and consequently to the world of the imagination. I was affected by it. But I also remained aspirational towards imagining life in its many aspects. Cinema also made me a dreamy person.

*

Back in 1990, Nagpur was a calm city. It was thickly populated with trees, even by the roadside. The roads were broad and unaffected by traffic, which was minimal. There were mostly bicycles on the road and public transport, such as government red buses. Very few people were seen with a scooter or a bike. For a five-year-old child, it sounds vague to capture these details in memories. But I told you, in my story, there are clues which not only connect but hold the story together. Movies are those clues. Back then, my father used to have a bicycle (he still has it—he has kept it safe). It was made by Hercules Cycle company, one of the oldest cycle companies originating in England. It was a strong bicycle. My father had fixed a small seat on the crossbar for me so I could sit comfortably and he could also keep a watch over me while riding it. Even after my birth, my father's visits to the movie theatres remained unabated. Every Sunday, after watching *Mahabharat*, he straightaway headed to watch a matinee show. I started to follow him. I insisted on going with him; I even cried. I started to like to be with him on Sundays.

It was with him that I entered the world of movie theatres for the first time. It was with him that I entered into that black box, full of a smoky smell, the smell of fried samosas, cool air and eerie silence. It was a gateway to an altogether new world for me, which was utterly colourful, enchanting, full of thrills and often dreamlike. For the first time, when my three-year-old eyes saw the movie on the vast screen, I was thrilled. My eyes were stunned, my brain mesmerized. *Qayamat Se Qayamat Tak*, a Hindi movie starring Aamir Khan and Juhi Chawla, was the first movie I watched with my father. It was released in 1988. I saw that in Alankar Talkies. The joy I discovered with him was unparalleled. It felt like communication without speaking. The movie theatre was the world of adults. I was probably the youngest person there. My father did not find it odd to take me there, however. I started liking that two-and-half hours' time, inside the black box, the theatre.

When the movie ended, we rode back home. The bicycle ride back home with him was the happiest time of my life. As he rode, I, sitting in front of him on the small seat, opened up my hands— like a bird opened its wing while learning to fly—and felt the wind against my palms. We rode across the charming streets of Nagpur, sometimes passing by Bajaj Nagar, Dharampeth, South Ambazari Road, Civil Lines etc. I started to see the city with him, taking mental note of it, in its bareness. He rode through shopping areas, food places, and toy shops. In those days, there were no shopping malls or multiplexes in Nagpur. There were only small shops and many famous single-screen theatres. Sometimes, we stopped by at our relatives' homes before going home. Sometimes, when I insisted, he bought me a toy. We did not talk much but we were connected. From Monday to Saturday, he left home early and came back late in the night while I was asleep. But on Sunday, I knew, we would be connected again.

Usually fathers take their sons to temples, mosques, churches, parks, but my father never took me to such places. He took me to the movie theatre, to bars. Yes, sometimes after the movie ended, he would drink before we reached home. He usually drank at two bars: Leo, which was somewhere in Bajaj Nagar, and Sher-E-Punjab, which was near our home. He drank whisky in those days, Officers' Choice. He got me a cold drink, Duke's Mangola, and roasted papad; I relished our moments together. I liked my drink—it was sweet and very mango-ish, pulpy. I liked crumbling the papad and then eating it. I also started liking the smell inside bars—that wispy smell, a fusion of liquor and cigarette smoke. With him, very early, I was introduced to what was supposedly called the 'adult' world. If to feel happy and secure and un-judged around a person is the proof of him being your friend, then my father was my first friend. Those moments were metaphors of our friendship. With him, I was free. I was complete.

*

My mother, Baby Wanjari, and father did not talk to each other much. Words between them were always need-based. Both were occupied with their responsibilities. There was only one time when we all spent time together. We had gone to watch a Marathi movie as a family—my grandmother, mother, my younger sister, me and my father. That movie was *Maherchi Saree* (Saree from the Father's Home). This movie had become tremendously popular among women back then.

I don't know why, but the thought of a Marathi movie made me feel annoyed. I did not want to watch it. I insisted on not watching it. So my father dropped my mother and grandmother in Janki Talkies where it was being screened, bought them tickets and told them to watch the movie while he took me to watch a Bollywood movie, *Phool Aur Kaante*, which introduced Ajay Devgn. I watched this movie in Variety Theatre in Sitabuldi; at this place stands Variety Shopping Mall and a multiplex theatre today. Back then, Variety Theatre was made up entirely of tin sheets. It had a huge parking space for cycles.

This movie was an instant hit, and I liked it for its action. It was 1991. I was five years old. By this time, Bollywood movies taught me that there is always a hero and there is always a villain. At the end, the hero kills the villain and love wins. In these movies, the enemy in love between two individuals was their richness and poverty. What they kept hidden from me was that in real life, we, the people who were living in the Dalit basti, were villains for this society when it came to our food, language, culture and our demands for our rights because, in real life, it was we who were the victim of atrocities. What these movies did not tell me was that love, for people like me, often had terrible consequences. I did not know the fascinating world that my father introduced to me as a child was a lie. I was growing up with this lie.

I have many recollections of my time with my father, but with my mother, I have only a few, maybe because the time I spent with my father in the theatre or when he took me to his workplace or bars where he drank was fascinating for me more than anything, and it has been carved in my mind so strongly that it has left no space for my memories with my mother. And with the three of us together, I probably have just one memory: a photograph. In 1988, when I was three years old, we clicked a photograph together in a studio—my father, mother and me. This was a colour photo. My hair was thin, my eyes had kohl and on my forehead, there was a small black dot. My father was wearing a black suit, his hair was shiny and neatly combed back. He looked handsome. My mother was wearing a pink saree, the *pallu* covering her head. She was young and gracious and looked elegant in it. The photo captures our charm well. This charm has faded over the years. Today, years of hard work have made my father and mother look rough, and their bodies are worn out. Later, for years after schooling, I was mentally disconnected from my family. In 2013, when I left for Mumbai to pursue my MA, I carried this photo with me, without telling anyone. And whenever I look at it, I think, sometimes, we remain together only in photos. Life inevitably separates us.

*

In those days, hunger was central to our lives. Not that we did not have enough to eat; but we never had any surplus, neither food nor money; we still do not. My father had to work, sometimes drive till late at night, to keep us fed. But as far as I know, he was generous in feeding people and spending money. He has this philosophy that we must cook extra because we do not know when a hungry person may knock at our door for food. Earlier, I thought he would say it for the sake of it. But maybe it had historical context to it. Maybe, in the old days, when Mahars (untouchables) used to walk from one place to another, one village to another, or travel long distances, they had to carry their food and water, because if it was revealed that they were untouchables, no one would provide anything for them. Besides, this revelation had terrible consequences. So the Mahars mostly knew the Mahars in other villages and went to them if they needed something. It meant that someone could come to your home without any prior notice (there was no way to inform people in advance in those days), and you had to feed them. *They should not go unfed if they visit your home* was the philosophy behind it. So the person, be it cleaner or conductor, who came with my father in the night, ate at our home. They were hardly paid by the owner of transport service and, hence, were unable to afford food.

I remember one man who worked as a cleaner with my father. His name was Bihari Chacha. My father said that Bihari Chacha ran away from his home in Bihar. He must have been forty years old when I saw him first. But because of smoking beedis for years, his face looked dull and aged. His nose was sharp, his hair silky— half black, half white. But what made him distinguished was a brooding silence on his face that was intensified through his eyes. He had no wife, no family. I did not know where he went after work, or where he would sleep. Whenever my father brought a trailer home if it got late in the night, Bihari Chacha, without forgetting, would bring for me a packet of Parle-G biscuits. Sometimes, he was too drunk to eat. But gradually, he too sank in the darkness of time, like all the other cleaners. All of them ran away from home, all of them were homeless and all of them, perhaps always, were in search of a home. Bihari Chacha became a character in one of my short stories, which was published in the collection *Flowers on the Grave of Caste*.[6]

*

Those were the days when life in the basti was carefree, harsh and undefiled by the sophistication of the dominant world. We had enough land around our basti to play, freely and limitlessly, until we exhausted our bodies and felt pangs of thirst and hunger. Sometimes, even though we were children, violence loomed over our lives. There was no way to understand how the violence I witnessed as a child changed me forever. I remember once, when we were playing, the eldest son of the Dhivars, a fisherman family from the basti, came to our playground, and we all started pelting stones at him. When he ran away, I aimed at him. The stone hit his head, and he started bleeding heavily. We all ran. I went to my home and hid under the bed. My mother came to know about this. She screamed at me and beat me up. When the father of the boy whom I injured came to my home, my mother begged him to forgive me. He did. But the sight of that blood pool terrifies me even today. In my life, at times, violence was not so explicit, but more subtle, more lethal and its effects more indelible.

*

From my childhood to my teenage years, I was closer to the world of my father than my mother. It may be because my father had introduced me to his world outside the home—theatres, bars and his transport office and garage, where he spent time with most of his friends and co-workers. He had worked for Chawla Transport for nearly thirty years. It was during the mid-1990s when my father first took me to this place. It was located a little farther north from the Santra Market, which is alternatively famous as Cotton Market, but whose official name is Mahatma Phule Bazaar. It was a busy place, with so many hawkers, shops, wholesale marketeers, a vegetable market. Ahead of it stood the office of Chawla Transport, and adjoining it was the garage where trailers and trucks of this transport service came to be repaired. And there was a chai shop, where all of my father's co-workers used to gather. My father generally took me there on Sundays. These were the people who were hard workers, the lumpenproletariat: drivers, cleaners, mechanics, porters, vegetable vendors, and mazdoors-labourers.

In my memory, this was a world unadulterated by the sophistication of the morality of educated people. These were people who were rough, intense, at times brutal, but knew how to extract the joy from life. I saw them playing cards, betting money, bullying each other, making fun at people, but all without any hypocrisy. This all used to happen in the chai shop of Ashok Kaka. Ashok Kaka was my father's closest friend back then. They used to visit each other's homes. He wasn't from our caste, my father used to say. Ashok Kaka offered me a cold drink or chai with bread or whatever I liked whenever I went to this place with my father. When a member of the Chawla family returned from the USA and joined the transport business, this world of the lumpenproletariat shattered. My father left his job over an argument about increasing his wages. Many drivers too left this transport service, while some were asked to leave. Ashok Kaka had to shut his shop.

Back in the late 1970s, my father had gotten selected for the job of a driver with the state transport. The story goes that his erstwhile truck-owner, his boss (at Chawla Transport), made him lose that job. This boss had some contacts at the state transport department and, through them, he got my father's appointment cancelled. Back then, my father was one of the few drivers who knew how to drive a trailer, a twelve-wheel carrier, so his boss did not want to lose him. My father showed us a state driver badge, which he still keeps with him. But he no longer had that job, which could have given him some security and comfort in his old age. There is something in him which convinces me to believe in this story and his meekness before the outer world. Because he survived, not to fight, but to tell me what failure means, and what it means to live with its consequences. In the outer world, he always remained thoughtlessly lenient. I would like to believe that this was the second time he was invisibly wounded.

*

A Dalit man is powerless in the outer world. It is true that there is a certain amount of power ascribed to him when he is inside his home. He lives in a duality of being, and with a complex psyche which is undecipherable for the language of the outer world. The situation of a Dalit woman in this sense is unthinkable. Whatever I have gathered later, while reading narratives of Dalit women from Marathi Dalit literature, I have begun to sense that no one has a moral potential and ethical power to free Dalit women other than Dalit women themselves. In their words, I found an ability to expose for me things with which I grew up but which my masculinity prevented me from seeing. In their words, I began to sense that every Dalit woman grows up with an instinct to break the chain of oppression if given a chance and, if not, she bequeaths this instinct to her children. Narratives of Marathi Dalit women made me see what I have not seen in my mother so far: *the invisible chain of sacrifices on which my ability to speak and write today has flourished.* It was undeniably there. Her life is a metaphor of it. Her labour to raise us and educate us is a symbol of her strength and vision. But my father was not this clear. He ceased to have a vision when it came to his children.

It had to do with the dilemma which is not uncommon for a Dalit man: *powerless outside the home, dominant inside the home.* He is cheated outside. He is humiliated outside. Though a man, he possesses no dominance in the national discourse. He is portrayed as a victim in the national imagination. But at home, he likes to dictate, he likes to control—he *intends* to be powerful. He becomes a twilight of dilemmas this country can hardly have a moral capacity to see and understand. It is the unhealthy *caste* that runs in the veins of this country that is responsible for this. He is located somewhere in between savagery and humanity. Often, he is too complex for himself to be normal and calm in the world's eye. He drinks, he blabbers. He murmurs senselessly, or sometimes curses as if talking to the people from the past.

This is how I have seen many men in my basti, who died alcoholics. First they consumed alcohol. Then the alcohol consumed them. These men were later judged and reduced to being called '*bewadas*' (drunkards). When they were sober, I found in their silent eyes the sign of horrified grief—complicated forms of grief that remained undetected in the autopsy of their lives. Alcohol may have been the reason for their deaths, but it was not the cause of their destruction. Much later in my life, when I started reading seriously about the role of society and crime, I told myself: *I know these men who endured failures but who were defeated by loneliness.* But earlier, I never had access to their emotional world, including my father's. For me, entering into their emotional world was only possible through the imagination when I started writing stories and they became my characters. *Sometimes, griefs are those wounds which leave a permanent scar on the skin. Although the wound is healed, the scar is its reminder—you have endured that pain, you have overcome it. You are a survivor; you are a victor.* My father is the wound; I am the scar.

Bollywood is a cataract in our world of perceptions. My father did not know this.

*

1993. I was eight years old. By this time, my fascination for Bollywood movies was rapidly increasing. I remember, it was during the same year that cable TV was introduced. One person in our basti had a huge, white, umbrella-shaped disc fixed on the roof of his building. Everyone said that it was from here that they telecast movies, but none of us knew how it happened. VCR was another sensation in our basti at the same time. Only a few households in our basti had cable connections. My home did not have it. I used to go to one of my relatives' place, who was a government servant and had a colour TV at his house. Everyday after school, around noon, I would go near his house, take a peek through the window. If I heard the sound of movies, I shamelessly knocked on the door.

On one Sunday that year, my father took me to watch a movie. It was *Khalnayak* (Villain), starring Sanjay Dutt, Jackie Shroff and Madhuri Dixit. We went to watch this movie in Sudama Talkies, situated in Dharampeth, a locality dominated by the Brahmins and Baniyas of Nagpur. As we reached as usual to watch a matinee show, we found the theatre crowded. There were long queues for tickets; people pushing each other at times, whistling, some were looking with enthralled expressions at the larger-than-life poster of the movie hung on the facade. There was a violent anxiety to watch this movie. They were mostly men, young and wild, who looked up to Bollywood stars, emulated their fashion, their mannerisms, their attitude. My father asked me to stand in a corner and went through the crowd. He returned after sometime with two tickets—he had gotten them in black.

Khalnayak was a little unusual story for the audience of that time. Sanjay Dutt played the role of Balram aka Ballu. Ballu is shown as a victim of poverty and his circumstances. Because of this, Ballu turns into a criminal. The masses were below the poverty line in 1993, and they were also the viewership of this movie. They easily related to Ballu. Seeing Ballu on screen, they felt powerful. In Ballu, they saw themselves, taking revenge against the system, against power. But this revenge was metaphoric, and so was the enemy. No movie of this time had ever tried to portray the reality of the source of oppression: the Brahminical value system. Bollywood wasn't honest nor intelligent in its movies. Ballu in *Khalnayak* was the symbolic self of the masses without any history of them, which for a long time wanted to take revenge against those who kept them poor and subjected them to exploitation.

My father watched this movie a couple of times later. Why would he watch a three-hour-long movie repeatedly? I wasn't surprised, given that I know about him as a person and why a few movies attracted him more than others—he related to the feeling of revenge lingering inside Ballu, who was agitated, frustrated, vengeful and an outlaw; but he was equally emotional and craved for the love and affection of his mother, who was left behind in the world that made a criminal out of him. It was the same year, in April, that Sanjay Dutt was arrested under Terrorist and Disruptive Activities (Prevention) Act (TADA), for his role in the serial blasts in Mumbai in 1993. It again pushed the popularity of the movie to another level. Sanjay Dutt became a 'khalnayak' in real life. Many stories about his relationship with his father and mother and his addiction to drugs later came out, which seemed to draw the sympathy of the masses. What attracted and appealed to the masses who watched this movie and made it the highest-grossing film of that year was the justification, his poverty and loneliness, that Ballu has for being a *criminal*.

But as I see it, whether in reel life or real life, Ballu was indicative of the lovelessness in life. And this lovelessness was very much present in my father's life. The idea of love that Bollywood promotes does not exist in society. Over the years, this idea of love with Brahminical notions attached to it has been served to society by movies. Outside the cinema hall or theatre, its audience only finds lovelessness, since caste keeps them separated eventually. In fact, this lovelessness is a part of Indian society. Later, as I got acquainted with people from many castes, including dominant ones, I witnessed this lovelessness was widespread in their lives and fractured the common sense among them. Why would it not? After all caste is pervasive; it separates one person from another; caste is the warden of the feeling of love. It makes one crave for the simple element which is an essential part of human life: *touch, the touch of love, the touch of affection* and *the touch of acceptance.* Caste prohibits a choice. Caste violates the will. What was more apparent in the life of my father was silence, not words, not expressions. But I wanted him to shout the essence of his life, I wanted him to tell me: *I told you, love is difficult to carry in your heart, because to carry it we need purpose and a person for whom it has to be carried. Most of the people, most of the time, carry hate in their hearts because they are yet to find the purpose of love and a person for whom they should carry love in their heart.*

I wanted him to share his insights, with which people like him become solid and survive; I wanted him to tell me: *The world is easy for those who carry hate within them, these people are ever-present in history. Those who have love to offer are like flowers who have sprouted after decades of nuclear attack on the soil. People who carry love in them are no less than a museum of hope. People who carry love in their heart are not weak; they are strangely tolerant.*

But my father did not speak. Or probably I am yet to develop a language to understand him.

*

I was growing up; the small seat that my father had fixed for me on the bar of his bicycle was growing smaller. My Sunday visits to movies with my father became less frequent. I hated it. My feelings were selfish, but they were mine, and I had no means other than them to make sense of the world around me. So when my father became reluctant to take me with him to movies, I thought he was being selfish. But this was not the entire truth. His own visits to movies had reduced. He was disconnected from the place where he worked for thirty-odd years. He started working for a new transport service, but he seemed to hate it. But to feed four growing, hungry mouths—me, my three sisters and my mother, he had to keep aside his likes and dislikes. Besides, he had no other qualification, and he had no experience other than driving a trailer truck. He had no privilege to make a *choice*. The Bollywood movies he watched all his life told him that people like him (Dalits) did not have stories, did not have choices and weren't heroes in any sense of life. Of course, the movies lied. But he lived with these lies, and surprisingly, to some extent, he believed in them. The movies he grew up watching, the movies which made him emotionally feeble, the movies which were the only source for a jolt to his imagination of the world, had something to do with it. Bollywood movies are emotionally crappy, unintelligent and pernicious for Dalit–Bahujan viewers. Because the very source of emotions of Bollywood movies is largely and predominantly Brahminical in nature.

I remember a day when my father took me to watch a movie. It was June 1997, and I was twelve years old. It was mildly cloudy, and winds were cool. The sun was lingering behind the clouds. But it did not rain. We went to Panchsheel Talkies to watch *Border*, a war drama. It was the last movie I watched with my father. It was the most popular and successful movie of that year. My father liked it so much that he took me to watch it for the next two consecutive weeks. And to me, this movie appeared to be a great experience of watching war thrillers; its dialogues were apparently patriotic and the audience whistled, clapped and shouted as they were being spoken on the screen. More than this movie, I enjoyed the bread pakora that my father fed me during intervals. They were delicious, so crispy and fresh with fried green chillies.

Border was a perfect blend of action thrillers, nostalgia and patriotism for the Indian viewership. The reason it became an instant hit was because it offered many in the audience a sense of fulfilment of being victorious against Pakistan. It was based on the 1971 India–Pakistan war, which India won. To see this victory in a theatre, as a story, with melodious music and songs of nostalgia, was an irresistible experience and a moment of bestowing on a person an identity of being an Indian; not just an Indian, but a victorious one. But was it true for its Dalit audiences? Was this victory meaningful in the lives of Dalits? The victory, or to be precise, the power of a powerful country, also seeps into the lives of its citizens. It sustains them and strengthens their lives culturally, politically and socially. In all these spheres of human life, this victory seemed to have been a paradox in the life of Dalits.

Border was released on 13 June 1997. On 11 July 1997, eleven innocent Dalits from Ramabai Nagar, Ghatkopar (Mumbai), were killed in the police firing of the State Reserve Police Force (SRPF). These eleven people included a small child whose skull was cracked open by a bullet. Most Dalits who were part of the audience of *Border*, cheering it for its patriotic zeal, were unaware of this brutality of the nation against their own community. Only those who were direct victims of it and associated with the Dalit movement seemed to feel any anger against this tragic and brutal incident. Bollywood movies made people forget the reality of their own circumstances, of their community as a collective consciousness, and replaced it with a pseudo-nationalistic identity. Sometimes, this forgetfulness lasts until the destruction of one's own identity and history. The people who are pushed to live on the edge when it comes to survival and only survival, become an easy target of oppressive aesthetics. Bollywood peddled this oppressive aesthetic.

*

In those days, our lives were like glass, which seems hard but is easily breakable. One incident that exposed to me this brittleness of our lives was the death of Kamal Akka. She was married to a person from Gaddigodam a Dalit-Muslim locality in Nagpur. It was situated a little distance from Bharat Talkies. Whenever we went to watch a movie at Bharat Talkies, it was a ritual for my father to take me to Kamal Akka's home. I was very fond of her as a child. The second youngest sister of my father, Kamal Akka got married when I was about six or seven years old. I do not remember this too well. But one fact is unforgettable. She loved me dearly. When she got married, I cried so much that I insisted on going with her to her new home. The people who came to attend the wedding assumed that I must have been *her* child. So my father must have thought that I should not lose contact with her, and that is why he took me to her home frequently. She was always happy to see us. She was slim and fairer in complexion than my father. A black mole on the edge of her chin added beauty to her personality. She was smart and, most importantly, cheerful.

I may have been in ninth standard at the time, but I do not remember the year clearly. My father was somewhere in another district, driving his trailer-truck. We got the news that Kamal Akka had suffered burn injuries and was hospitalized. My mother and grandmother rushed to the hospital. When my mother returned, she informed people at home that Kamal Akka was dreadfully burnt; it was so bad that one could not even look at her. Maybe in a day or two after that, Kamal Akka succumbed to the injuries and died. Some said it was an accident that took place while lighting the kerosene stove. Others said she had been immolated. The truth in this case remained unsaid. But looking at the cases of the burning of women in Indian households, it is not difficult to draw conclusions. It is difficult to say whether at the suggestion of the family or if he decided so himself, but my father did not go to see her in the hospital. And I do not remember whether he attended her funeral or not. My own memory of this horror is unreliable. It was only when I started to write poems that I gathered courage to recall this incident. Poems gave me the courage that people did not.

Fifteen confused and dreadful years had to pass before I could revisit that horrible incident. It revealed to me a side of my father which was as complex as the hidden mysteries of this galaxy. I wrote the poem in Mumbai, newly graduating from my MA course, struggling to find a job. It was 2016. I was hardly in a position to send money home, and my earning from writing news stories for TwoCircles.net was too meagre to support myself in the expensive life of the city. My father was becoming more and more frail by then. He was around sixty-three and still driving a trailer truck.

My father was not someone who believed in teaching. I do not even remember a moment when he taught me or my sister to do this or that. Unlike many fathers, he never tried to discipline us. In this sense, he did not tame me to any particular practice or habit. Later, I saw many people, especially from dominant castes in university, recall how they were disciplined by the family and were hurt in the process. I thought about it: *Disciplining meant hurting.* I had no experience of it. I was not hurt; I was just neglected while growing up. As a result, I felt free but I grew up fatally confused in my teenage years.

It was my mother who made sure to fine-tune the home and the people in it, like a musician does with their instrument. She beat me up when I argued or tried to use my privilege as a boy over my sister. I was the only son, among three sisters, and the eldest too. As a boy, I mostly played outside, and my sisters remained in and around the house. While growing up, I had certain privileges which my sisters did not have. I was allowed to go out and watch movies, first with my father, then with my friends. I was allowed to stay outside home till late in the night and when I returned,

I was not questioned. For a long period in my life, I mistook the 'privileges of being a man' for freedom.

No one in my family was a graduate. When I reached the moment of crossing the threshold of school, there was absolutely no one to suggest to a direction my life could take. It was a life full of invisible chains. Sometimes, you are not free just because the law of the country declared you free. You must *feel* that freedom, and to feel that freedom, you must be privileged to make choices in life. Not only did I not have the freedom to make choices, but I had no social capital which could immediately inspire me to lead a life of freedom. By this time in my life, Ambedkar remained a part of history, a story. He was yet to become a *force*.

*

Our financial situation was weakening. My father kept losing jobs with new transport services. I entered the tenth standard. It was the year 2000. After a few months, in March 2001, I appeared for the SSC board (10th standard) examination. The result was awaited. We had our summer vacation, the last vacation of school. After this there was no more school. I thought of it as some kind of freedom. Most of my friends from school came from an *Adivasi* background, and they decided to work in a factory in Maharashtra Industrial Development Corporation (MIDC). I joined them too. I was just fifteen years old.

I got a job in a cardboard-making company. This company manufactured corrugated boxes. It was fifteen kilometres from my home. This meant I had to ride a bicycle for an hour in the month of April and May, the hottest months in Nagpur, when the temperature went up to 45–49 degree Celsius. It was my first step into the world of transactions: sweating it out and earning wages. It was my first lesson in the value of time and labour. It was my first experience in witnessing humiliation, enduring it and surviving it. Since we were first-timers and had never worked anywhere, we were given the task of arranging cardboard sheets into an L-shape and sticking it with Fevicol. We sat outside the factory, under the shade. To stick cardboard into an L-shape, we had to use our fingers furiously and feet to press the cardboard down so it would stick firmly.

We were working under a contractor called Mishra, a Brahmin from North India who was not educated at all. Every now and then, he kept a watch over us, overseeing if we were working properly. If our pace appeared slow to him, he cursed us. We showed as if we did not mind, but it hurt inside. Sometimes, when some permanent employee was absent, he would take one or two of us inside the factory and order us to unload the corrugated sheets from the machine. A single sheet was lighter than air. But if hundreds of them were piled together, they became heavy and slightly dangerous, as while holding them in our bare hands (they needed at least two people to hold them from both ends), they cut the skin if they slipped. During the two months of my work, I got several bruises and cuts on the skin of my hands. 'They are part of the job,' everyone said over there. Wounds were part of my job.

Our daily wage was Rs 30. Thirty rupees for eight hours of work. This added up to Rs 780 for twenty-six days in a month (we had one weekly off). These were not the lowest wages. It was an indicator of the degree of misery and helplessness with which many people live their lives. They had such low wages because there were people who had no choice but to accept this demeaning wage to survive. To reach the factory at 9 a.m., I left my home at 7.30 a.m. I met my friends on the way, and we all rode to the factory, reaching fifteen minutes early to prepare for the work. To reach late meant having to bear Mishra's cursing.

We were paid weekly. When I received my first weekly payment, I felt a sense of self-worth. I learnt what it meant to sweat, to endure pain and to earn a wage. I dreamt of buying a new bicycle with the money I earned. In these two months, my body became used to working hard, to tolerate abuse and to listen to curses without reacting only because it came from people who were in a position to pay me for my work. It was my first job, and I learnt that the way to one's dream in this world was not easy. The only thing that relieved me in these two months was the thought that I was going to work in this factory only for two months, until my exam results were out. In a week or two after I started working, my father lost another job. He did not get any job for a month. I had no choice but to give all the money for that month to my mother for household expenses. This incident pushed into I growing up prematurely, and I hated it. I began to hate family responsibilities. I had suffered a fresh wound to my dream of buying a bicycle. I was thinking selfishly. But now, I empathize with how my father worked all these years, and what he must have suffered. How many of his dreams were buried under our hunger, needs and demands? He must have witnessed miseries I could not imagine. And while working in the ruthless air of the factory, I began to feel scared, wondering if his misery was going to be mine now.

*

Lost and Lonely

my body is the poisonous flower
no one has ever dared to touch me
they didn't know: I am the door
to the dream they killed mercilessly

A bird whose wings are clipped is still a bird, but it is unable to fly. Many of us spend life like a bird with chopped wings. We hardly aspire to fly. In our case, our dreams are those wings. If we follow our dreams, we fly. But in the case of Dalits, caste-society acts like a butcher. The agonies in the life of a Dalit person whose dreams are butchered are difficult for language to understand. To me, the most evident factor in our inability to comprehend the meaning of pain in our lives is our lack of introspection and our fear to see and reflect on our own failures and mistakes. Our biggest fear in life is the fear of looking at ourselves in the past and thinking that we could have been different, or perhaps happier, if things could have been different or avoided. To me, this fear was real. It emerged from my weakness, or perhaps from a habit of avoiding pain. We tend to forget pain. I was no exception. But I also did not know that healing from it is no accident. It is a work of sheer determination and of developing a habit of facing the pain, of looking beyond it.

Healing is important, if not necessary. But it is also true that you don't heal unless you suffer enough, and to suffer enough you need inscrutable strength and the ability to see your pain, not in isolation, but as a part of the world. Because when you see pain in this way, you also decide to fight it. My pain is nothing but a part of the world I belong to. My world is largely a part and parcel of my ancestors who, for most of their lives, were never known to society at large, neither as stories nor as history. And to decipher our stories, society needs to understand the silence underlying them, not their voice. The silence in our lives is cruel, violent. And one of the first institutions in India that silences the stories of Dalit community is the school.

*

My first school was Brahmin-Baniya school in which I studied till the fifth standard. The name of the school was Bharatiya Vidya Mandir. It was just a kilometre from my home. The school made us recite the Gayatri Mantra and the national anthem every day before classes began. It was a small school with a few Dalit students from my basti; the rest were mostly from dominant OBCs. Back then, in Nagpur, it was a dangerous, if not deliberate, practice by schools to make every student recite the Gayatri Mantra so that they could imbibe 'Hindu' values. But for us, it was an assault on our newly embraced and carefully protected cultural values: the Navayana Buddhism of Babasaheb. This was around 1996. In that school, my only vivid memory was to learn the history of Maharashtra and Shivaji Maharaj. No other subject excited me.

I was an average student. And I barely had anyone around me whom I could call a friend.

After the fifth standard, my parents decided to put me into a 'good' school. I was admitted to Dharampeth High School, again a school run mostly by Brahmins. I used to walk to my previous school, since it was at a short distance away. Dharampeth High School was in the city, far from my home. So I had to take a bus. It was on the side of the city where I never travelled alone. In this school, the Sanskrit mantras scared me, the big building filled me with the feeling of seclusion and I felt feeble around the students there—they were evidently elite and came from the dominant classes and castes. Soon after I joined, I knew I could not survive there. Often, humiliation or discrimination does not come with visible noise. It comes with the environment being completely alien to yours, in complete and haunting silence, and you begin to sense that one day, this silence will engulf your ability to speak. I felt there was a kind of pompousness in the air in this school, in the speech of the students and in the body language of its teachers. Every activity in this school, as they claimed, was to create discipline in the students. I hated the word 'discipline', for I always felt that discipline meant taming. So, I was frightened by the overall atmosphere. The students and teachers there were still strangers to me, yet I feared them silently. I sensed that they were not the people around whom I would be comfortable.

I stopped going to school after a month.

My parents were clueless about my reluctance to go to Dharampeth High School, as was I. Overall, I knew that I felt secluded in this school, because I did not have the language and lacked the cleverness to mix with the other students. What I did not know was that it was too early to feel scared, that too in a school. I did not realize that this fear would be there to stay with me, forever. It was not the fear of people, new places or different environments. The fear came from my own weakness to be able to make friends, especially when they were unlike me. I stopped going to school, and seeing me sad, my parents did not force me either. Instead, I told them that I could study in the nearby school, which many boys and girls from my basti attended. It was Awale Babu High School. In this school, only students from SC, ST and a few poor children from the OBC backgrounds came to study. As if it was *reserved* for them. In Nagpur, there are many schools and colleges which were built by the associates of Dr Babasaheb Ambedkar. Mr Haridas Awale was one such.

It was not a school like what today we imagine a school to be, whether government or private. Awale Babu High School was about two kilometres from my home to the west. It was like a big house, with four rooms, with high walls. The school had no boundary walls and only a few houses around it. It had plenty of open space, where students used to roam and play freely. The roof was made up of English tiles, and it was often broken as mischievous students used to pelt stones at it and run away after the end of the school day. Most of the teachers in this school were SCs and OBCs, and only one or two were Brahmins. I did not have to put any effort to mix with the students here. There was no insistence on 'order' here. In this school, the word 'discipline' was rarely mentioned and hardly put into practice. I felt *safe* here.

The full name of this school was Karmaveer Babu Awale High School. It was known for accommodating 'dumb' students. Of course, public opinion about a school which was built by Dalits, where most of the students were Dalits and Adivasis from Vidarbha, could not have been any different. This is what we understand today, but back then, even I used to think the same about the school in which I was going to spend five years. However, no one cared. In terms of study, the school did not help develop any interest in me for reading or writing.

What you were supposed to learn in school, I learnt—the state-designed syllabus. That was a time when schools tended to contribute only one thing in the life of their students, about their after-school life. It led to an unresolvable paradox: the majority of the students could not relate to what the school taught them because the realities of their lives were in conflict with it. When I matriculated in 2001, with 60.26 per cent, I felt this paradox as a very real, decisive force that had misled many people. I was misled too. And my path to books and writing had to cross years of confusion, disappointment, insecurity, mistakes and loneliness.

*

'When pestered with questions, memory is like an onion,' says Günter Grass in his book *Peeling the Onion*, 'that wishes to be peeled so we can read what is laid bare letter by letter. It is seldom unambiguous and often in mirror-writing or otherwise disguised.' I can fully understand the existence of memory in this way, in the life of people who at least have a history preserved for them by their ancestors, in stories, in parables, in songs and passed to them through texts. By the time I stepped out of school, I had no such memories that could guide me any further. My memories were not linear. My memories were as complex as a spider's web. Besides, I had not learnt to question. Although they were complex, the memories in my life were neither unambiguous nor disguised. In fact, they were as solid and adamant as a rock in the river that does not move an inch, no matter how strong the stream of the water. From early childhood till very late in life, my imagination had been fed on Bollywood movies. They told me that only certain lives or cultures are worth aspiring for, to be nostalgic about. I made the mistake of thinking of my memories as *insignificant stories*. And this mistake gave birth to an invisible man.

In 2001, I had the last summer holidays from school. During this break, I worked in a factory for three months. I hated it. And I decided never to work in factories. But I did not have enough privilege to make choices. I did not know this. This was the same year my father started losing jobs, one after another. So my mother decided to work—in a factory. A woman, our neighbour in the basti, had been working in a plastic bottle factory. The bottles were used to pack insulin. My mother, along with a few women from our basti, got a job there. In India, men and women are paid unequally; this inequality also varies according to the caste of the men and women. The wages on paper are different. Wages on the ground are decided according to the misery and need of the worker. The wage of Rs 25 a day paid to my mother was not only low but also discriminatory. In addition to this, the factory environment was toxic, in the absence of any safety equipment or health guarantees. I often heard from my mother how women fell unconscious while working. But my mother had no choice. There was only one thing in her sight: our growing, hungry stomach and our needs.

When she got late for work, in the month of May, my mother would ask me to drop her on my bicycle. The month of May in Nagpur is the cruellest month, with unimaginable heat. As I would pedal the bicycle, I would be completely soaked in sweat and feel intensely irritated. At such moments, I hated my life. The sweat also ran down my face. My body would literally emit heat, as if I had been freshly taken out of the oven. And it was only 9 a.m.

On one such day, when the sun was scorching hot, the electricity connection of our home was cut off because we did not have the money to pay the bill. My father was away, working, and he was not in the least interested in home affairs. When my mother returned from the factory in the evening, exhausted, she was angry at seeing the house in darkness. But she could not afford to lose her cool. She took out the only gold jewellery she had and mortgaged it to the local jeweller. Then, she went into the office of the electricity department and paid the bill. At last, the electricity connection was re-established at night. The light in our home was rekindled by her suffering. There were many such instances in which she took matters in hand and kept things running at home.

My mother's hard work for us emanated from a vision, unlike my father's. While he lived in the house, he was never *at* home, never emotionally present. Quite contrary to this, my mother *was* our home. I denied this fact to myself for a long time—until I sat down to write this book, in fact. My mother took care of each of us with undivided attention. I remember she took me to Dr Pathak's clinic every week for a few years when I was a child. I do not remember what was wrong with me. We took a red government city bus from our stop of Takli Sim to Shankar Nagar. Then we both walked to the clinic, with her holding my hand. Dr Pathak was a chubby man, from what I can remember. His hands were always cold, soft and sweaty. After the check-up, he would give me a chocolate, taking it out from the drawer of his table. On the way back, sometimes, I insisted on eating *pani puri* (in Nagpur, we call it *gup chup*). I could not resist the temptation. She was worried about my health and diligently followed Dr Pathak's advice. I remember that green file in which my mother religiously arranged all the prescriptions and test results in chronological order. She was determined to fight all the pain coming my way.

My father, on the other hand, introduced to me the pleasures of life. His existence grew fascinating for me and my mother's dull. Whatever I read or was asked to read for a long period of my life did not teach me to value or find worth in my mother's small caring acts. No one told me that people like me are products of such 'small' acts. The school did not have stories of people like my mother and their 'ordinary' lives. The result of this was that I grew up unsure of how to understand my own people through books because they were simply not there. Today, when I look back at pedagogies of schools in India, I cannot stop myself thinking that school as a system meant to fail us: Dalits.

*

After school, it was time for me to take admission into a college. I was unable to decide the course I wanted to pursue. I acquired slightly above 60 per cent in my board exams for class 10. I thought I had a chance at science. But, before applying for the course, I had to get my caste certificate issued from the district administration authority. It was the first time my caste was going to be attested, on paper, and gradually embed itself in my thoughts. The caste certificate was going to be a document that, in a way, would officially connect me with my ancestors. The certificate was mandatory to avail the reservation and compensations reserved for us against our historical exploitation. Of course, at the time, I was totally unaware of its political connotations. I was ill-informed about the 'reservation debate' and how this very word is despised and hated by those who are deliberately ignorant about our history and largely insensitive to the ideas of social justice, which the Constitution of India has promised to many communities on whose sacrifice and labour this country has been built.

State governments love to change the list of required documents needed to make a caste certificate every year. It was in the scorching summer of 2001 that I stepped out to make my certificate. Those boys from basti who already had it offered some information on how to make it and where to make it from. Everyone directed me to the zilla: the office of the additional collector. The premises on which the additional collector's office was situated also held a district court and several other government offices and department blocks. In the month of May, when schools would declare the exam results, the zilla office would be filled with faces of Dalit–Bahujan students, who would just about to taste the sheer bitterness of the government apparatus, along with countless lawyers in black-and-white clothes. The heat muffled my breath.

After asking several people the way to the office, I finally found it. The list of documents required to make the certificate included the legal evidence of my family's residence in the city since 1950. 1950? The only year in relation to my immediate history I recalled then was 1985, the year of my birth, engraved into my mind by my school certificates. When I came back home, disappointed and anxious, I asked my mother if we had any such document. She dug through a jumble of papers in the almirah and found my father's school certificate. 1954, the year of my father's birth. Mahar, his caste. That was the first moment I read the year of his birth and caste, on paper. 'We are here since 1954,' I muttered, 'and we are Mahars.' In the absence of stories from the past, this moment was no less than a revelation to me of having some semblance of a history or, at least, some traces of it. But it wasn't enough. The certification required a document that could prove that my family was in this city before 1950. My father's elder brother, Ramchandra (whom we used to call 'Dada') was at least ten years older than my father. When the search for his certificate began, amidst tattered papers, I found his school leaving certificate, typewritten, with a stamp of the school, faded by the dust of years—1946 was his birth year, and Mahar his caste.

I was issued the caste certificate in a month. It meant that I could now prove that I had a history in this city since 1946. I had evidence that I belonged here. For the first time, I consciously uttered who I was historically. I was now out in the world, as an individual, with a certificate of my caste and, with it, carrying the past that I had never consciously thought about. But what I had still not thought about and did not know was this: *The caste certificate was going to be the prologue and epilogue of my story, of my life and death.*

I was seventeen. I think seventeen is an age when more than *knowing*, you rely on *feeling* to understand the significance of things happening in your life. Back then, for me, a caste certificate was just a document required by thousands of students to pursue their journey into education without obstruction, to avail the opportunities that had been hitherto denied to them. I did not understand that the most crucial aspect of the certificate was to facilitate the strength of representation of those communities, whose presence in all aspects of the national imagination had been deliberately restricted. *Reservation is responsibility, not welfare.* But those who hate the very existence of the word 'reservation' choose to perceive it otherwise. They do not wish to acknowledge that *reservation is bloodless reparation that is owed.* Their choice to see it otherwise originates from their fear of seeing Dalit–Bahujan communities studying, working and excelling at par with them. The oppressor never wants to see the oppressed as their equal; their critique of 'reservation' is just an excuse. What they also do not know are the dilemmas with which a person who possesses the caste certificate lives throughout their life.

This dilemma was so real to me that I lived with it for fifteen years. Maybe it was just the commotion in my head. But this pain wasn't mine alone—it was historical; it has consumed many generations.

*

June 2001. I got admission in Dr Ambedkar College, Deekshabhoomi, Nagpur. It was located at the place where Dr

Ambedkar had converted to Buddhism in 1956. Eight years after this historical event, one of his closest associates, Dadasaheb Gaikwad, founded this college. On my first day at college, it was raining. It was my first step into the larger world, amid people who were not necessarily aware of my world. I felt strange being there, not because I was new to this place, but because I was yet to learn to argue for a place for myself. Although a BSc was hardly a difficult course, it did not interest me. I started avoiding going to college. Eventually, I dropped out of this college and got admission into another college in another course, BCom. I dropped that course too. The colleges and courses were not the problems. The problem was me and my inability to mix with people. I did not know it then: I was defined by loneliness.

For most of my life, I struggled to know my interests. I grappled with this challenge. I imagine that this is part of the life of so many Dalits. In the absence of someone who can fill them with inspiration and guide them, they grow up like a wild tree in a jungle, against all odds. Some survive, some do not. Those who survive learn survival the hard way, carrying many wounds and hurts. They grow tough and become too hardened to be understood by those who grow up with all the nourishment they receive because of their privilege.

When I dropped out of the second college, I was not sure if I was ever going to study again. Confusion overpowered my vision. So, I decided to work at a telephone booth, which was just a few metres away from my home. Mobile phones had not yet become part of everyone's life. People who came frequently to make calls at the 'STD booth' were truck drivers, small businessmen or lovers. Other than them, other people needed to call only in case of extreme emergency. I was paid Rs 10 a day, amounting to Rs 300 a month. My job involved counting the number of calls, noting them down in a register, taking money and keeping a record of everyday transactions. When the owner of the booth was not there, boys from the basti came to sit, chat and pass the time. Books or literature were not part of these formative years of my life.

Then my mother's elder sister's son, Suresh Bhau, told me that the industrial training institute (ITI) had a scope in terms of easy and skilled employment. 'You might get a government job if you have an ITI diploma,' he said. I believed him. He was one those many men I knew who, years later, succumbed to alcohol and died in Hyderabad, alone, away from home. He held the electrician diploma from the ITI and aspired for a job in the electricity department of the state. He never got one.

After a year, I applied for the course of fitter, to train in doing fittings, as he had suggested. I got the admission. On my first day at the ITI, which was just next to the Deekshabhoomi premises, surrounded with thick trees and their silence, I stepped into replica of the world that I hated and had decided to shun. The ITI campus was the miniature version of industrial terrain of the city, the MIDC. I had worked in one of the factories there and had decided not to go there again. This industrial terrain was bleak. Its factories reflected a world that was devoid of any beauty: dark, black smoke flaring from chimneys, chemical smells from some factories, dust, workers with dejected faces and worn-out bodies.

The ITI campus replicated this for me. In it, there were various departments, such as fitter, turner, machinist, welder, electrical, sheet metal, etc. The ITI was a state invention, to produce skilled workers for various industries. It was not the place one would find hope in when it came to a fulfilling life or a bright future. I disliked it at first sight. I asked myself: *Do I want to be a part of a plethora of those nameless workers that society does not care about?* The ITI was an institute where the majority of students were from Dalit–Bahujan castes, hailing from remote villages of Vidarbha, joining it with a hope of obtaining a 'secure' livelihood. The ITI made a class out of themselves, a class of workers with skills, a class whose working hours are determined, whose wages are determined, whose free time is also determined when they join factories. These thoughts would run through my head. I had no idea why. Within a couple of days, I felt out of place. The atmosphere demanded a certain kind of roughness that I knew I lacked. I dropped out of the ITI.

In those days, Suresh Bhau was doing an apprenticeship at the Maharashtra State Electricity Board (MSEB). He was convinced that, after his apprenticeship, he would get a government job there. He was disappointed when he came to know that I had quit the ITI. I remember we both went to Khurajgaon, to my mother's parental home. I think he had some farm- or land-related work to discuss with my uncles. 'If not this, then what you plan to do in life?' Suresh Bhau asked me. 'You have screwed up a good chance,' he said. His empathetic, blunt words disturbed me. I was convinced I had made a big mistake. For the first time in my youth, I cried before someone. All I could say was: 'I'll try next year.' Within a year, I had changed two colleges, one institute and three courses. Was I confused? Today, I am convinced I was not. I was in search of something else without knowing what it was.

The next year, in 2002, I applied to the ITI again. I got a seat in the turner course. I was going to learn to operate the lathe machine and to make mechanical parts, from screws to nuts and bolts to gears. Guilt was silently pushing me into the harsh world I had intended to shun. This time, I stayed on, for two years.

There were twelve students in this course. All were boys. Out of twelve, six were Dalits. We called ourselves '*Jaibhim wallah*' (people who hail Dr Ambedkar). Maybe because we were in the majority, maybe because of our common history and growing up in Dalit bastis, I did not feel as alienated as before.

It was a part-applied and part-theoretical course. Our instructor belonged to a carpenter caste. He was good at teaching us the procedures for fixing mechanical parts at the lathe machine. He would take a metal bar, fix it to the lathe wheel and ask us to observe silently while he explained each move and why he was doing it. During most of the classes, he was drunk and reeked of alcohol. But no one seemed to mind. Once he left, we poked fun at him. There was none among us who had not been slapped in the face by him. He hated being ignored. And initially, we undermined his authority. In the theory classes, he would come, speak for a few minutes, then give his copy to Sumedh, one of my classmates, and ask him to read aloud what was written in it, so we could jot that down in our books. And he would leave, either to chat with the other instructors or to go off drinking.

Sumedh was one of the six Dalit students in class. His father had served in the military, in the Mahar Regiment. After retirement from the army, he was given a job at the General Post Office, Nagpur (GPO). When I met Sumedh, his father had retired from the GPO. This way, he had two pensions. He, too, would drink every day, like my father. Because of this, money at home was never enough. Sumedh's mother had died when he was still a young boy. Despite growing up in this emotionally challenging environment, Sumedh managed to learn to make a way for himself in the world. While still in school, he started working to pay for his studies. This made him street-smart very early in life. I secretly admired him because of how he dealt with things and how he handled situations, something at which I had never been good. He was five years older than me. His was a tale of one of those people who are forced to mature before their body can accommodate the maturity.

It did not take much effort to get along with him.

*

If you don't plant the seed of a dream in a child's mind, then, sometimes, their barren mind begets weeds. Confusion was the weed that sprouted in my mind for a long time. I swayed with its natural rhythm, going wherever it took me. I did not see things as moral or immoral. The only criterion for me to do a thing was the pleasure principle. I liked all those things that excited my body and imagination, which intoxicated my senses in all possible ways. Sumedh was somewhat like me. I was seventeen, he twenty-two. One day, we students were sitting at the chai *tapri* (a tea stall) outside the ITI and he suggested we all drink. I had never tried alcohol until then. All others refused. I was the only one who neither refused nor consented. The very thought of drinking excited me. I had seen my father drinking all his life. I wanted to experience what it was about alcohol that made him weird and talkative, as if he had two different personalities. There was only one problem. Neither of us had the money to buy alcohol.

Sumedh was an artful planner. He had already thought of how to arrange the money. Every day, while cycling to the ITI from his home, he noticed a scrap shop on the way where you could sell old newspapers and defunct metal things. His plan was to hide the metal components that we made on the lathe machine as a part of our practical lessons in our bags and sell them at the scrap shop. He knew the price of various liquors and had already inquired about the rate for one kilogram of scrap. Accordingly, we filled our bags. We sold the metal and bought beer from a nearby shop. Surprisingly, I felt no fear. It was thrilling. There was a small piece of empty land behind the ITI. It was green, bushy and had many trees. If we went a little deep into it, we disappeared from the world. Sumedh had already zeroed in on this place. That was the first time I tasted beer. The first sip was bitter, acidic, and it tickled the fabric of my brain. It also wildly increased my appetite. We stole and we drank. Nothing was as thrilling and freeing as that.

We did this once or twice in a month. On other days, we planned for movies. The nearest cinema hall from the ITI was Panchsheel. In those days, the rate for a balcony seat was Rs 30, reserve Rs 20 and front Rs 10. We could not afford the balcony nor reserve. My father had introduced me to this theatre. *Border* was the last movie I had seen with him there. It was also the last time I had gone to that theatre. That was in 1997. Five years later, I went to watch a movie there with Sumedh. Now it was *my* life, without him—to seek an escape from the 'life' we had inherited. In those two years at the ITI, we went frequently to movie theatres. It was our favourite pastime, the only way to feed our imaginative faculties.

Then one day, Sumedh suggested that we should get laid. He said, 'We should go to Ganga Jamuna and fuck.' Ganga Jamuna was the infamous red-light district in Nagpur. 'Decent' people reserved contempt for this word. But we did not see things as good or bad, moral or immoral. Also, we were at an age when one tends to challenge all conventions and morals of the world. And with Sumedh, I was learning to explore the various dimensions of fear, which often made me certain of my needs and desires. I tread into labyrinths of desire in which I chose to get lost and find myself anew. Besides, for us, morality and immorality had been defined by the very same society which defined us as *untouchables*. No, I did not know this then. I was only certain about my needs, my desires, my pleasures. And this certainty was no less than a rebellion against the world.

Sumedh knew the way to Ganga Jamuna. We decided to ride only one bicycle. Since he knew the way, he rode and I sat on the carrier. We passed through the railway station, Gandhibagh and Central Avenue Road. As we neared the place, my heart started beating fast. I was excited. Afraid. Finally when we turned left, off the main road, we entered the district. It was a different world—a world within the world, a small world shunned by the dominant world. Women and girls stood on either side of the road, wearing striking make-up and fancy clothes, influenced by the latest Bollywood movies, to allure customers. They were whistling, calling and signalling to the men who stood by the paanshop and those who were passing by but could not take their eyes off them. Most of the men there were drunk. It was a world to which you are immediately drawn. It was not the idea of having sex that attracted men to the brothel but the gloomy eyes of those sex workers, whom we call 'prostitutes', in which men seek love, acceptance and solace from loneliness. We were there, driven by the unbearable absence of loving touch and care in our lives. Each customer there is a consumer of flesh. But he does not know that each time he consumes the flesh, he also consumes the darkness of this place. My eighteen-year-old self knew only one thing: *we were hungry for sex, and sex workers were the ones who could feed us.* I was restless to know how it would feel to see and touch a naked body.

We parked the bicycle. We went into one of the narrow alleys. The women's existence was fascinating, their eyes sullen. Some of them were sitting as if posing for an artist and waiting to be drawn, eternalized into a painting. Sumedh pinched my hand at one moment. I was lost until then. He signalled me to stop. 'We should ask her,' he said. She was wearing a white t-shirt, with her cleavage overtly exposed. A whiff of her

strong perfume incited my sense of smell. Her big eyes had
a glimpse of emptiness in them. 'How much?' Sumedh asked
her. 'Fifty rupees for each,' she said plainly. We had Rs 70 in
total. But he was persuasive. 'We have only seventy rupees in
total. We did not know the rate. Will that do?' He told her this
with desperate and shameful honesty. 'Do you think you are
standing in a vegetable market to bargain?' she replied, eyeing
us with an expression of surprise and disgust. The air was
heavy with clouds of weed smoke and incense sticks, turning
the atmosphere into intoxicating festivity in which the path to
one's pleasure goes through another's grief.

After a while, she agreed. '*Andar aao* (come in),' she said
dismissively. We entered the room, which was narrow, messy
and smelled like a dungeon. Humidity and heat made it
suffocating. Posters of Bollywood heroes and heroines alongside
gods and goddesses were ceremoniously hung on the badly
painted wall. She turned on the light, but the murkiness of the
room did not dissipate. '*Pehle kaun aayega* (who'll come first)?'
she asked, without looking at us while taking off her jeans. 'You
go,' Sumedh said. 'You go,' I retorted. '*Pehli bar kar rahe ho kya*
(are you a virgin)?' she said. Sumedh stepped in. A sheer curtain
separated me from them. She ordered him to remove the pants.
He did. She made him wear a condom. She then lay down on
the bed and spread her legs in the air as if opening her wings.
She took hold of his penis and aimed it at her vagina. Sumedh
started stroking himself. He ejaculated, sooner than he expected.
He put on his pants and went outside. Then it was my turn.
My heart was beating fast, but my body was working at a steady
pace. 'You should not take this much time,' Sumedh said when
I came out.

It was my first touch of a woman's naked body. I had no idea
that she may have been *forced* to allow my touch as a part of her

subjugation in a brothel. I had no idea about all these conspiracies of men against other human beings. After that, we went to Ganga Jamuna a couple more times during the course of the two years at the ITI. Each time I went, I returned with a sense of pleasure combined with a nagging feeling of emptiness. On my return, I had already forgotten that face. It was not like what I had seen in porn videos. It was not like what Hindi movies portrayed. It was something the world had hidden from me. Back then, it was too profound a mystery to be solved—the mystery of patriarchal men when they want to feel women but at the same time hurt them in so many unimaginable ways.

A decade later, when I started writing poems, I reflected on this phase of my life. I was convinced that I lacked the ability and vocabulary to understand what had led me or us there. Curiosity? Excitement? Sexual urge? Pleasure? It was not that simple to put into a few verbs or adjectives. Maybe it was possible through metaphors. Maybe it was possible for poetry at least to decipher the unseen force or untold needs that I carried within me. A decade later, I wrote a poem about this, and in it, I criminalized myself without intending to do so.

An Unknown Crime

In the age
When no school taught
The language
Of grim eyes

He paid money
And saw
The naked vagina
For the first time

A child
Unaware of a murder
Tasting the blood
Of an unknown crime

                              *

I began to like staying away from home. I liked to think of myself
as an individual, having no family, no one—just me, alone,
wild, boundless and free to do what satisfied my senses. My
imagination was moving into strange terrains of pleasure. I began
to like being alone. By the end of the first year at the ITI, I started
to work in a factory. My first day at the gear-making factory
was uneventful. In fact, no day in the factory is ever eventful. I
reached the factory an hour prior to the shift. Since it was my
first day, I needed to be oriented about the work and procedures.
The man from the earlier shift received me with a rather sceptical
look. He was short, wore a pair of spectacles and had a short
white beard. He spoke less than I expected. Rather, he asked me
to silently observe him doing the work. I did not find it difficult
to operate the computer numerical control (CNC) lathe in his
absence. But the work required physical strength and alertness.
Every two minutes, I had to de-clamp the finished gear and
clamp on the material for the new one. One gear weighed half
a kilogram. My hands turned black and coarse with the dust of
iron by the end of the shift. It was only for a week that I worked
in the afternoon shift. Since I had the ITI classes during the day,
I had no choice but to work in the night shift. Typically, workers
hate night shifts, especially those who are married. I was rather
excited. The other operators were glad to hear me ask to work in
the night shift for all weeks. I acquired the smell of the factory as
days, or rather nights, went by.

For Dr Ambedkar, the cultivation of the mind, the life of intellectualism, was the highest form of life. Factory work made the mind too tired to realize this quest. It did not spare me either. I remember how, in my basti, old people used to keep time with the factory sirens. The industrial area was near us. I had grown up seeing people from my basti working in factories, from Thursdays through Tuesdays. Wednesdays were off. It was the routine of their lives. There was no thrill, no newness in it. Working for years at factories made their bodies stiff, their loneliness grotesque. I wondered if it was possible to conceive any dream in such an existence. They were diligent workers, but the kind of atmosphere in which they worked prevented them from realizing the relevance and urgency of Dr Ambedkar's words. It was like coming out of the old prison because it was dilapidated and entering a new one and being relieved by its newness.

I had been working at the factory for a year. I appeared for the last examination of my course at the ITI. I failed the theory paper. From my class, I was the only one to fail. They said the ITI was all about practical learning. I was good at that. But because I had failed the theory paper, it meant I had failed the entire course. I got frustrated. I remember I drank that day with Sumedh. The next day, I went to work. I worked for two more years. I changed three factories. All these factories looked the same, and people in there too had the same temper. The majority of these workers appeared to me helpless and choice-less. For me, the workers' struggle or agitation was only a story from the past. Until then, I had not witnessed any workers' union or any agitation for their rights. All of them seemed satisfied with having work and being able to earn money to survive. When I recalled the conditions I had seen, been a part of, I was compelled to believe that the wages we were getting were below the minimum guarantee and undermined our dignity. Yet, I had heard no voice raised against it. The 'old world' of industrial capitalism that Marx talked about: I was part of it. I knew this world. I was there. I knew: When the body is tired, mind is unable to conceive anything, let alone liberation. Working for a few years at factories deprived me of two things: sleep and silence. I began to sense that the world of factories was not what I was in search of. I developed an aversion for them. Factories were tough and harsh. I desired company, affection. I felt lonely at home; I was not understood. Sumedh had left Nagpur and gone to Pune to temporarily work at a shopping mall. I had no other friends. Like never before, I felt the need to escape the home.

I left my job and went to Pune. It was the winter of 2004. Sumedh was working at a newly opened shopping mall in Bund Garden. He helped me find advertisements for work at several malls and arranged a few interviews. I did not get any of those jobs. So, I spent a month in Pune with Sumedh, drinking, roaming around or watching movies. I soon ran out of money. I returned home, burdened by a sense of failure. It was not clear to me what I wanted. I did not have anyone who would listen to my doubts. At home, we did not talk about such things. Maybe I grew up like this, or maybe I inherited this way of being. The ability to deal with pain is an instinctual pattern you inherit from your parents as much as you inherit their blood. And you start growing as an individual the day you realize this. Because then you break this pattern. Some break this pattern early. For others, it is only possible through an escape from home. For me, it was possible only after facing the fear of being alone.

*

Men Don't Cry?

I think of myself, being born like that child
Who has lost in light, found in darkness
Who has walked like a hermit in the forest wild;
A flower, plucked from the tree and put into a vase

It was 2005. I was twenty years old. I was growing up, lost, without any idea of the work or studies I wanted to pursue. But there was a growing sense, a voice inside my head as if it was shouting: *escape*. I started searching for options. One day I went to an internet cafe to search for an option for a career and a field of study. I was always fascinated by the idea of leaving home, to go outside and make my own life. But there was simply no one to tell me how. On the wall of an internet cafe, I saw an advertisement printed on plain white paper. It said: *Join Merchant Navy & Sail Around The World*. I jotted down the number given with this advertisement. I phoned the number. I was told to come over to the office.

It was a home and not an office that I saw when I reached there the next day. The man introduced himself as an officer from a merchant ship, now on vacation. He must have been in his early thirties and appeared to me a secretive man, hiding behind his covert knowledge about sea life. He claimed that he wanted to help young people join the merchant navy. He told me thrilling tales about ships, voyages, sea travels and the money crew members earn on ships. Everything sounded impressive. It sounded like the idea of life I wanted to live. Little did I know that it was not as easy as it sounded for people like me. In fact, it was difficult from the beginning. Money was the first difficulty. He said that to complete the course from a marine academy, I had to pay about Rs 60,000. His commission was 10 per cent. He was one of those agents across India who got young boys admitted into such marine academies and earned commissions from it. They had unwritten pacts with the academies. These agents sold alluring dreams of being seafarers to young boys and then abruptly cut themselves loose from this dream. It was a huge network of marine academies, agents and candidates. I discovered this when after finishing the course I tried a few times and visited offices in Mumbai that provide marine jobs, only to discover that to find a decent job in this field, you either need connections or money to begin with. I knew nothing of it then, as I was living in the negation of truth. All I desired was escape at all costs.

Asking my father for the money was out of the question. He was not in the least interested in my career and hardly aware of what I was studying or doing. So I asked my mother. 'Sixty thousand!' she said in a voice that filled with worry and anxiety—worried because she never had that money and anxious because she was thinking that because of the lack of money, I may never be able to pursue the training at the marine academy. After fifteen years today, if I imagine her expression in that moment, the moment which seized her face with worry and fear, I feel guilty. I was blinded by selfishness. I was persistent and pressured her emotionally. So she borrowed the money from a Dalit woman from our basti who used to lend money at 10 per cent interest. 10 per cent monthly of 60,000 was 6000. Even the interest amount was huge. Nevertheless, my mother borrowed the money for a period of six months. The course at the marine academy was for three months. I was putting her into a big financial burden, but I was barely conscious of it. I was living the fantasy that after the course, employment in the merchant navy would pay huge amounts. And the more fascinating idea than this was the thought of getting away from home.

*

In the winter of that year, I booked a train ticket for Mumbai. My training at the marine academy was to begin two days after I reached there. My mother could hardly afford any extra money. So I had a demand draft for the fees and enough money to travel to the academy once I reached Mumbai. I did not have a single rupee extra. I did not dare to ask my mother. It was my first time in Mumbai, and the very idea of the city, constructed in my mind by Bollywood movies and tales from people who had been there, kept me excited until I reached there. The agent who arranged my admission there instructed me about the routes of buses and local trains to reach the academy. It was situated in CBD Belapur, Navi Mumbai. He said that from Thane, there was a direct bus to CBD Belapur. I followed his instructions. When the train left Nagpur, I was excited and equally scared to think of what was lying ahead. As the night advanced, the chilly winds furtively invaded the compartment through gaps in the windows and doors. As the train moved ahead, one world was disappearing behind me. I was reaching closer to another world I had never seen, the world in which

I would be alone, the world in which I desperately wanted to lose myself.

*

B.P. Marine Academy was a ten-storey building. To my eyes, it felt like an unimaginably huge structure because it was the first time I was entering such a building. Some floors had administrative offices; other floors were classrooms and hostels; there was a huge terrace which had a cafeteria similar to the structure of a lighthouse. The interior of the building was designed like that of a ship. Walking across it for the first time, the building *felt* like a ship. The day I entered the building, I did not know that it was only after four months that I would exit it.

On the day when training began, we were allotted hostel rooms, beds and uniforms and given instructions that were meant to be followed strictly. Candidates were allowed two day-time holidays in a month, on Sunday. I was not privileged to enjoy those two holidays, because I simply did not have the money to travel or spend on anything. My course here was on saloon rating. It was a training associated with kitchen tasks on the ship. In the classroom, we were taught recipes, about the functions of the onboard kitchen, the responsibilities of a saloon cadet etc. For most of the course, we were taught recipes and the etiquette of the merchant life. Here, etiquette mostly meant following the rules, protocols and maintaining discipline on the ship. We were also taught about the methods of cutting the vegetables and meat, how to use utensils carefully and how to be alert all the time, because, as they said, life on a ship is a life of alertness. Only once did we get to cook in the kitchen, towards the end of the course.

Each day was scheduled in the academy. We awoke at 5.30 a.m., and reported at 6.30 a.m. Apart from forty-five minutes of physical training, we had six hours of classes, punctuated by specific timings for tea, meals and rest. Muster time was at 7.30 p.m., when all the cadets came together to start with their physical training for the day. We went to bed at 10 p.m. Except Sunday, each day was defined by this rigid schedule. Everyone had formed their groups on the basis of their linguistic identity or their class, their social status. There was an invisible wall between them and me, which stopped me from being seen and heard. And it was the same wall which prohibited me from entering their world.

For me, Sunday was timeless, like eternity. On Sundays, while all the others went out to explore the city, to roam around, to eat at restaurants and watch movies, I was there waiting for Monday so I could camouflage my loneliness amidst the noise of people who made me invisible. I was there, but I was simply nobody, probably because I did not have the privilege of language or smartness or boldness which the better-off and dominant-caste boys there had. They spoke loudly and were physically well-built. They called it *being tough*. Almost all of them came here with a legacy of having someone from their family in the merchant navy. They knew the profession, they had the money and they knew someone who could help them get a job on a ship. I had none of that. As the days passed, I became more conscious of this fact. Here, only the clock kept me busy from the hurt of being excluded. There was no female candidate in the academy when I was there. It was a man's world. Boys from all linguistic backgrounds and majorly from the dominant castes were there. Their confidence, affluent clothes and gadgets reflected their background. There seemed to be nothing called 'caste' here. And yet, it was at the very root of the social fabric all around me in the academy. We were all aspiring seafarers. And we needed to be tough, physically and mentally. To be mentally tough here was to tolerate and ignore curses and abuse from the seniors—these were part of sea life, we often heard from instructors. I remember that one of the instructors, who was a Christian and known for his strict behaviour and discipline, called me 'Kaliya' (blackie) on more than a few occasions. My complexion was much darker back then. Whenever he said 'Kaliya', I felt he utterly hated my complexion more than my mistakes.

The physical training never interested me; I wanted to learn to cook, but the course was more about adapting to a sailor's life than what I had imagined. I had no one to turn to, so I stuck to the schedule. By following the timetable, I felt I was simply approaching the day of my return home, which I had marked in my diary. One cross for each day. Each night, when I crossed off the day, I told myself: *One more day has gone. One more day nearer to returning home.* This was the only feeling, the only thought, which made me happy during my four-month stay at the academy. Strangely, I started to find comfort in the idea of home. Something in me drastically changed, and I did not know what it was.

On every Sunday, we were allowed to make a phone call at home. There was a pay phone installed on one of the floors. Each one-rupee coin allowed a minute of talk-time. I had saved some coins: my only privilege to talk to the ones at home in real time. Many boys who talked over the phone with their families seemed to have happy conversations. Some boys never called home. They seemed to have everything that made them feel comfortable. We did not have a phone in our house. So I used to call my neighbour's phone, exactly between 6.30 p.m. and 7 p.m., when my mother would be waiting there, anticipating my call. Whenever she asked 'How are you?', I replied 'I am good.' It was a lie. Now I understand that I was not 'good'. We really did not converse much. Sometimes my mother would ask me if I needed money. She did not have any, but she had the vision to ask if I needed any, and she meant it. She would have arranged it if I needed it. Knowing that she had arranged the money on interest to pay my fees at the academy, I could not gather the courage to ask her for more. I felt guilty. I began to sense that I had put her into financial problems. But she seemed to have perceived things differently. She said, 'If you study well, this problem will no longer be there.' Listening to this, I could not help but feel the need to cry. But I did not. Here, at this place, we were being trained to be *tough*. I suppressed the need to cry. But I was not wrong to feel that way. I was right in feeling the need to cry. I, who imagined an escape from home, was homesick. I felt emotional, I felt real—as if I wanted to cry for centuries. Sixteen years later, I wrote a poem, reminiscing about this moment from the academy. Surprisingly, I titled this poem 'Cowards':

> Since I am a human being,
> My eyes get wet invisibly
> Whenever I must leave my parents
> To find my 'life' in a strange city,
> But no tears roll out
>
> I was taught by cowards that
> Men don't cry

This poem brought me clarity about myself, about the side of myself that I have always protected from everyone. Cowards. Yes, I called those men cowards who taught us to be tough, because they defy the simple truth: the gift life has given us of expressing emotions. Revisiting those moments, I imagine that men are indoctrinated by society and institutions to hide their emotions, which make them appear feeble. I have witnessed this in the academy. It was all in front of my eyes. This poem was access for me to the institutionalization of men into reacting subjects. I began to sense that each suppressed emotion transmutes into violent energy in men. I feel one of the reasons men turn coarse and insensitive and dominating is because they are taught by society and its institutions not to respond to their emotions in a generous way, to give expression to their emotions freely. Men are taught to cling to their outward toughness even though they are shatteringly weak inside. Sometimes, to express the weakness is the biggest strength one can exercise. Sometimes, we need to weep, but we are trained not to. And in this society that treats men according to their castes, we all are psychologically terrorized. And men here cling to their toughness to the extent it crushes them as human beings.

The reason for my homesickness at the academy was not merely the absence of love or attention. It was the existence of unkindness around me. In my home, in the Dalit basti, I was not 'a part apart'.[1] I was a part of the whole. In the academy, I was a part apart. When many boys were able to buy food in their free time from the canteen, I simply looked at it and cursed the rising desire to eat: I did not have the money to buy any. Hunger was relentless at this age. The days were busy with physical activities too, which helped quickly digest the food from the academy's cafeteria, which was prepared with a generous amount of soda. I ate at 1.30 p.m., but I was hungry again by 4 p.m. I learnt to suppress the hunger to the extent I later became capable of distinguishing between needs and desires and to the extent I remained trapped in the tussle between need and desire for a long time.

I was neither sad nor happy when the day of graduating from the academy arrived. I was scared. In the academy, no one bothered about how we received the training and what it made of us. This place was intended to train us into the same creatures, who learn to take orders and respect hierarchies. The reason I developed fear is because I failed to develop interest in the idea of the world that the academy instilled in me. I sensed that I would not survive in this rough and tough world. The burden of money for my mother was going to be more real and heavy now. But all I thought about was myself. I hardly thought of her and how she would repay the money. My selfishness kept me immature and insensitive for a long time. But I consciously I refused to see it.

Sometimes, I think I never even went to the marine academy. Maybe because it needs two people to create a memory, and I remember virtually no one. My memory of the time at the academy is mostly eroded. What is left is the interpretation of my feelings, emotions, reactions and silence from this place.

My mother had sent me a money order of Rs 400 two weeks before the end of the course to buy a train ticket. I bought a ticket and, after two weeks, I was back home, more lonely and even more lost that before.

*

Khairlanji: Know My Place

I am a dream, a song, of that historical tree
Who didn't beget fruit but a wounded history,
But I sheltered those birds who will break this cage
Despite being erased like a wrong word on the right page

Of all the things I learnt at academy, the sense of my being unfit in the different cultures was the most decisive one for me. The academy was a cultural shock, and it was also the experience that taught me that the world outside my basti was insensitive to my existence. Yet, the world outside was the reality I had to step into, one day. How would my mother repay the huge amount of money that she borrowed for my fees? This thought kept recurring. I decided to give the merchant navy a try. So I found an agency in Nagpur that advertised in the paper about recruiting for positions in the merchant navy. I visited their office.

The person there was a lean, young-looking boy, sly but polite while convincing the candidates. His name was Mr Chandel—a Rajput, he told me. He asked for some Rs 30,000 as his fees to get me a job on a ship. I told my mother, and she again borrowed, anticipating that I would get a job after this. I paid him the money. He kept calling me for this and that matter. Sometimes, he would say that my weight wasn't enough to be recruited on the ship. So I went on increasing my weight. Then he gave a few more excuses. Months passed. I got frustrated. He told me that they had a marine academy in Hyderabad where I should go and work for a couple of months. In that way, I would be busy and remain in touch with marine job updates, he said.

I went to Hyderabad. The academy was situated in a residential building. Its director, Mr Sharma, they said, was in Dubai. I worked there for two months, but nothing positive came of it; I was not paid a single penny. Eventually, I got depressed and asked the agent to return my money. He gave me excuses and tried to convince me that I would get a job. I was insistent. He then gave me a cheque, which bounced. I smelled something fishy. Then, my mother and I made rounds of his office in Nagpur innumerable times. Finally, we succeeded in getting some money back, but not the entire amount we had paid. He was arrested by the police for several cases of fraud, I learnt many years later. A year had already passed while we chased after him for the money. I could hardly imagine what my mother was going through. Despite this, she was resolute in bringing things on track. She asked me to take up some job. It would have been cruel of me to refuse. I thought of focusing on my own study once again. But, my situation demanded me to sweat and earn, to wipe out the guilt in my heart. At this point, my father became invisible from the crucial affairs of my life.

*

I got a job as a data entry operator. My new office was situated in Shankar Nagar. It ran in three shifts: morning, afternoon and night. I preferred the night shift. I liked the deserted road at night, the cool breeze and the silence that impregnated the sense of time. It was 2006, the first week of October. I would return early in the morning from the night shift. One day, I remember I was sleeping and suddenly I woke up to cacophony—there was the sound of burning tyres, rushing vehicles, shouts and cries of people, the siren of police jeeps and slogans, hailing Dr Ambedkar. It was a noise of discontent. I went to the door and saw that the entire village was gathered on the ground in front of my house, where the Buddha Vihara was situated. Back then, it did not have compound walls. So the entire scene was naked to my eyes. There was a frenzy in the air. My parents asked me and my sisters to stay inside. The previous night, when I had left for the office, the basti appeared to me as it has always been: slow, monotonous and bleak. A couple of days earlier, on 29 September, a Mahar-Buddhist family in the village of Khairlanji in the Vidarbha region was brutally raped, tortured, paraded naked and massacred by caste-Hindus: men and women of that village who belonged to Kunbi and other OBC castes.[1] What I was witnessing now in front of my eyes was the eruption of rage against this heinous caste-atrocity.

This eruption was justified. Nonetheless, it was unorganized. It was spontaneous. The Khairlanji massacre shook the Dalits (Mahar-Buddhists) to the core, and many such outraged eruptions sprung up across cities and villages in Maharashtra. It shook other Dalits outside Maharashtra too. But it did not even touch the conscience of most non-Dalits. Because if non-Dalits were shaken by it, then Bhaiyalal Bhotmange (the lone survivor of the massacre) would not have died awaiting justice. In my basti, I saw young boys and women stopping vehicles, burning tyres on the road, shouting slogans—in protest. Their loud cries gave the impression that their own family had been raped and massacred.

Even the description of the killing and rape of Surekha (mother), Priyanka (daughter), Roshan (son) and Sudhir (son) causes nausea. Imagine the insanity of people who committed this crime? While giving his statement to the authorities, these were Bhaiyalal Bhotmange's words: 'The entire village was involved, sir. Entire village.'[2] The entire village included both men and women. This is the undeniable fact. No upper caste or OBC women from this village raised their voice in protest against this massacre. The reason was simple. Their complicity in this massacre is more than apparent.

Almost a decade later, when I went to one of the premier institutions for social sciences in India for my post-graduation, I witnessed that such instances create a small ripple of solidarity among many Brahmin/Savarna boys and girls and nowadays in social media spaces. And then these ripples wane with their flights to foreign universities or their return to their caste-ghettoes. They fail to understand the dynamics of caste crimes because they never honestly contemplate the relationship between their privileges and caste-atrocities. They presume solidarity between like-minded people from all castes, even Brahmins. But when it comes to Dalit atrocities, it is Dalits against entire India. This is the bitter truth. History tells us that only Dalits were forced to make sacrifices for the cause of Dalits, barring a few rare exceptions. This is a caste-nation. No superior caste can liberate the caste below it because the existence of the superior caste relies on keeping the caste below it inferior. They don't understand that caste follows those Dalits who intend to annihilate it to the grave.

The day of protest in my basti was the first mass agitation I witnessed in my life. Things had been planned, although they did not seem to be. Men and women were hauled inside police vans and taken into police custody. The police marched inside the basti with lathis and equipment meant to deal with riots. I saw lady police constables pulling women by their hair and taking them into custody, while the shouts of the people continued, demanding the arrest of the rapists and murderers involved in the Khairlanji massacre. According to some estimates, across Maharashtra, thousands of Mahar-Buddhist men and women were taken into custody and charged with false cases in the post-Khairlanji protests. This was obviously an assault on the spirit of the protest and protestors, who were demanding justice. The violence of the police that day exposed to me the place of my basti in this society, and consequently mine too.

This memory has grown inside me. It has become a memory of who we are in this society. That day was the first time I witnessed our powerlessness before the state. How we perceived ourselves was not the way the state saw us. We were mishaps, blunders in their eyes, especially when we demanded justice. Our idea of justice was their defeat. The Brahminical state and society was fully aware of this. The Brahminical state was too powerful and pervasive to be defeated by mere protests; we seemed to have forgotten this.

Back then, I saw this incident in isolation. It was only after leaving Nagpur for many years that I came to know that there is a Khairlanji in every Indian state. Khairlanji takes place frequently in this caste-nation. Such massacres are so frequent that maybe another one is taking place even as I am writing this. So much energy, years of youth, time, emotions and feelings have been invested by thousands of Dalits across the country to fight for justice. Yet, we wait, for it seems to be never-ending. The story of Khairlanji is the story of many such atrocities. Caste-Hindus involved in such atrocities hate Dalits who pursue the life of the mind, who refuse to live by caste rules. Caste-Hindus outnumber Dalits in villages. In urban spaces, they deploy other means to erase the presence of Dalits and, if needed, stigmatize them.[3]

Two years after this, in 2008, the book *Khairlanji: A Strange and Bitter Crop* by Anand Teltumbde, one of the leading intellectuals and academicians in India, was published. It laid bare the intricacies of caste violence, of which I was not aware earlier. I read it a year later. But except feeling anger and reactions inside me, I did not understand much of the book. For me, caste violence was still a distant reality. I was wrong. I marked a few lines in the book. At that time, I did not fully understand their implications in making me aware of caste violence. But the *subconscious* of a Dalit, born and brought up in a Dalit basti, tends to get formed differently. It sees what is hidden. This is because it is the subconscious of one who has been made invisible by society. When I picked up the book later, my earlier annotations revealed this to me. More than a discovery of what and how I think, it was evidence of me acquiring clarity—about myself in relation to caste-society.

These are those lines I have marked from the book:

At the time of the atrocity, Khairlanji had a population of 787 distributed among 181 families belonging to OBCs, dalits (Scheduled Castes) and adivasis (Scheduled Tribes). The OBCs (kunabi, teli, kalar, lodhi, dhivar, vadhai) constituted an overwhelming majority with about 750 persons; there were 10 gond (adivasi) families. The village had only three families of dalits excluding the Bhotmanges—two belonging to the mahar and one to mang (matang) castes respectively.[4]

I labelled this paragraph with these words: 'the greater the number of caste-Hindus, the greater the degree of violence in caste atrocity'.

I further imagined: 'These dalit families lived in the terror of the shudra-OBCs of Khairlanji.'[5]

This I interpreted as: 'No Bahujanwad (intercaste solidarity) is possible between Dalits and OBC Hindus, unless OBCs abandon Hinduism and embrace a religious teaching which advocates equality, rationality and a scientific attitude.'

'Politically, the village is said to be in the grip of the Hindu nationalist Bharatiya Janata Party.'[6]

I decoded this sentence with these words: 'No party led by Brahmins/Savarnas could put an end to atrocities on Dalits. The Congress was ruling the state at the time of the Khairlanji massacre. Dalit atrocities were happening before the existence of the Congress or the BJP. Party politics does not change how caste-Hindus think about Dalits.'

> The Bhotmange land, being close to the village's Pench canal, was irrigated. However, owing to caste discrimination, it was never easy for the Bhotmanges to get water from the canal. They would draw water from the canal either during the nights or at daybreak to avoid problems with the villagers. The Bhotmanges laboured hard on their farmland and lived a contented life in their thatched hut built at the edge of the village on panchayat land.[7]

I read this in this way: 'Dalits are hard workers, and their ability to digest the poison of caste is unparalleled, especially when they are nurturing a vision for their children.'

'The family reportedly also faced discrimination in accessing drinking water at the village well. The Bhotmanges raised their four children in this hut under such adverse conditions.'[8]

I imagined: 'Dalit parents who carry the vision of education for their children and toil for it sow the seeds of liberation on this casteist soil.'

'In 2005, Surekha had bought a bicycle for Priyanka, who rode it daily to her junior college. All these features, coupled with the family's fierce refusal to conform to the expectations of the caste-Hindu villagers, generated envy and resentment.'[9]

I jotted down: 'Caste made Savarnas so pathological that they could not digest a fearless and rational life being lived by Dalits. The Savarna's mind is caste. Caste is the Savarna mind.'

'Bhaiyalal Bhotmange was a simple and mild-mannered person and would keep quiet—but not Surekha. More often than not it was Surekha who stood up to the caste-Hindu tormentors and tried to pay them back in their own coin.'[10]

I thought: 'Savarna men hate Dalit women who are assertive, so much so that they nurse gruesome feelings of violence against them, which translate into the rape and murder of Dalit women.'

*

After this, I no longer remained the same person as I had thought of myself earlier. *What I think of myself is not what the world thinks of me*, I told myself. This was the first realization. Khairlanji became emblematic for my generation to remember our vulnerabilities in caste-society. But I hated to remind myself of my vulnerabilities. I refused to acknowledge them for a long time. Perhaps, that is the reason why, for a long time, I deliberately withheld myself from getting involved with narratives of Dalit atrocities. I felt I would sink into the darkness of its stories. Bhaiyalal Bhotmange, the sound of his name, his face, his eyes, became engraved in my mind as the bleakness this country carries in its life. His world, his family, had been destroyed. Even if he would have got justice, what could he have done with that? He died in 2017, of a heart attack. I never gathered the courage to look into his eyes, even when they appeared in the newspaper or on TV. His eyes were a gateway to the pain and sadness this country has been carrying for centuries. He died without receiving any justice. Perhaps there was no justice available on the earth for what he had gone through.

Seventeen years later, I went to watch a movie in a theatre—*Asuran*. It was a Tamil movie, starring Dhanush in the lead role. I did not know Tamil. I went to watch it alone, under the impression that it would have English subtitles. It did not. In that engrossing darkness of the theatre, I sat amid a Tamil-speaking audience in Mumbai. After a while, I felt no need for subtitles. I was following the story. I was *into* the story. It was a story I had heard, which was engraved in my memory as a part of growing up. While watching *Asuran*, I could not help myself from imagining Khairlanji in front of my eyes. *Asuran* was the extended version of Khairlanji, with the vision of Khairlanji coming into reality. I proposed its review to my friend Krupa, who was working at silverscreenindia.com. I simply wrote that review as an extended version of Khairlanji, not as an event, but as a story that had a dream, and that dream had come to realization through the movie. Maybe for the first time, I felt the strength of storytelling through cinema. The visual imagination of *Asuran* had transcended for me the meaning of a brutal event. Probably for the first time, I experienced cinema as an integral part of my memory and not as an imagination defeating my memories.

A year later, my friend Kunal Gaikwad sent me his poem about Khairlanji, written in Marathi. After reading it, I was no longer scared to remember Khairlanji. It helped me move beyond the darkness this incident carried in its womb. It asserted that there was a life there once, a life full of hopes and dreams and wishes. This is the poem:

The ghost of Surekha Bhotmange
must not be haunting people from Khairlanji village,
after the death, Dalits do not become ghosts,

their shadow is absent even when they are alive
after her death, in which mansion will her ghunghroo tinkle?

And
I have not heard of any folklore
saying 'a village is under the wrath of a goddess
after a woman is paraded naked'

But I have seen pervert old men
taking sadistic pleasure by assassinating the character
of a murdered woman

Sometimes
she too must have held the sun from the grass by her hand,
she must have bloomed, poking the tip of grass at her shadow's
shape,
listening to her screams, a tree was dried,
said the eyes of Bhaiyalal in the court.[11]

After reading this poem several times, my imagination of the
Khairlanji massacre rested in the grave of understanding. I
remained restless, but I gained the courage to look at the massacre
anew. My fear was replaced by the sense to look at human
existence, beyond darkness.

*

I Am Not Your Buddhist!

I am the sun; I follow my wild instinct
On the light's path through darkness,
I am a wounded deer, preyed upon by its own footprint;
I am a beautiful flower blooming in the wilderness

I had been working for six months now as a data entry operator. At this stage, I had lost the taste for academic education. My mother managed to return the interest on borrowed money as well as the principal amount. Paying huge interest on the loan hurt because it left us with no money. All my earnings and my mother's savings had gone into clearing this loan. I had no money in hand and no educational degree to speak of. I was simply working to rectify my mistakes. By this time, unlike in my childhood and even when I was at ITI, Bollywood movies had ceased to be important to me. A huge distance had grown between my father and me, simply because he had no idea of what I was going through. Equally self-defeating was the fact that I had never seen my mother as a reference point of my memories or my life.

It took me a while to feel wanted in the office where I was working. Not that I liked the people there, whose mannerisms were overtly Hindu/Brahminical—they were overtly ritualistic, orthodox and pushed their religious beliefs on to others. But I managed to give them the impression that I was not *like* them. I liked to work in the night shifts. And when we took a break, somewhere around 3.30 a.m., to have a chai and poha at Shankar Nagar square at Mishra's tapri, I would feel alive as cool winds touched my skin, the silence of the night made my feelings audible to me and I would reminisce that these were the same roads, the same neighbourhood I had once crossed with my father.

In that office, I got acquainted with Abhay. I liked him from the beginning because he seemed more empathetic while talking to people. Unlike me. He was not demeaning to anyone but he was also smart at getting things done. He was outspoken about his views. I envied that. We began to talk. I discovered that he was also a Mahar-Buddhist. And the more I talked to him and came to know him, the more I realized that he had this fine balance of emotions and reasoning while dealing with things in everyday life. And then, when he noticed that I had become interested in his ideas about Buddhism, which he frequently brought into our conversations, he introduced me to his Sangha life: a sect of Buddhism he was following and was part of, which was conceptualized and controlled by white Westerners, who called themselves *practising* Buddhists.

The night shift would end at 7 a.m. One Sunday, Abhay took me to meet his Sangha friends. There was a flat in the north of Nagpur where his Sangha friends used to meet every week. They called it a 'chapter meeting'. The flat was a calm place. It had a couple of small busts of Dr Ambedkar, portraits of the Buddha, *mala*s of beads, books, calendars and pamphlets with mystic pictures on them that I did not understand. Abhay told me that these were symbolic Buddhist pictures of Tibetan Buddhas and Bodhisattvas. It was fascinating how he explained those pictures to me. However, their resemblance to images of Hindu gods and goddesses was disturbing. I was arrested by the air of calmness that filled the room. One by one, his friends arrived. He introduced me to all of them. Candles and incense sticks were lit. In a while, they sat and began to recite Panchsheel and Buddhist prayers. Followed by it, they began to chant Tibetan mantras, which were totally alien to my ears. Then they began meditation. The bell rang softly; as its echo faded, the voice started guiding us through the process of meditation: *Now relax, watch your thoughts, let them go, look at your breath, feel your body, take a breath, let it out* etc. I followed the instructions. After twenty minutes, the voice asked us to open our eyes. Then they chatted about things, events and subjects which were new to me and sounded amusing. What had fascinated me in that room was the aura of mysticism around everything they talked about. They talked about meditation, the birth and life of the Buddha, the wisdom of Bhante (Sangharakshita, the founder of this sect) and their spiritual progress. Ambedkar as an idea or a subject was absent. They seemed to eulogize Dr Ambedkar. Unlike in Dalit bastis, in the Sangha, Ambedkar was never presented as a force in relation to justice, liberty, prosperity. Here, he was associated only with principles like compassion, wisdom and spiritual growth—principles that were practically useless and redundant for a majority of the Dalit population. After this, they cooked food and we ate. I felt I was at home but without the weight of home bearing down on my mind. It was comforting. I suddenly had a desire to be embraced.

Trailokya Bauddha Mahasangha Sahayak Gana (TBMSG) was the name of the sect of which Abhay was a part. In England, where it was founded in 1967 by Sangharakshita, whose Christian name was Denis Lingwood, it was known as Friends of Western Buddhist Order (FWBO), and they called themselves Western Buddhist Order (WBO). Around 2018, they kept one name globally: Triratna Buddhist Order (TBO) or, as it is called in India, Triratna Buddhist Mahasangh (TBM). Of all the things they seemed to offer to a person, the most appealing to me, as I felt then, was the scope of spiritual development and their stress on individualism. In their world, everything was reduced to greed, hate, anger or morality, compassion, friendship, forgiveness and containment. To me, they seemed to have the answers to all the problems of the world. It fulfilled a subconscious need I did not know I had.

But I failed to see how this worldview obscured social issues. Erase society and its oppressive systems from a person's mind in relation to his problems, and he starts putting himself in the position of the perpetrator. This is how spiritual/religious sects create a force of men who work for their agendas at the cost of forgetting their own history of oppression. At that time, morality seemed to offer the answer to my problems. I never thought that my problem was poverty, the inability to develop intellectual aspirations, confusion in pursuing education and my alienation from myself and my family. No one told me that the root of these troubles lay in the past and our present was defined by it. Abhay, though intelligent and conscious, did not mention any of this. I was totally taken in by whatever he said about spiritual development, TBM, the *Dhamma* (Pali term for Buddhism) life, Sangharakshita and how all these changed his life. I envied the smile and contentment on his face. I wanted to be able to smile like that one day; I wanted to be that happy one day.

One day, Abhay suggested that I attend the upcoming youth *shibir* (retreat), organized by youngsters associated with TBM. It was December, and it was cold. Early one Sunday morning,

Abhay arrived at my house on his motorbike. I told my mother that I would return by evening, or maybe in the morning the next day. Until that day, I had not crossed Nagpur in the west beyond Hingna. The road we took led us to Wardha through hills, jungle, villages and natural serenity. We passed through a few villages. The cool and romantic morning winds hit my cheeks and hair. On our way, I saw vehicles, herds of goats and cows, empty green fields, brooks and then mountains. That trip was transporting me to a world where the noise of my old world ceased to exist.

The place where the retreat had been organized was called Huen Tsang Retreat Centre. It was located at the small mountain, which could be seen from afar. Down the hill, there was a huge water dam, and Bor National Reserve forest. As we rode down the hill, the green terrain was clear and plain. Abhay pointed his finger in the direction of the Buddhist stupa, almost three kilometres away, the central infrastructure of the retreat centre, which was situated on the hill. As we approached the stupa, it looked grander. It felt as if the stupa was a door to a completely different world. And I was prone to drift towards the idea of any world that made me forget mine.

Since Abhay had been a part of this sect for a long time, he knew people in the retreat centre. The people here met me with a smile on their faces. Yet, it seemed that their smile was a part of some sort of compulsion. It was as if they had been trained to smile. Nevertheless, a smile wasn't unwelcome. Slightly higher up on the hill were a few dormitories, strong buildings constructed with cement and bricks, in which full-time residents stayed. The whole vicinity, with dense trees, charming birds and a few species of animals, surrounded by hills and its echoing silence, muffled by the serenity of the jungle, drew me in. I was haunted by the beauty of the place. To witness and feel the unabated peace around me, I realized I had longed for it secretly. Maybe because I was born into noise, a noise which often deafens people and makes them forget the sound of their own voice. Growing up in the basti, I had witnessed almost a chronic need to shout. As though to be alive meant to shout, to curse. Women cursed and shouted, drunken men cursed and shouted, children cursed and shouted. All homes in the basti were the same. As a child, the curses around me were loud; affection was muted.

A decade later, I read Vasant Moon's autobiography *Vasti*. In this remarkable book, he described the emergence of Dr Ambedkar as a mass leader and its effects in Mahar-wadas across Nagpur. In this book, Dalit bastis appeared to have a vibrancy of a new thought, the thought of liberation, inspired by the emancipatory ideas of Dr Ambedkar. The culture I read about in this book was missing in my basti. In my basti, Dr Ambedkar was present as a historical figure, but he was absent as a thought and force behind living. In TBM, I found Dr Ambedkar was eulogized in an empty way. Here, he was a project of representation, not of persuasion. But there was no one there to guide me about this. Most Dalit people make their way in life by following their instincts simply because there is no immediate legacy around them to guide them through generational changes. I too had my instincts. The only danger in following the path of instinct lies in the uncertainty of reaching the other end of the road.

*

I did not inform my parents about it in detail. I did not know if I was going to stay here for a days or years. The youth retreat lasted for seven days, spent in utopian discussions around constructing a new world, without being pestered by worries of survival, future and education. Hundreds of Mahar-Buddhist youth and a couple of white people were there, practising what they called 'friendship', without any reference to their histories or their pain. Spiritual sects work in this way too, especially in the life of people who are historically exploited. They negate the histories of people and their struggles and propagate a path of 'happiness' or 'self-realization' without addressing the instrumental needs of their lives: justice, education, opportunities, equal treatment etc. Dr Ambedkar's idea of Buddhism, however, addressed all of these. It took me many years to realize this distinction. With that youth retreat, I was influenced to think uncritically that home is irrelevant as well as an obstacle in one's spiritual development. I was made to think and feel and be like a spiritual Buddhist. In this persuasion, I was made to forget my small dreams, my needs, my aspirations (which they labelled 'greed' here) and my responsibilities towards the family. I too had given up because looking back at the life in basti, I could see nothing but bleakness. For a long time, I refused to accept this darkness as a part of my life. Probably that is the reason I hated life in the basti while growing up. Probably that is why I was enchanted by the peace at the retreat centre. And precisely for this reason, I decided to immerse myself into the world of TBM, where Buddhism was merely about spiritual development, individualism, beauty, friendship, happiness and the life of containment.

*

Life at the Huen Tsang Retreat Centre, which was also called by the people as Bordharan Retreat Centre, was adorned by silence, undisturbed by society and people. There were birds and there were flowers, rejuvenating the air all the time. We were seven to eight men staying in a monastery, which the people here called 'community'. All of them were Dalits, and they all had stories of pain and despair from the past. Yet, metaphysical and spiritual sermons they had received from the white members of this sect came up frequently in their conversations. At times, there were retreats for which we needed to arrange logistics, food and accommodation. During retreats, the centre used to be a lively place, because there were new people to see, to talk and exchange words with. When there was no retreat, there was harmless solitude all around.

There was always something to do. Sometimes, we dug the soil and planted trees. Sometimes, we watered plants. Sometimes, we cleaned the huge stupa in which our voice echoed. Sometimes, there was absolutely nothing to do except eating and sleeping and waiting for the day to end. Here, days were long and nights were longer. In the night, the silence was gothic and if you walked alone, from the main gate to the community place, you could feel what it means to live in the jungle, among animals and silence. There were leopards in the jungle and, often, people from the village downhill told us how their goats had been hunted by one the previous night. The sound of a leopard roaring at night was not uncommon in the summer, as it was a dry season and it needed food and water. It did not take me any effort to adapt to this life. I was immersed in it. Silently, my aspirations for education and survival and a career were being erased from my mind; because of this place, I no longer felt the need to think about outside life. I had food and a place to stay. Sometimes, that's all you need. The life here demanded no efforts from me to be alive. In this place, my body got food and my mind received stimulus from spiritual ideas. The spiritual conversations were intriguing. At least I thought so.

*

Staying with Abhay in the retreat centre helped me know him closely. He seemed more inclined to the spiritual side of life than the material or pragmatic. On more than one occasion, he told me that he wanted to dedicate his life to Dhamma. He was a Dhamma-Mitra (literally, the friend of Dhamma) as they were called in this sect. His mother was Dhammacharini (which literally means 'a practitioner of Dhamma'). Dhamma-Mitra is a beginner in this sect; Dhammachari or Dhammacharini is the person committed to the practice of Buddhism. 'Dhamma life is beautiful,' he frequently said. Peacefulness, calmness, patience, soft-spokenness, forgiveness, kindness, silence etc. Were considered beautiful in this sect. He desired nothing different.

Once, we went back to Nagpur for a day. He took me to his home. On the way, riding a bike, he narrated an incident from his life as an example of the discipline and seriousness of TBM to practise Dhamma. His father was an employee at Indian Railways. As a first-generation beneficiary of reservation policies, his father was a sensible, hard-working, aspirational Mahar-Buddhist. He was fond of prawns. One day, some members of this sect visited his home, and found out that they were eating prawns. They told his mother, who was going to be Dhammacharini, that they had to quit eating non-veg to commit to the life of Dhamma. Being an employee at the railways, his father required protein for the work, which demanded robust mental and physical exertion. Besides, prawns were a delicacy his father savoured. But for the people in TBM, Dhamma meant practising 'purity' in the consumption of food. For them, becoming a *serious* Buddhist meant consuming vegetarian food. Abhay narrated this to me proudly.

At the centre, when there were white participants in a retreat, milk, cashews, almonds and eggs were provided to them in breakfast. I never saw eggs being provided to the people who worked at the centre, maintaining it with their blood and sweat, day in and day out. No one seemed to have found any hypocrisy in this. But yes, I sensed a palpable jealousy among a few who also noticed this. But white skin has fascinated all there, including me. In the centre, I saw many Dalits becoming jovial while talking to the white people, but while talking to their own people, their bodies emitted a sense of bitterness and detachment. Whatever their reason, none seemed to recognize the existence of colonization. In fact, no one there understood what colonization was. Whatever the white people preached as Buddhism must be of extreme significance, was the widespread perception there. I was no exception.

We did not consider the white people's history of colonization, which clearly suggested that they could distort even 'religion' to imagine a world of their convenience and interests. It was impossible for them to decipher our world, let alone lead us towards better lives.

Many years later, when I expanded my circle of friends at Tata Institute of Social Sciences (TISS), who came from various states, and cultural, linguistic and religious backgrounds, I learnt that food has nothing to do with religion. I discovered how oppressive the idea of a vegetarian diet is for Dalits, as we are the toiling masses of this country. Depriving us of good protein and wholesome food and restricting our food choices with a religious veil was to deprive us of our biological health.

*

Often silent people can be subtly violent. I just needed to look back into my past. I remember the evenings in my childhood. My grandmother used to take me to Buddha Vihara in our basti. During the recitation of the Panchsheel and Buddhist prayer, I felt as if the sound was coming from a different world. That smoothly flaring smoke of incense sticks, those calmly burning candles, that monotonous sound of prayer, those Buddhist parables, that profound stillness on Buddha's face—beside it, there was the brooding face of a modern man wearing a suit and spectacles, holding a pen: Dr Ambedkar. Totally in contrast to this was my mother. She is an atheist. Unlike my grandmother, she did not go to Buddha Vihara everyday. Nor did she perform prayers or recite the Panchsheel. My mother was hardworking. She knew how to take care of the home with dignity and sheer labour. Unlike my grandmother, who had prevented my father from making decisions for himself, she did not stop her son from pursuing the life he wanted. When I realized what my grandmother had done, I could not help seeing it as the violence that killed my father's dream. The world in which I grew up, being *religious* equates with being *superior* or *socially upright*. But my grandmother, while being religious, was also *selfish*.

Religion sometimes becomes an excuse to impose one's ideas and views onto others. In TBM, I had begun to sense that caste realities were totally absent from the discussions. When history is absent from the conversation, it is the beginning of colonization. And the one who shows you a utopian world by ignoring your history is a colonizer. Colonizers can never see your wounds. And our wounds were much more complex than the world could ever imagine. Because the wound of caste is not visible. It can only be felt. Those who can never have these feelings, can never have the ability to comprehend which spirituality is fit for our liberation.

*

I had been in the retreat centre for a year by now. It was a different life. All the conversations centred around meditation, spiritual growth, transcendental experiences and the history of metaphysical Buddhism in India. We were encouraged to form friendships with senior Dhammacharis to learn how to become one of them. Dr Ambedkar's intellectual fervour or his views on Buddhism were absent. Only his photos, his books (government-published volumes) were here. Often, Abhay evoked the tales from Tantric Tibetan Buddhism. This fascinated me and at the same time perplexed me, because I could not feel its relevance in my immediate life. But sometimes, the fascination for abstract things overpowers the ability to connect the past with the present. Maybe because we are scared to look at our wretched reality and to escape this fear, we seek freedom in the abstractions. In spiritual sects, the creation of fascination for abstract things without taking different social histories of people into account intends to create a new man who will *obey* the order of that spiritual world rather than *think* about his world.

Religious propaganda preys upon an oppressed person quickly and easily. You tell an oppressed person that his problems are rooted in his own idea of the world, and he is ready to kill for that idea to be happy; he eagerly listens to an idea that could free him from suffering. Then religious dogmas follow through the mouth of spiritually 'superior' beings. He forgets to listen to himself and to peep into his immediate history; he is turned into an experiment in the process of forming the spiritual world that the oppressors imagined for their convenience and to maintain their dominance. It is bloodless violence. Organized religion is a bloodless invasion into the consciousness of an oppressed person. It hides his history and replaces it with a spiritual vision of a life without sorrow, and he is ready to dedicate his life to his spiritual masters. I began to sense this gradually. This mental tension began to grow within me. Yet, I did not make it explicit to anyone. I sensed the fear among Mahar-Buddhists in TBM, which stopped them from seeing the Buddhist life outside the sect. Somehow, I had stepped into the world of TBM only to witness that this fear of freedom was real.

This is when I began to read. I found more sense in reading than doing meditation. For this reason, I started being called lazy. By this time, back home, after realizing that I would not be taking care of family responsibilities anytime soon, my mother began to work as a housemaid. Not even once did she stop me from doing what I felt right for my growth.

If I recall that period of my life today, then I feel deeply affected by thinking about the power of loneliness in defining the self. Because for a long time, loneliness has been an integral part of my growing up. I know it was loneliness because I know there was an instinct in me that stopped me from sharing my feelings with others. Loneliness is not being alone or being abandoned. It is a condition to grow perennially isolated from social norms. This loneliness is widespread among *thinking* brains, because their isolation is determined to defy these social norms, at the cost of being hurt by the silence of boycott by society.

*

The sexual urge is real. And at a certain age, it is almost everything. In the retreat centre, they said that humans commit crime (they called it here *paap*, sin) in three ways—by the body, by speech, and by the mind. Sexual fantasy was a crime, considered as committed by the mind. They said that it has repercussions. I was twenty-three years old and to my mind, this notion was as convincing as the fear of death. How can you rectify this if you cannot control your mind? They had a system. The person who is in the process of becoming or willing to be Dhammachari should have a Kalyanamitra (a senior Dhammachari as friend) with whom this person could share his spiritual growth as well as mental 'sins', not only sexual, but of all kinds. They called it *Paapdesana* or confession. To be a Dhammachari, a person was kept under checks *and* balances. The whole order of things here was indicative of suppression rather than liberation.

Even academic education was actively discouraged. One of the Dhammacharis whom I had befriended told me that once he had enrolled for a MA course (he later dissociated himself from me knowing that I was critical of this sect). A few senior Dhammacharis reached his home, asking him his intentions behind joining that course and intended to know whether his intellectual needs were being fulfilled in this sect. This was absurd. But all weird and absurd things can be easily planted in the life of ex-untouchable (Dalits) communities, if executors are disguised as liberators or allies. If a white man tries to work for the good of black people, he is seen as who he is and recognized as a descendent of enslavers. It is as clear as that. But if a white person tries to do the good for Dalits, he is seen as a well-meaning foreigner; he is revered for his white skin and hardly regarded with caution, let alone suspicion. This is where caste has hidden fangs. And this is where our historical vulnerability lies. Because, the history of Dalits with white people is neither that of kindness nor that of unkindness. This history is that of consumption of the Dalits' labour. The bitter truth is that a victim of an oppressive social system is the first target of any type of colonization, whether cultural, intellectual or spiritual, because in him, the colonizer seeks the cheapest labour so he can thrive. Under colonialism, we were given space, wages, education and respect because we were of some use to them. Our humanness was not self-evident. Nor did our shackles become a matter of disgust for them. Our shackles were invisible to them. The white people looked at our shackled feet, but not at our mind, capable of breaking free.

This is how I began to think about things around me, but I was fully unaware that I too was not immune to this spiritual intoxication. I was yet to see it as propaganda. But there was a voice in my subconscious which was saying: *I am not your Buddhist— the Buddhist you want to make out of me.*

*

A Kiss, a Touch and Love

I am not in fear of loneliness
For I am protected by it from getting hurt,
I am scared of your cruel gaze
That can't see a blooming flower in the dirt

I began to read at the retreat centre. This was my way of defying what I did not like there. I developed an inexplicable fascination for the English language. The mere sound of it transported me to a world I eagerly wanted to be in, the land of cold and snow. So far, I had never had the privilege of owning a book, nor had the time to sit with it and enter into the world of words. My life had just not been like that. To spend money on books was simply not something my family could have ever afforded. But here, amid the stillness of this retreat centre, I encountered books.

The majority of the books that I found here were published and printed in England. Their scent was foreign. They were published by Windhorse Publications, a publication founded and managed by TBM members in England. All the books I laid my hands on were authored by white, English members of TBM.

I loved the smell of those pages and their covers. I felt elated, merely thinking that they came from England. In those books, I smelled England. Since Sangharakshita (*Bhante*) was the founder of this sect as well as an illustrious writer and poet, it was impossible not to read him, if you were interested in reading, while being in this sect. I read his autobiography, his memoirs and his poems. I also read his books on Buddhism. These were my initiation into reading. I was naive as a reader. But even if I was naive, what I was reading was deep meditation on life and living. At this time, he was the first author whom I read who had an impact on how I thought about life. Throughout his books, life was present as a subject, as a principle, not as object or practical. *Man* was present in his book, but *society* was largely absent. I related to the man he has depicted in his books; but the society in which I grew up, the society which had defined and continued to define me, affecting me, was curiously invisible. Because of his books, I began to see life as a subject, same across societies, countries and continents. His books taught me to simply *believe*, whereas what people like me needed to learn from books was to *question*.

Because all I was reading during this time was in English, I began to get a taste of this language. English was being dissolved like a drug on my tongue. I liked the hallucination this language was providing me, in which none of my caste-realities were visible to me. The books and the propaganda of TBM were affecting me in many ways. Maybe out of instinct or some subconscious voice, I have avoided, even silently resisted, reading anything in Marathi. Maybe because reading Marathi meant reading life around me. And the life around me was inevitably painful and full of bitter truths. I sought an escape from this. In these English books, I found it, and I savoured it like a drug. Every drug has its own language. When you consume it, it speaks through you. But language as a drug is a two-edged sword. At this time, this drug called English was shaping my mind to express my feelings and emotions through it. I was consuming its vocabulary and its sound.

*

When loneliness is widespread in life, we accept illusions more quickly than reality. Because in illusions, we find the love and acceptance that is denied to us in reality. In these words, I summarize my time in the retreat centre. Loneliness creates a deficit of love. With this deficit, one can become so vulnerable that we find love where actually hurt awaits. But again, driven by instinct, one can hardly come to this realization until one is hurt. Seven kilometres away from the retreat centre to the south, there was a village called Seloo. To access the market or buy groceries, we had to go there every week. It had a small internet cafe. In 2007–08, I opened my Facebook account for the first time. Then I started adding white English TBM members to my Facebook account. It was during this time that I randomly added Carol, a Dhammamitra who was then associated with the Sheffield Buddhist Centre in England. TBM was the common factor between us, nothing else. It was my fascination for the English life and people I had seen in movies that led me to her profile, and I, without thinking for a second, added her. What was pushing me to do what I was doing? I did not have any inkling of it. The only thing that concerned me then was if it helped me feel the sense of being heard or accepted. Besides, it was an age when sexuality is the director of our actions, but we hardly see its face. Also, what I was reading at this time was silently affecting my emotional world. The imagination of the English world was growing under my skin. Do words have potential to create desire in you for the distant world? I think they do. They did to me. How could they not, when I intended to shun the darkness next to me?

Two weeks later, when I visited internet cafe in Seloo, I found a message from Carol. She had written: 'Hi Yogesh, thanks for connecting. Good to know that we are part of the same sangha, Carol xoxo.' I replied to her message. I only had Rs 15 to use the internet for an hour. I browsed her profile. I scrolled through her photos, which provided me the taste of a different world that was soothing to my eyes. That cold weather, that snow, those winter clothes, that gleaming sun on the blanket of snow, those unpopulated streets, pleasing greenery in the vicinity, those white faces—all attracted me. The life in those photos seemed tender and desirable. That photos can lie too, I was yet to learn. I mistook them for the truth. People whose access to other worlds is conspiratorially prohibited mistake anything for anything. They mistake hurt for love and needs for wishes. I was a need for someone, not a wish. This never occurred to me. To desire love, acceptance and reciprocity is not a crime. Being a Mahar-Buddhist, to desire all these is even justifiable. But for me and my ancestors, this has been a crime. Caste ripped all opportunities from us, in this sense. But it was not able to destroy desires within us—the desire to live, to love, to touch, to feel the bodies in love that were separated from us, to fall in love with someone or to be destroyed in love. This is the enigma of being a Mahar-Buddhist. When Carol's message came, from across the seven oceans, I felt irresistibly thrilled and fascinated. It was suggestive of nothing. Yet, I was destructively curious to talk to her more.

We started chatting over Facebook whenever I visited the internet cafe. England was about five hours behind us. So when it was afternoon for me, it was morning for her. I had never imagined the world in this way before. This difference made my mind travel into different time zones in the world. Suddenly I started thinking about the difference we had yet how we were the same in so many ways. Then, Carol shared her phone number with me one day. I was using a mobile phone, but this was the time when I hardly had any money in it to make calls. Also, this was the time when there was no one in my life with whom I could talk romantically or share my sexual desires. A simple text message back then cost Rs 5. And I could afford only two messages a day: *good morning* and *good night*. It was Carol who used to call me. The more we talked, the more the desire to talk grew irresistible. It seemed reciprocal. And reciprocity in the field of feelings and emotions in my life was a rare event.

Carol was a hairdresser by profession. I had never imagined a woman as a hairdresser and that too pursuing it as a profession. Besides, in caste-society, certain professions are recognized as unworthy or though important, demeaning. In India, hairdressing has been one such profession, perceived as being degrading until recently. Yet, when Carol told me about her profession, I felt curious as to where she worked. She was trained with one of the world's leading hairdressers, Toni & Guy. This must be distinctive to the western world, I thought, women choosing to be hairdressers. What made me feel close to her was when she told me that coming in contact with TBM in Sheffield had changed her life. Buddhism changed her life. By this time, my reading of Buddhism, especially of TBM's narrative, was broadening. And whatever I had read convinced me about her realization. But then, this was the tip of the iceberg. The major or heaviest part of her life was below the surface. As far as I remember, she was the daughter of working-class parents from Sheffield. She had not been to university. She had hardly been to college. And she had started working early in life. She had one son, fourteen or fifteen years old in 2008, and a daughter, maybe five or six years old in 2008. Her son was grappling with a drug problem, she said. Her daughter was growing up, spending five days in a week with her and two days with her father. Her son was from her first partner, and her daughter was from her second partner, with whom her relationship was in decline, emotionally and consequently physically. This was a different life, and I certainly did not have any social understanding to process and comprehend this, because the society in which I grew up was the society which was too morally and ethically dubious to understand such individualist, scattered and unbounded lives.

But this did not concern me. With Carol, I was increasingly feeling wanted. It was my only concern. Talking to her over the phone, listening to her foreign voice, her accent, and facing difficulty in grasping the social context of what she said, yet feeling welcome, were a few things that made me feel emotionally alive then. She told me many things, about her life, her relationships, her experience with Buddhism and the demanding life in England. I understood very little of it. Carol was thirty-nine years old. I was twenty-three. But age does not bother you when all you look for is touch, of love, of care and acceptance.

Living without the physical touch of a person is living a memory, whose map is drawn on the paper of imagination. Such memories are drawn with the signs and symbols of desires and needs. They are defined by urges to consume rather than a struggle to know the person. And yet, they are so real. Carol was an idea, a voice to me. I had seen her in photos; photos can evoke many feelings but not someone's real presence, the current state of the body, the smell of it. I had not touched her with my hands, not felt her on my skin. Besides, for a twenty-three-year-old boy, a Dalit—who hasn't identified himself but is already identified by society and hence pushed to live in a systematic isolation from the other gender and from the touch of passion of flesh and bones and blood—a little bit of affection is no less than nectar.

Me and Carol had been talking for months now. And one day, she messaged: 'Yogesh, I think I am falling in love with you.'

This was precisely the message. These words were engraved on my mind right at that moment when I uttered them to myself. I kept my feelings, romantic and sexual, secret within me and, furthermore, I intended to keep them secret because the thought of being rejected had dominated my entire world of emotions, always. I always thought: *I am not someone whom anyone wants to love.* But here she was, proving me wrong, and destroying my long-preserved sense of inferiority. What could have been my answer? Did I have a choice? Was I privileged to have a choice? I was true to my desires and needs, if not feelings and emotions. But what did I know about these, especially when I belonged to a people to whom the world had always been unkind, cold and cruel? *I also feel the same,* I replied. But what I meant was: *I need you, now, more than anything else, come and make me forget myself, I want to get lost in you.* Often we disguise need as feelings. I did not know this. *We are in love; I am in love; Carol is in love with me*: I uttered these words to myself and, suddenly, my anger for things around me evaporated. I shared this with Abhay, and he seemed to be happy about it, yet there was a vague scepticism in his eyes about the possibility of anything further.

We continued to talk for the next few months. It had been nearly two years that I was in the retreat centre. I liked the space it had provided me, in which I witnessed my needs and desires very closely. Yet, I remained illiterate about feelings and emotions. I liked the peace preserved by the hills here. And I liked the birds here, chirping intermittently throughout the day, influencing me to think that there is some beauty still left in the world. Carol's presence, via her voice and texts, was the only charm in all these in my life. When a person grows inside our head as an idea, as an image, a voice, we want more of it; we want their skin, their bone, their saliva, their warmth, and perhaps we want to test their ability to hurt us. I could no longer be patient. There was a strong craving in me to see her, in front of my eyes, to feel her skin against mine. I did not know if she felt the same. I told her this, and she said that she too could not wait to see me.

Apart from our romantic and sexual anxieties, we discussed a project she suggested to me. She wanted to help students from my community to learn computers. She came up with the idea of raising funds there in Sheffield so we could start a small computer centre in Nagpur. I told her that I have a small empty space in my house where we could do the project. She agreed to this.

To work on the project and to repair the empty room in my house and convert it into a computer room for children, I shifted back home. But I couldn't stand being at home now—the chaos there, in the basti. I hated it because it reminded me of the bleakness it inherited, and to be in contact with it was to be in a hopeless world. That's what I thought. Staying two years in the retreat centre, amid peace and in a socially isolated environment, with its spiritual reveries and metaphysical indoctrination, alienated me from my home and people. I started hating the noise of life in the basti. I often told myself that the basti is the place of chaos, hopelessness and low life. I did not learn to see the history in it, the history which was my inheritance and the only thing for me to belong to in this sad society. No white person or Indian Dalit member of TBM cared to bother about the past of the Mahar-Buddhists. They only cared about showing us a spiritual state in which the world would be blissful and peaceful. I believed them. I kept going back to the retreat centre to stay there for a few days intermittently. I thought life in the basti was not a *meaningful* life.

During the same period, talking to Carol became the most important event of the day. I was talking to her in English. The language was growing inside me. She nourished it, helped it grow inside me without controlling it. She wrote 'luv' for 'love', 'wot' for 'what' and 'gal' for 'girl'. I thought it to be some typing or spelling error. But she said that that's how many people write back in her place. This was a discovery of sorts for me, that the language I was attracted to had also been conveniently changing in its place of origin as per people's style of speaking and writing it. I remember my earlier encounter with English and how grammar fanatics almost took sadistic pleasure in correcting spellings and accents and what not. With Carol, my fear while pursuing this language found a freedom and consolation. *If she, being English, can speak and write English the way she wants, I too can do it*, I thought. Love overpowers fear of any kind. If it does not, it is not love at all. And with Carol, love was happening in the background, like jazz; there were few words, but the music was profound.

*

When the renovation of the place for the computer centre began in my house, I got so involved with it that I no longer missed the retreat centre. Carol had received almost 500 pounds through her fund-raising campaign; she offered haircuts for this and people contributed. She sent me this money and to my surprise, her own money, to buy myself a birthday gift. I do not remember if I had ever received a birthday gift before. I never expected it too. I remember it was October in 2009, my twenty-fourth birthday. I bought myself a computer. For a month, the renovation work went on. The walls were rebuilt, the roof was fixed, the floor was constructed; tables, chairs and computers for the computer centre were bought. Everyday, I told her the progress we were making. And then, she surprised me with one more thing. She had planned her visit to India. 'I will see you soon my love; I cannot wait anymore,' she told me.

Things I had never imagined would happen with me were happening. The degree of happiness was unbearable. Loneliness was not a problem for me, affection was, simply because I did not know how to handle it. Simply because I have never had an opportunity to learn that. A person is mostly the product of how he was treated by his father or mother while growing up. I was no exception. I was mostly treated with silence. And the people who are treated with silence carry storms inside. A child neglected is the adult often hurt in love: I could summarize my entire life so far in this sentence. Carol was the first lesson in this sense.

I do not clearly remember the exact date when she came. But it was the season when mornings were foggy and chilly, when the sun was as pleasant and tender as the skin of a newborn child. I bought a bus ticket to Pune, and from there I planned to go to Mumbai. In the bus from Nagpur to Pune, all I was thinking was what would I do when I saw her? What do people do when they meet each other for the first time, but are already in love without ever meeting each other? I could imagine that it was not how most people function in society.

I reached Pune early in the morning. I had a friend from TBM in Pune. He later became a spiritual fanatic, upholding the view that those who do not do meditation and practise Dhamma are inferior beings. I had breakfast at his place and took a bath. Carol's flight was coming early the next morning, at 2 a.m., which meant I had to reach Mumbai past midnight. I took an evening bus from Pune to Mumbai. It was midnight when I reached Mumbai. Even at night, this city was energetic enough to make you feel alive. When I reached the airport, I was mesmerized by the lights, the people, the colours and their distinct smells and the fusion of smiles and silence of waiting. It was my first time seeing the airport, being there, being very close to the gateway of migration to the sky and foreign lands. To my eyes, the airport was the republic of migration, of hopes, of belonging.

I spent two hours learning the rituals of this place, from where people arrive, from where they depart, from where they were received, where to look for flights arriving and departing and so on. Every now and then, I looked at the screen displaying flight details with utmost focus. The numbers and names on the screen kept changing. It was 2 a.m. The number of the flight which Carol had given me flashed on the screen: *Flight XXX arrived*. My heart started pounding in excitement. After an hour, my eyes captured her, making her way through the passengers, nervously searching for me. It did not even take a moment for us to recognize each other once our eyes met from a distance. Our smiles were evident. She came; she hugged me. It felt as if some kind of storm inside me had abated. Her smile was the smile of a woman who had seen a lot in and of life. She had that smell of a cold country. Her smell, her touch, her presence and the fact that she was there, everything started to dissolve in my bloodstream. With her hug, the inferiority complex inside me disappeared. I grew up with a dark skin, the type of which has been disliked in this country and considered as *undesirable*; besides, there was my caste—if people came to know about it, it created repulsion in their casteist minds. With her arrival, something changed. I felt worthy. Love resurrects self-worth. It was a discovery more than a feeling. Feelings are universal, but discoveries are personal and hence political. Discoveries are made by those who desperately feel the need of it, but most importantly by those who have been deprived of the need of it. Touch kills prejudices, and perhaps the inferiorities which make us perceive ourselves as unworthy too.

We had planned our trip to Bhaje, a place near Pune, where two-thousand-year-old Buddhist caves with engravings were located. We had a plan to stay overnight at the TBM centre there, which was situated at the foothills in Bhaje, surrounded by a fort, rice paddy fields and a village. From there, we planned to go to various cities and towns, including Nagpur, to see the development of the computer centre project. Then back to Mumbai, and from there, she would fly to Heathrow.

*

We talked for an hour or two outside the airport. She touched my hands frequently. The soft coldness of her flesh was melting in me, soothing my flesh and bones, as if my body was thirsty for that touch. We talked, drank coffee. To go to Bhaje, we had booked a Meru cab. It came at around 5 a.m. It was still dark and breeze was cool; it became colder as we reached outside Mumbai. We were moving swiftly on the Mumbai–Pune Expressway. In the car, we exchanged words, words that came out of a necessity to talk. Her eyes indicated to me to come closer to her. I obeyed. Carol kissed me. We kissed. It was the first kiss of my life. More than being sensuous, it was comforting. I felt as if I was being embraced the way I was, as if I was accepted for what I was. *Love is embracing*, I told myself.

Don't we all define love in our own ways? According to our own convenience? Love is embracing. Because the opposite of this is hate. Hate is rejecting. But when I think this way, I feel scared to think further. Because I struggle to recollect a moment in which I have been embraced for who I am, and if I have not been embraced, then I am defined by hate. Those who are defined by hate are victims of intrinsic loneliness, which is dangerous. But since I am writing this, I feel the greatest virtue of writing is *knowing* it, and knowing that this loneliness is not only mine to bear. I am not the lone traveller on this path. Love may not have made my life beautiful and perhaps never will, but writing this will certainly make my life meaningful. I saw people surviving without love, but mostly go insane by the end of their lives in the absence of having the ability to prescribe meaning to their lives. My father's example is in front of me—later turned paranoid. And I think precisely for this reason, when Carol kissed me first, I felt: *Love is embracing, nothing more, nothing less.* Because the history of 'being rejected' runs in my community for centuries. This sense of history was subconsciously rooted in me, so that I imagined love was all about embracing and being embraced in all possible aspects of life, even in the smallest way possible; love is the opposite of rejection. In that moment of the first kiss, I felt I regained my lost personality, because the acceptance, for the first time, came from outside my caste.

*

We reached Bhaje, the village situated at the foothills of Bhaje caves. City sounds ceased here. We were now being buffeted by alluring cool winds. To reach the TBM centre, we had to cross rice paddy fields and farmlands. It was a walk of about two kilometres. It was the perfect season, with the crops and flowers in bloom. I felt the richness of colours and silence around me affecting me surreptitiously. We were surrounded with huge mountains, the witness of Deccan Buddhist history. We crossed two brooks where the water was flowing musically. Birds were chirping frequently. Insects were going about their activities without fear. The soil on which we were treading was sublime. From time to time, we stopped and kissed. From last night, I developed the greed to kiss her; I developed a craving for her touch.

We reached the TBM centre and settled in our rooms, facing the tall green mountains. There was a deep chasm between us and the mountains. It felt as though we were uprooted from the mundane life for good. Carol needed to know something. 'Yogesh!' she called my name. I went to her room and she kissed me. It was a long kiss; it was endless. Time was evaporating instead of running—a moment of uninterrupted concentration. She undressed me. My chest was sweetened by her tongue and saliva and warmth. I was learning the objectives of the human body newly. She drank me in. Piercing my eyes with hers, she said, 'Let's make love.' *Does she mean sex*, I thought. Carol was experienced in this domain. I followed her urges, translated through her body, her eyes, her moans. When I ejaculated, she embraced me, as if caressing me after I had allowed myself to be driven by our needs. She hugged me as though I had been wounded for ages, and now in her arms I found consolation. I knew how depressing it was to be unseen and avoided by the person with whom you are having sex, being driven by desire, and in the process, just refusing to see the pain in those eyes in which you wish to see acceptance of your violent lust. In a brothel, one can never be anything other than a body, a body that has needs, a body that is desperately anxious and a body that has destructive desires. That's it. One can hardly find consolation there. I began to sense the power of feelings and acceptance when two bodies, two hearts interact with each other. Ever since Carol arrived, I felt a sense of maturity within my body, distinct from the way it had acted before; this I had never felt before. I began to learn the difference between kinds of touch. There is a difference between the 'touch' you pay for and 'touch' that is *for* you. Touch in love makes you feel special; touch in prostitution makes you feel like just another body or perhaps nobody, and if you are thoughtful, then it makes you feel guilty too. Right after Carol kissed me first, and now since we made love, I felt this in my nerves. Love makes you worthy of being alive. Love makes you feel that you are *needed*. This was a new feeling for me.

*

The next day we went to Pune. We halted at a place for a day, where we had planned to meet a few people and see the city. We made love again, several times, from morning till afternoon. Then, hungry, we went to German Bakery in Koregaon Park, Camp area. Looking around the faces there, I felt myself as an odd number among them, unfit in the high-class place, an unwanted presence. The contrast between my skin and Carol's seemed to surprise a few people, including the waiter. It was apparent in their eyes, unkind and cold. Carol was calm and surveying the Indian-ness around her, decorated by hippy white foreigners from Osho's commune. My heart was pounding out of inferiority, which I felt as soon as I stepped in there. At night, when Carol suggested that we should go to some nice place for dinner, I said, 'I am tired. We can bring food here if you want.' I lied. I did not want to feel unwanted in those 'nice' places.

*

The flight from Pune to Hyderabad was the first flight of my life. It was the first time I was in the sky, with society beneath me. I found the airport chaotic, but since Carol was with me and she was well acquainted with airport hassles, I did not feel the need to learn much. In two hours, we were in Hyderabad. We had to catch a bus for Gulberga. At the bus stop, we ate idli sambar, the best I had ever eaten in my life. Carol was having a hard time dealing with the spices in it. The bus was to start in an hour, so we waited. The suspicious eyes of people were unavoidable, especially when they rested on me, seeing Carol beside me, holding my hand.

The bus took double the time as expected to reach Gulberga. On the way, it stopped for passengers to get fresh, to have food. Carol went to pee in the public toilet. 'It was filthy,' she said when she returned. Eventually when the bus dropped us, a couple of young boys, the organizers of the TBM retreat here, came to receive us. We went to a government rest house where our accommodation had been arranged. They asked me if I was her tour guide. I felt bad. I did not respond. Once we settled in the rest house, we made love twice, once before and once after bathing. The feeling of being embraced by her during our lovemaking was so irresistible and addictive that I wanted that feeling to last, maybe forever. At night, we went to see the newly built Buddha Vihara in which a retreat was going to commence from the next day. When we returned, we made love again. Tired and drenched in elation, empty as if the body had fulfilled all its desires, we slept, so carelessly as though we did not exist for each other in that room.

*

The next morning, we woke up early and made love. Making love had become a ritual now, a ritual to forget the world around me, an intimate ritual to affirm my belief in my existence. In sex, we both sought a relief for our silent grief. Those moments were just the beginning for me of this painful realization.

The retreat began. Carol and I went to the Buddha Vihara. One of the senior-most order members of TBM from England was leading the retreat. He had a white male assistant recording all his talks. Carol was the third and the last white person there. The uncritical fascination of Indians, across all castes, for white skin has always been amusing if not disgusting. I witnessed this throughout the day while I spent my time with Carol in that retreat. The order member who was leading the retreat received an abundance of reverence from the Dalits who participated in it. He spoke in English and a Dalit man translated his talk in the local language. The talk was held in the basement of the Vihara, which was a beautiful construction, sensibly constructed under the patronage of a prominent Dalit politician from Karnataka. The white man was delivering 'wisdom'; all Dalits were uncritically receiving it. That was the time when I was yet to learn to decipher hierarchies in any given event and actions of life. That is why I found the proselytization of Dalits by a white person—in the context of Buddhism and Ambedkar, around me—so normal. And why not? I was yet to learn the difference between normal and abnormal when it came to our lives.

The next four days were going to be frantic. It was like a dream I had seen, but now I could not remember all its details. We went back to Hyderabad from Gulberga by bus. When we reached Hyderabad, it was late in the night. We needed a place to stay. We were very tired. At the bus stop, we asked the autorickshaw driver if he knew any hotel nearby. He dropped us at one hotel that looked huge from the outside but was gloomy, lonely and haunting inside. The first room we shifted to was found unclean by Carol. She asked to change to another room or shift to another hotel if that was the standard across all rooms. I had never been to any hotel in life until then. The hotel manager shifted us to another room which was bigger and which Carol found clean. Once we settled in, she seemed impatient. She held me, kissed me, undressed me. I had grown accustomed to her body language. We made love. I saw the blood on the sheet when we were done making love. On the white sheet, the bloodstain looked like a rose petal. It was remarkably big. *Don't worry. My period has just begun*, she said. She went inside the bathroom and took a bath. I followed her. She said she was not hungry, so she went to sleep. I was craving food now. So I called room service and ordered food. I was twenty-four. My craving for sex and food was as real as could be imagined. I ate, without bothering to ask her if she would like to eat or want to eat later. I was unaware of other people's needs for a long time in my life.

Carol woke up in the middle of the night and asked me how we planned to reach Nagpur the next morning. We had not booked any flight or bus. But we had to reach Nagpur the next day because after two days, we had a flight to Mumbai. So, tense, I went down and asked the hotel manager if there was any way by which we could reach Nagpur by that evening. He said that there were flights, but they were booked for the day. There was also a cab, which would take the same fare as the flight but would drop us in Nagpur by the evening if we left the hotel by 6 a.m. The cab charged Rs 8000 from Hyderabad to Nagpur. Having slept only for four hours, we started at 6 a.m. and reached Nagpur by 7 p.m. The journey of eleven hours included constant dust, heat, spicy food on the way and constant back pain, caused by the car jumping at countless potholes on the road. It was a nightmare for Carol. Her face could not hide it. I did not know how to console her because I was ignorant in this matter. We had a puncture in between. We were getting increasingly annoyed with each other. By the time we reached Nagpur, we were so irritated that we did not talk to each other for an hour. We went to the Central Point Hotel in Ramdaspeth, but there was no room available there. The only other hotel I knew was Tuli International in Sadar because I had seen it whenever my father took me to watch movies in theatres in that vicinity. We got a room in Tuli International. We settled in. Without words, we resumed our rituals: seeking comfort in each other's bodies. I was back in Nagpur, but I did not inform my parents. In fact, the thought of them did not occur to my mind.

Carol called me from inside the bathroom. I went. She was bathing. She looked at me with a conciliatory smile on her face and said, 'Come inside the tub.' I removed my clothes. The water was lukewarm, so pleasing to the skin on that winter evening. We sat inside the tub, facing each other, naked, scissoring our legs.

We caressed each other's flesh as if trying to locate the source of our emptiness that had evaporated in each other's presence. We fondled each other's genitals in the warmth of the water. The candles she had brought with her from England were now burning smoothly with fragrance in the Indian hotel bathroom—they gave those moments a sense of elegance. This whole atmosphere was new to me. We remained in the tub for an hour or so, like cattle do. We experienced and touched our bodies with a sort of mature curiosity, like a painter creates brushstrokes on canvas. When we came out and dried ourselves, that freshness somehow compelled us to make love. We did. I felt all desires and needs and fascinations running out of me now. It was like a big chunk of pain had been released through my body.

While Carol was getting dressed, rummaging through her rucksack, something ignited a strange curiosity in me and I went to the window, and pulled the heavy and long white curtains. Down, through the thick window glass, I saw the busy street, vendors, shops, vehicles, lights. They were so familiar to me. 'I never saw this world like this before,' I muttered. I had walked on that street many times and I was a part of this crowd. I was one of them. I remember those silently rooted memories, in which I had looked at this hotel many times, seen its windows and the dim yellow lights inside. I had seen people inside, behind the window glass, moving like shadows. It was a glimpse of the world that attracted me then. 'Yogesh, let's go for the dinner,' Carol said, looking at herself in the mirror. Her voice brought me back to the present. I felt as if I had travelled decades in a moment. I felt as if I had grown up by decades in one single moment.

Carol and I went to a posh restaurant on Mount Road that I had seen many times but could never afford to go inside. Now inside the restaurant, sitting among people who were so unfamiliar and with strangely hostile eyes, Carol ordered wine and pasta for us. I nodded to everything she suggested simply because the names on the menu were not a part of my world, and I was ignorant about them. Some of the names were unpronounceable to my tongue. I liked the wine, but the food did not satisfy me. By the time we returned and were done with making love, I was famished. As Carol went to sleep, I ordered food from the hotel: Dal fry and jeera rice. I ate furiously, like a dog.

The next day I took Carol home. It was a brief visit. Carol saw the work on the computer centre. We ate at home. I told my family that Carol came from England and she was involved in the computer project. From home, we headed up to Nagaloka, a campus developed by TBM for people to study Buddhism. Carol was mesmerized by the tall Buddha statue in a walking posture. And then we paid a visit to Deekshabhoomi, the place of Dr Ambedkar's Buddhist conversion, about which Carol did not know much. I am unable to remember our conversation because there was hardly any. There were hardly any words shared between us which affected me. There was a long and perceptive silence between us which is the language comprehensible only in pain.

That was Carol's last night with me. In the hotel room, she gave me a haircut. She made me sit on the chair and placed a towel across my shoulder. She had brought her haircut kit with her, which was rolled and wrapped inside a cloth that felt like leather to my fingers. She sprinkled water on my hair and ran her finger through the strands as if they were woollen threads. Her hands moved gracefully while she cut my hair. I felt as if I was being taken care of. It was a significant feeling for someone who has been judged for his birth, skin complexion and caste. When she was done, I looked in the mirror. It felt different; I felt I was not ugly anymore. Maybe, in giving me a haircut, she gave her sight and her perception to me, to look at myself newly.

The next morning we boarded a flight from Nagpur to Mumbai. At the airport in Mumbai, we waited for an hour or so. We exchanged a few words. But mostly we were silent and anxious. I had slowly graduated in my emotional world and felt *attachment* for the first time. But my twenty-four-year-old self did not have the words to articulate my feelings. I not only lacked language but emotions as well. Not that I was scared of being alone, but to feel *insecure* was the horrible discovery for me. Carol's eyes turned wet as the time of her flight approached. The feel of her skin and her smell were now coated on my body. She kissed me. We hugged. 'I will bring you soon to England, my love,' she said. She disappeared into the crowd of people, leaving me with a few promises and hope. Little did I know that it was the last time I was seeing her.

*

The same night, I took a train back to Nagpur. I had already started imagining myself in England, in the snow, walking across those silent gothic villages. I felt myself free as I imagined this. It was the only way for me to feel free. The source of my fascination for England was deeply rooted in my pursuit to escape my world, my immediate life, my stories. But I did not know this then.

The next day Carol messaged: 'I've reached.' That was it, nothing else.

Days went by. Her messages became less and less frequent. She said she was keeping busy. But she assured me that she was in the process of bringing me to England, to her, to be with her. She asked me to download Skype, and once or twice, we chatted. I was seeing her for the first time after she had gone from India. She explained to me about the demanding life in England and how she was trying hard to bring me to her. She said that she had been speaking to one of the best immigration consultants in Sheffield. 'The consultant's fees are high, but she is the best,' she said. She also forwarded me their conversations, in which they discussed all legalities and my prospects once I reached England. I had no qualifications and I had no idea what I would end up doing there if I went. But going to England excited me. At this age, my decisions were driven by my fascinations and not by thinking.

The life I had inherited from the basti was not the life in which one is educated by elders about the world of emotions and feelings. Here, experience was the teacher and wounds were the lessons. Here, one learns about the intricacies of emotions and feelings when one is deprived of it. Here, between one generation and another, there is a long excruciating silence. But here, deprivation leads us to imagine a world in which love and justice are inseparable principles of human society, maybe because you seek for the world what you didn't get yourself—and this must be the *idea* of liberation. For a Dalit person, to seek justice is to seek love and to seek love is to seek justice. How can you love someone without accepting them as equal to you? How can you do justice to someone without having love for him? This uniqueness of vision has historically existed in a Dalit person's life because this deprivation makes him realize the importance of the emotional nourishment of tender minds. I was to discover this much later. But back then, there was no one to tell me the difference between longing and belonging. I longed for something I had never belonged to.

Now, whenever Carol messaged, she mentioned how stressed she was while doing all the paperwork for my immigration to England. My response to this was silence. Then her messages suggested that we should rethink all this, about *us*. In a few days, her voice sounded empathetic, as if she saw the hurt coming. I felt powerless even to speak. So I started writing her emails, long emails, begging her to explain to me what had gone wrong. Her replies became smaller and smaller, and less and less frequent. Then there was silence from her side. A bleak silence. That silence is unabated, even today. And the worst thing about silence is: that it grows inside your nerves, like a tumour, but you cannot see it.

*

I started watching English movies on rented CDs. These movies, mostly dubbed badly in Hindi, somehow seemed to comfort me. They consoled an empty corner inside me carved after Carol ceased to talk to me. Subconsciously, in those movies, I searched for the functions of Carol's world, the white society, their culture, how they love and why they separate. Watching these movies slowly turned into an addiction. I used to watch four movies in a day, sometimes more, from morning to night, until my eyes gave up. My calls and emails remained unanswered. There is nothing more painful. I was yet to learn to interpret the various signs of rejection. People who are not hugged in life pay a huge price for the little bit of affection they do receive. For me these movies were the only access I had to the world she hailed from. I watched all kinds of movies: thrillers, romances, action movies, dramas, adventure, suspense etc. My only relief was to be in the imagination of her world. I felt closer to her when I watched those movies. Yet, these movies never offered me the clarity I was looking for. In fact, I did not even know that I was looking for clarity regarding the situation I was in. Movies had reappeared in my life, not as entertainment but as a revelation.

Abhay had some movies with him, downloaded on his pen drive. It was the time when I was on the hunt for movies. I copied all the movies from his pen drive on my computer. One of the movies was *The Reader* (2008). It was a story of Michael and

Hanna set against the backdrop of Holocaust. Michael is fifteen years old, Hanna thirty-six. The moment this age difference was revealed, I was immersed in the story. I related to every bit of anxiety Michael felt in wanting to be close to Hanna, her body, her presence, which educated him on his hunger for making love and having sex. This story was set thousands of miles away from me, yet it appealed to my feelings and emotions in every way possible. I grew up watching movies, but none had had an educating effect on me. What all these Bollywood movies had done to me was to shape my mind as patriarchal, manly and reactive. *The Reader* was a revelation of my own feelings, desires, greed, stupidity and loneliness. But it gave me courage to overcome the loneliness, to follow the still vague instincts and to grow up, to move on. When Hanna, with silence, without saying anything, departs from Michael's life, he feels anxious, sad and scared of being alone. I felt this anxiety, this sadness and fear. This movie told me that I am not alone and my pain is not exclusive. And you grow up fast as a human when you cease to see your pain in isolation.

*

Learning to Read

I walked in the world of words
To search for my story, to search for my sky
Alone, away from the flight of birds;
My story is not defined by what, but why

The first impression, or rather, a realization, that I got after I began reading for a year or so, was that of my having been imprisoned until then. I felt it in my gut. Reading had introduced me to that acrimonious rage, which is silent but is essential for acquiring an understanding of one's own suffering and place in society. Reading offered me two major revelations: first, stories can immortalize the ideas and histories of man; second, stories can also erase the existence of an entire people if told by those who believe in the existence of oppressive systems. The latter was keenly applicable to my life. Reading made me reflect. Of course, it was a subtle process, and I was totally unaware of it then. Although somewhere I knew I was unfree, I did not know what the prison was. I felt free after I began reading.

It took me five years to discover which prison had held me captive. If my getting into reading, especially English texts, was correlated to my tendency to escape my reality, then my beginning to write was triggered by my first break-up, with Carol. After she had gone and I accepted the impossibility of her return, I was submerged in a kind of loneliness which pushed me to search for avenues through which I desperately sought a sense of fulfilment and worth. I did not know that reading and words had much more than this to offer me. I began by writing poems, abstract and romantic; none of them are with me today. But they helped fill the emptiness within, through the ideas sparked by my feelings. It was only after five years of a continuous writing practice, when I could imagine my history, politics, identity and my intellectual pursuit in relation to poetry, that I began to identify the source of my imprisonment. It was not the absence of choice. Because I have seen many people surviving without choices in my community. My imprisonment was essentially about remaining aloof from the world of books for years. In 2016, I wrote a poem. Unaware of what exactly it was about, I wrote it thinking of my relation to books and what they had come to mean to me. This two-line poem, titled 'Imprisonment', appeared on the page in less than five seconds. It was published in my first poetry collection, *The Bridge of Migration*. It reads:

I grew up for long
Without any books

It was the moment when I understood that in my life, poetry was increasingly becoming a vehicle of revelations, both intellectually nutritious and emotionally painful. But I chose this way of life. Or, maybe, I was in search of it.

*

You give a little bit of affection to an orphan child, and learning to live with detachment becomes a cruel process for him. He might hurt himself while accepting the inevitability of detachment while growing up. When I finally gained the courage to think beyond my break-up with Carol, I realized I was standing at a bleak corner of life where I had no real education and hence no real job. I had no money and my family had no legacy of any sort; so far, all the people in my family as far as I knew were mazdoors, and the work they did was literally called *mazdoori*. I was twenty-five years old by now. It had been two years since my mother had started to work as a housemaid. And I was still a long way away from unravelling the source of my alienation. By 2010, however, I was increasingly becoming involved with books: stories and the understanding they had to offer me about the human mind, its weirdness, its absurdities, its cruelties and its beauty. In May 2010, I went to Dr Ambedkar College to get an admission in a BA course. The procedure of admission was simple: Take the prospectus, select subjects, submit documents, pay minimal fees and admission was done. Being away for almost ten years from any formal education, the BA course (with English literature as one of the major subjects) was my conscious choice, but this choice had no promises in terms of a job. My choice was defined by my clarity that by getting into this course, I was going to formalize my passion into education. I was not wrong. And to finally have that clarity was no small feat after wandering in confusion for almost a decade.

That day when I returned home, after registering myself in the BA course, after cycling for twenty minutes under the 47-degree hot sun, with sweat running down my face, chest and back, I felt remarkably empty inside. The future looked blank. Yet, I was hopeful because there was a sense that what I had chosen was something with which I could never lie or be dishonest. Literature drove away the lies from me. The heat wave invaded my home through door cracks and roof tiles. In the month of May in Nagpur, not only water but all hopes of life blooming seem to dry out. This month resembled my life. But then, in June rain descended on the dry soil that emanated petrichor, a symbol of hope amidst dread.

*

Dr Ambedkar College is situated in the premises of Deekshabhoomi. In old photos, from the time of Dr Ambedkar's conversion, this place appeared to be a vast empty ground. It was at this place that nearly half a million Mahars in 1956 embraced Buddhism, following the path of Dr Ambedkar. This was the loudest message given by a people against the caste system. It was at this place that half a million Mahars proclaimed that they would no longer be defined, dictated to and directed in their psycho-social–cultural life. It was at this place that half a million Mahars cut themselves loose from the culture that psychologically terrorized and pathologized and enslaved millions of people in the name of caste. It was at this place that Dr Ambedkar declared the arrival of an anti-caste consciousness, at the heart of which there was a vision of Begumpura—'the sorrowless city'—which Dr Ambedkar referred to as 'Prabuddha Bharat'. It was at this place that the silent revolution of embracing Buddhism, after its decline for centuries, took place. It was the only meaningful revolution that took place in modern times on this side of the world because it gave birth to a *new anti-caste man*. And it was at this site that in 1964, Dadasaheb Gaikwad, known as Dr Ambedkar's lieutenant in his movement for the annihilation of caste, established Dr Ambedkar College. What a remarkable assertion it was: People who were despised and prohibited by Brahminical society and their institutions to acquire education went on to establish educational institutions for all in modern India.

Not that it was my first time entering Dr Ambedkar College. I had been here in the past. But in 2010, as I stepped in here, it was different. This time, I had a purpose. I was going to be here for three years, but I intended to be alone, away from people, irrevocably determined to drift into books. I did not know in what way they would affect me. My inability to connect with people was replaced by my ability to connect with books. I began to learn about people through books. The atmosphere of the college, its gate that resembled a stupa of Sanchi (a historical Buddhist place), the photos of Dalit-Buddhist icons who were proponents of education, apparently filled the colours of democracy in its vicinity, and it felt like a remarkable poetic resistance, especially in the time when educational institutions were increasingly becoming spaces in which casteist culture was cunningly spreading its roots. And when I looked far beyond the college buildings, I saw a gloriously standing stupa of Deekshabhoomi. *It was here that my ancestors put an end to Brahminical slavery*, I thought. In Dr Ambedkar College, I felt at home. And once you feel at home, it becomes easy to deal with pain. The home becomes the door to the journey to your history, to your roots.

So on that day in college, when clouds were darkly thick in the sky and warning of rain, I once again felt something was wrong with me. I thought that I should have been here eight years ago. I just felt odd. This feeling came from the realization that I had lost eight years of my life, wandering aimlessly, doing things without knowing why I was doing them. Sometimes, I feel: *there is no bigger violence than being in ignorance; ignorance kills the enthusiasm to bloom, to grow, to dream as a human being.* The fear of the future was now real to me. But, this fear somehow made me determined to go ahead with the choice I had made. On the first day of college, I did not attend any lectures. I sat in the canteen and tried to read with a cup of sweet, sticky milk tea, amid the cacophony of students. I felt a distraction, sexual in nature, growing inside me. I do not remember which book I held in my hands, but I forced myself to stare at the words. I was still vulnerable to my desires.

*

The library at Dr Ambedkar College was the first library in my life where I learnt to browse books. The English literature section became the avenue for me to discover stories in which I could find the meaning to my vagrant life or perhaps, overcome my vulnerabilities. I avoided reading anything in Marathi during this time, because there was a subconscious feeling in me that reading them meant reading my reality, being aware of the harshness of it, hurt by the insensitivity around it. So without any inkling as to where this blind trust in English books would lead me, I began to invest my emotions in its pages. A person who is vulnerable to social norms, especially when they are against his history and identity, receives incredible comfort and strength from books, which are essentially stories in pursuit of truth and love. Because these books do not judge him. Because these books put their trust in him. Because these books tell him that now he is not alone and he has stories to belong to. These were my instincts. My instincts did not deceive me. It had been a month since the college started. One day, in the library, I remember I had spent an hour or so in browsing books. Amidst books, time seemed to vanish. I would take a book from the shelf and put it back. I did this with several books. I liked their covers and how their pages felt to the touch. But more than this,

I savoured the smell in their pages, developed over the years, the smell that spelt timelessness and the survival of stories. It was that day that I issued Charles Dickens's *Great Expectations*.

It took me around three months to finish *Great Expectations*. It was the first novel that I had finished reading from cover to cover. I saw myself as a 'late' reader. I began to read at an age when I desperately sought to find meaning in books for my own life, for my own stories, the ambiguity which had puzzled me for a very long time. Initially, I read *Great Expectations* as *language*. I was fascinated with English. But to read a novel, a single complete story with so many characters, to understand the complexities of human emotions and to be affected by it and grow with it, was something altogether different. A lot of the vocabulary was new to me, so I had to keep referring to a dictionary. I read *Great Expectations* three times. In my first reading, I attempted to jot down meanings of all words I did not understand. In my second reading, I focused on its characters and how they make sense to each other and are an integral part of the single story. In the third reading, I read it like I was reading a story of people in whose lives I might also find some insight to make sense of my own life.

My first impression after I finished reading *Great Expectations* was that reading a novel is laborious. And the labour pays off. I had just learnt to see the stories behind people's actions. I learnt that all humans are prone to fall prey to their needs and desires; all humans at the end of their lives are the sum total of how they take care of their needs and how they deal with their desires. The learning was my wage, the reading my labour. One of the reasons I was pulled so much into this book was because the themes of love, rejection and poverty which recurred in it, were also, to an extent, part of my life. I empathized with Pip. I felt *close* to him. How strange to feel close to this stranger with whom I neither shared language nor culture, who belonged to a world completely alien to me. His pain made me aware of my own. Was this the strength of stories? Stories which tell us that we all share something in common and hence are worthy of respect as human beings. Stories which make us believe that our pain is not exclusive and our despair not permanent.

After *Great Expectations*, I read other works by Dickens, including *A Tale of Two Cities*, *A Christmas Carol*, *Bleak House* and *Nicholas Nickleby*. Dickens became the first literary voice that irrevocably pushed me to believe in the stories of people who are considered 'lowly' by society. Then I turned to Victorian poetry. I read it but, somehow, I did not like it. Then one day, I discovered D.H. Lawrence and more than his novels, I was enchanted by his poems, especially his poem 'Piano'. 'Piano' was the nostalgia of a child within a man, about his mother; there was longing in the poem and pain, but there was comfort too. I liked it because, as I see it today, somewhere I could feel the urge of this child, his longing to belong. I think it was right after I read this poem that I sensed an unstoppable force in me to write a poem. I copied Lawrence while writing my poem and utterly failed.

In college, during those chilly mornings when the sun was shadowed by buildings and there was hardly any open space to be secluded from the crowd, the only place where I felt comfortable to sit and read, quite paradoxically, was the canteen. In the morning, by 8 or 9 a.m., the person who owned the canteen used to fry samosa and green chillies, whose delicious smell attracted anyone standing around. Whenever I had the money to afford a samosa with chai, I would enjoy them and read; all around me were girls and boys and their impulsive laughter and conversation, which by then had ceased to distract me. I was swept up by the newfound joy of reading about the complex nature of human emotions, in stories, in poems and the lessons they offered me in the field of pain and pleasure. One year passed. I started dreaming of becoming a writer. And when I thought of my family, I wondered whether I was holding on to an illusion.

*

All of us at one point in life have dreams. Many of them we kill while growing up, and the rest of them are killed by the society in which we grow up. The idea of 'growing up' itself indicates developing an instinct for murdering our dreams. That is why writers who leave the world restless with their words, with their stories, are mostly disturbed minds, are antithetical to religious morality and live with an uncanny consciousness. Because they need to defy the violent order of the world, because they need to protect and nourish their dreams. The more I thought of this, the more I realized the impossibility of my dream becoming a reality. And to be a writer writing in English, with this legacy, seemed liked I was trying to mock myself. Besides, I knew that writers were not the people who could be breadwinners for the family. And this was the beef my father had with me. I had been jobless for three years now and, for a year, I had been doing nothing but reading in the seclusion of my room, oblivious to the affairs at home. I was never *interested* in the home. My father seemed to know this. But he could not digest the fact that I was doing nothing. He was wrong. I was *reading*. But in his world, reading was doing nothing. Because it could not fetch bread and butter.

He was right in his own way. He had never heard of anyone who ever made or earned money by reading or writing. In his world, to survive, one had to toil, tolerate bruises and endure pain. Although my parents worked hard, they barely made anything that could offer them a semblance of security for the future. Besides, they were nobodies in the eyes of caste-society. Seeing this, I grew up with a sense of defying this insignificant legacy. I increasingly wanted to be in people's mind as a literary imagination because *an untouchable* was hardly seen as one. I had decided not to cut my hair until I graduated to test my own determination. When my father came home at night, drunk as usual, seeing me read provoked him to curse me, abuse me, call me unmanly and impotent. My reading was worthless for him, and my rebellion 'abnormal'. In those moments, I hated him. I took it as an assault on my dream. I felt a repulsive anger because I did not want to become *him*. And yet, what did I know about raising a family, feeding them, protecting them? That too being Dalit mazdoors. At that time, I reacted with, 'I won't even come to light your funeral pyre.' His response was, 'Go fuck yourself, no one needs a useless person like you.'

My father belongs to the generation of Mahars who, during 1960s and 1970s, had recently transitioned from the baggage of caste-identity to the freshly embraced legacy of Buddhism. But for many of them, it was nothing more than a shift in referring to oneself with new names and having a new cultural identity. Those from this generation who remained lumpen proletariats in a real sense of the word could not translate this new identity into politics for their liberation. For them, survival from caste-bullies and hunger was a real fight—they fought it every day. They were hard workers. But their labour had always been undervalued, undermined and at times, maliciously despised. I have seen them toiling beyond human capacities, bearing all those humiliations and mental tortures against which they fought in their own ways. My father belongs to this legacy, to this generation and to this atmosphere in our basti. He saw an entire lineage of men who were outwardly so tough succumb to the systemic loneliness emerging from caste-society. Those who became active participants of the anti-caste/Dalit/Ambedkarite movement learnt how to come out of this historical darkness of being. But those who did not remained afflicted by self-destructive forces. My father was not immune to them.

Sometimes when drunk, my father would blabber about how his mother stopped him from joining the navy. Today, when I reflect further on my grandmother's actions, her selfishness or what I earlier referred to as 'cruelty' may have had some other basis. Having lived for nearly ninety-five years, she had seen Mahars break down from the trivial social norms and hateful behaviours of dominant caste people. Maybe she wanted to protect her children by keeping them close to her. She was not just a woman; she was a Dalit woman who, while standing against the viciousness of society, perhaps inherited some cruelty from it. As a Dalit woman, this was an understandable instinct. She was cruel in the right way. But she was protective of her children in a wrong way. My father is perhaps the product of this condition, which in turn, is largely responsible for what he is today.

Once I began to read literature, I would get much more irritated with my father's drunken abuse, but I also began to see him more closely. Whenever I reacted by telling him angrily that his *unimportant* life was the product of his being uneducated despite him having had a chance, he would reply, 'We were kept at the last bench. Teachers were inattentive to us and they used to beat us. We were ignored.' These simple anecdotal references suggest the trauma he faced at school, which eventually deteriorated his interest in studies. At the school, where he was supposed to be taught a lesson of equality, fraternity, love and compassion, he was made to feel a prisoner of his past and that his identity was a matter of rejection and abomination. Not all among us Dalits learn to fight this. A single act of discrimination in childhood can define the entire course of a life because it grows inside us as an invisible tumour. Only words can detect and diagnose it. But in literature, he is present as an *experience*, not as a *story*.

*

A year or so after I joined Dr Ambedkar College and was gradually immersed into the joy of reading, I accepted the fact that my father would perhaps never understand my dream to be engaged with words, to read them, to write them. I was learning that his stern disagreement with my choice was rooted in his fear of my survival in this society, financially and otherwise. I think this clarity released me from feeling the *burden* of it. I was becoming increasingly more concerned with books than people at this time, especially after meeting Meghdoot.

Meghdoot hailed from a small village from Vidarbha region in Maharashtra. I became acquainted with him a year before joining college. Meghdoot was not his birth name, which was Rajendra. When he came in contact with TBM in his youth, he decided to renounce material life to dedicate himself to TBM and learn and spread Buddhism; so when he was ordained (became official member of TBM), he was given the name Meghdoot. He had recently returned to Nagpur after staying about eight years in England. The common chord between us was our affiliation with TBM. When I met him, he was in his mid-forties. He knew about my relationship with Carol and how we broke up. He came to India with his white English wife, who was also associated with TBM in England. In India, his wife gave birth to a girl. And I think after staying in India for a year or so, she left for England, never to return. In a year or two, they were divorced. It was during the time when he had just begun to adapt to living without his wife and daughter that I met him for the first time.

I was silently thrilled to see so many books at his place, which he had brought with him. Those books smelled of England. I smelled Carol in them.

*

Somewhere around 2011, I began to write poems. I copied English poets, not only their style but also their subjects and, to a great extent, their poetic imagination. Little did I know then that I was not only not writing poems but also, in the process, erasing my history. These poems were abstractions in which I found literary thrills. These poems were desperate attempts not to be a poet but to become the *English* poets I was reading at that time. Meghdoot seemed to have a taste for poetry. He was the first person to whom I read out my poems. He praised me, was uncritical. In the absence of any English literary peer group or movement around me, Meghdoot was important company. We often discussed books and movies. This kept me connected with the faculty of literary imagination which, otherwise, was prone to be disrupted by my father at home.

Whenever Meghdoot reminisced about his time in England, I liked it, maybe because, through his memories, I felt a connection with Carol. But I liked it even more whenever he described the peculiarities of English people and their culture and how they were incapable of understanding us and how they, in general, liked to *dominate* things. But despite everything, in his opinion, English people were *genuine* and *committed*. To justify this, he gave me examples. The understanding of colonization and racial discrimination were absent from his narration. I, too, was yet to learn about the darker side of the white world for which he had such admiration. I had my own share of ignorance, which made me believe his every word.

So to speak, the problem was not his fascination for English books and culture but his—and in a way mine too—unwanted alienation from our cultures of resistance.

*

There is one memory; I could not forget this incident, because it turned out to be a paradigm shift in my thinking of my identity, history and TBM's version of Buddhism. In 2012, in college, a Brahmin professor was teaching me English literature. Meetings in which Meghdoot and I discussed literature had grown frequent. So, we decided to invite different people who could possibly be interested in having those conversations with us. I told Meghdoot about my Brahmin professor. She agreed when I told her about our literary meets. I reached Meghdoot's house early. He welcomed me with his typical calculated smile. 'At what time is she coming?,' he asked me. '5 p.m.,' I told him. It was a winter evening. He stood up from the sofa, reached towards a small shelf beside the TV and lifted a photo of Dr Ambedkar which was placed there. He went inside the bedroom with the photo and returned, empty-handed. 'I do not want to upset her if she sees that photo,' he said as his face grew paler, as if his confidence had been ripped away. This confused me. But I knew something was wrong. I was aware of this act of hiding who we are. What I did not know was *why* we hide who we are.

*

By the time I became acquainted with Meghdoot, much of my loneliness had been replaced with a blooming fascination for books. As far as I knew, the public libraries in Nagpur had disappeared and I had no money to buy books. I felt guilty asking my parents for money. One of the reasons I liked Meghdoot's company was his collection of books and our discussions about literature. When you are isolated from people out of the fear of being hurt, a book can be the sole refuge. Books protected me not only from feeling lonely but from seeing myself in complete darkness. *There is a light in me too*, they told me. I was writing poems regularly. A year later, somewhere around December 2010, Meghdoot introduced me to R.S. Thomas, a Welsh poet, who left an everlasting impact on my mind about various meanings of *being* a poet.

That was a cosy, comforting winter evening when I, as usual, went to meet Meghdoot on weekends. To meet him at his home meant a bicycle ride of around forty minutes, crossing two small hills, Ambazari and Botanical Garden, and wayward traffic in between. What kept me enthusiastic all the while was the thought of borrowing a new book from him. That evening, as I read him my poems, he abruptly stood up and said, 'Brother I have something to show you. This might interest you.' He went to one of the bookshelves and fetched a book. 'This. Have a look,' he said. It was a hardbound book; its cover looked dull; on it, there were two quotes in praise of the book. A man on its cover, an old man, was slightly bending forward, looking afar, so pensively that the seriousness of his eyes could immediately arrest your attention. Behind him, there was a church-like house. A barren tree was lurking in the background. The title was *The Man Who Went into the West: The Life of R.S. Thomas*. Byron Rogers was the author. Until then, I had never heard of them. R.S. Thomas was to become my first serious lesson in poetry. I smelled the pages of the book. It was like beginning to love, freshly, with new hope. 'Can I borrow it?' I asked Meghdoot. 'Of course,' he replied.

Not only did I savour the prose of Byron Rogers, I felt consoled by his words as they attempted to make sense of the strange, self-determined and isolated yet intellectually stimulating life of R.S. Thomas, a recluse who wrote in English but always desired to belong to Welsh, as a language, as a land, but could not, because English had invaded a large part of his mind. Some lines from the book I read twice, three times, always going back and reading them again and again, hearing their sound echo in my ears. I would tell myself, *yes, I know this feeling, this desire to be alone yet defy the loneliness of being, to become a part of the history yet remain detached from it, writing about my life in the language of a stranger, trying to articulate my feelings and emotions in the tongue of colonizers.* There was one particular sentence in the book that made me think about the purpose of poetry more seriously. While astutely summarizing the essence of Thomas's poems, Rogers writes, 'There was no comfort in his poetry, and no answers.' I muttered: *Poetry is the beginning, not the end.* This was so true about me. In Thomas' poems, and in Rogers' intrinsic understanding of this recluse poet, I found a strange wisdom about poetry that eventually freed me from the fear of *how* and *what* to write. It was as if I had reached myself and found a way to write my poems without being bothered by the language I was writing in.

R.S. Thomas, who until yesterday was a stranger, whose name I had never heard before, became the first poet in my life who guided me, through his poems and the story of his life, in the otherwise hopeless world of English poetry in India. He became a heavy influence. So much so that I printed a photo of him, placed it in a wooden frame and kept it on my table. He was watching birds in that photo, like a poet hunting for a poem, of hope, amidst the hopelessness around him.

*

Meghdoot was not a man who could be understood merely through his appearance or his behaviour. In fact, no Mahar-Buddhist man is easily understood in this way. In his mental world—as the Dalit movement transitioned through many ideological, political and literary changes—a lot of things were constructed, things to which he often felt he should not belong. When I started expressing my critical opinions about practices in TBM, I was shunned by their silence. I witnessed their quiet rejection of me for a long time. Eventually, Meghdoot too told me that he had to stop contacting me. How can having a different opinion be the reason for being rejected? But back then, in 2010, Meghdoot was different. He listened to these differences and did not deny them. In fact, it was he who introduced me to many practices within TBM that were an antithesis to the struggle of Dalits, which later confirmed my speculations. But in spite of all, he remained a part of TBM. In him, the fear of freedom was real. His hiding of Dr Ambedkar's photo from a Brahmin, his sharing the truth in person but shunning it in public, his following the metaphysical explanations presented by TBM yet knowing that it was Dr Ambedkar who could offer him the real liberation—these were all symptoms of indoctrination. His sense of being a Dalit and the accompanying inferiority were replaced by the abstract identity of being 'just' a man, a man without any caste and history, hence a man socially and politically dissociated from the community struggle. I think he understood that he was in a trap. But what made him adhere to this spider-web-like-life, I suspect, was literature—the only thing that sounded genuine in him, between us and in our discussions. And then interestingly, the books I borrowed from him, and the books for which he had a lot of praise, became my guiding maps to understand the origins of his entrenched complexities. For example, in the winter of 2010, he introduced me to Pankaj Mishra's *The Romantics*.

I was emotionally arrested by the story. Not that it was a great story, as I understand now, but because when I read it, I was lonely, I was new to the feeling of a break-up and I wanted to escape its pain. *The Romantics* is the story of a Brahmin boy, who sees himself as poor, who is perplexed yet fascinated by white people in Varanasi, and according to whom, as the novel suggests, Brahmins are the new 'victims' in democratic India. His views in the novel about reservation and casteism seemed to suggest the victimization of Brahmins. Yet, when I read it at first, after Meghdoot had praised it endlessly, I overlooked all these aspects. I was yet to read Dr Ambedkar. I was yet to learn to see the story behind the story. In 2010, I was in love with *The Romantics*. I secretly felt an irresistible urge to write prose and commentaries like Pankaj Mishra. I frequently went to an internet cafe, from where I took print-outs of all the articles that I could possibly find written by Pankaj Mishra on politics, books and culture, and I read them studiously. I learnt vocabulary from them. The temptation to hate yet desire white culture, the feeling of loss, the nostalgia in the novel—I made them all mine and I felt relieved. It was a myopic reading of *The Romantics*.

Four years later, in 2014, I read and understood *The Romantics* differently. The novel with which I had been in love then appeared to me a story in which lay the history of my oppression. I wrote a scathing review of the book that was published in *Round Table India*, the platform created by Dalit–Bahujans, with which I started my journey of writing regularly. This review reads:

Rajesh is shown as a product of penury which is apparently a result of the land reform policies imposed in the Nehruvian period in which Brahmins' lands were taken away (I do not understand by which hard efforts Brahmins attained land in the first place if they ever tilled them with their own labour). These reforms seem to have shaken their pride of owning material wealth which is yet another sociological distortion created by Mishra for the readers. Mishra forgets that this penury has been an unbearable fact imposed by the caste system on Dalit lives. And yet, Dalits have created a different space for themselves and have tried to get rid of this penury by democratic struggles through the expressions of various Dalit movements. Though it is apparent that his character Rajesh has a real life origin, yet in the novel, Mishra fails to give it a creative end. The reason is simple. Mishra's own Brahmin consciousness seemed to have prohibited him from offering a creative end for Rajesh's struggle.[1]

Yes, my language and tone were harsh. But problems of caste cannot be dealt with in analytical, jargon-filled language. Today, caste is a complex entity, hence the exposition of its subtle violence must be as direct and clear as it can be. This novel is filled with many psychological underpinnings that revealed to me the mental world of Brahmins. Rajesh is one of the Brahmin characters in the novel who gets involved in criminal activities since, according to Mishra, Brahmins' prospects in democratic India have worsened due to the reservation of jobs for Dalit–Bahujan people. Rajesh was an alter ego of Samar and consequently of Mishra. In the review, I further wrote:

To maintain the evergreen image of Brahmins being seekers of knowledge, Samar, in *The Romantics*, on the one hand tried to establish empathy with Rajesh from time to time and, on the other hand, silently (using no direct words) refused to justify the route Rajesh had chosen. Mishra describes the world in which Rajesh lived as mean and hard, and through this, overlooked the fact that this hardness and meanness has been the creation of Brahminised notions of society that has victimised Dalits for centuries and continues to do so. Further, Mishra mentions Rajesh's discovery of the 'underside' of middle-class society, whereas the truth is the society in India has been caste-ridden . . .[2]

I had started to learn to see the bigger picture behind literature in India, especially in English. The reason for this accidental discovery was Dr Ambedkar.

The learnings from the college classroom did not fascinate me. Prof. Kharat, who was the senior-most professor in college, had many times seen me sitting in the canteen, reading, unbothered by the people around. He was a professor of Marathi and an eminent Dalit short-story writer and a literary scholar. We knew each other. I had never attended his lectures, and he did not seem to mind it. He seemed to have an idea that I attend only one lecture: English literature. One day, in the canteen, he came to me and told me to come and see him.

A couple of hours later, I went to his cabin. He offered me tea. I smiled. 'I always see you reading something, what do you read?' he asked with curiosity and joviality. I replied, 'Novels, poetry.' Becoming more serious, he told me, 'I heard from your English professor that you write too.' He continued, 'What do you write? In what language do you write?' I told him that I write poems and I write in English. 'Why in English? Your mother tongue is not English. Besides, poets prefer to write poems in their mother tongue because that is very natural and spontaneous and in fact genuine too. Why did you choose English to write your poems in?'

His questions were provocative, yet they had a point. I knew the trouble of imagining *life* in a language I had just begun to learn, to write in. Until then, I had never reflected on this fact, and I had felt no need to do so. The only thing I knew was that

English fascinated me and, for me, it had already opened up a new imagination of life through literature. I had never thought until then that language is political, hence the writer hence his stories. Prof. Kharat's questions stayed with me for a long time. It was only in 2017 that the roots of my fascination for English became visible to me, and I began to see the politics behind my choice to write in English. A poem opened it up for me. That poem is called 'Politics', I wrote it in 2017. It was published in *The Bridge of Migration*, and reads:

> Everybody has the right
> To defend himself
> And if necessary, attack.

> Hence, I write
> But not in my mother tongue.

It was clear that I was thinking about two things while writing this poem: English and politics. But why did I write what I did and exactly from where did I get to imagine this correlation between language and politics? By then, as I had started to contribute essays and poems on various subjects to *Round Table India*, I felt an unstoppable and irresistible urge to write everyday. It was as if I wanted to show something to the world. To shout out my stories, my mind, and tell the world that I could also *think* and *write*. And when I passed this urge and writing became a discipline to me, I was haunted by those old questions, left in my conscience by Prof. Kharat about *why English*. As I continued to publish my writings, in English, I started to receive various responses on Facebook, in email, from all kinds of people, people whom I had never known and never seen before. I was being read, no matter how little. I started to feel the strength words have. The majority of these people did not share my mother tongue, yet I felt, through my words, they felt connected with my story, my life and my thoughts. The advantages of writing in English were slowly being exposed to me.

But I was not writing about what I had mostly read in the English literature course. I was writing from my imagination, of my world, of my people; I was writing *us*, which hitherto seemed to have had no sound in the English language. For years, I had read novels, stories, all those so-called texts in English which were praised by the Savarna world and its literary mechanisms. I had read these narratives as a reader. The moment I re-read *The Romantics*, not merely as a reader, but as a *Dalit* reader, I acquired the perspective that made me see the story behind the story. This changed everything for me. When I wrote this poem, I intended to convey that, as a Dalit, I would also pursue this language that represents and defines status. I wanted to proclaim my arrival in a language in which I was a secondary citizen and at the mercy of translators. By writing in English, I wanted to tell that Savarna and elite world that I was here and I would stay here with my story now. I wanted to tell them that the same language in which I was being mocked until now, I had turned into my weapon. By writing my stories in it, not only would I defend myself, but if necessary, attack as well.

*

Prof. Kharat belonged to the generation that has been instrumental in the making of Dalit literature. He was a man who believed in discussing literature. He was, apart from being the first generation of Mahar-Buddhists in his family to enter into school and university, also one of those Dalit men who adopted the style of being clean shaven and wearing clean, ironed and gentlemanly clothes from Dr Ambedkar. When we started to meet in his cabin, discussing literature for hours, my fidelity to literature grew much stronger. I could see the potential of words and stories in liberating the minds of people. If with Meghdoot I had discovered the transformative power of the literary imagination and Western books and literature that kept me connected with the foreign world, with Prof. Kharat, I was being initiated into a world that had always been close to mine, which was my world, even though I had failed to see any meaning or beauty in it.

Sometimes when our talks on books, literature and the Dalit movement seemed to be never ending, he would invite me to his home for coffee and to continue. Those talks were a real education about human life. Not only because we talked about books, but also because, intermittently, Prof. Kharat would unravel the story of his life, how he came to Nagpur, how he studied and those processes and moments that gave birth to his short stories. In other words, he was telling me his journey of becoming a Dalit writer. I was learning to see the making of a writer and what it meant to be a Dalit writer. Until then, I had assumed that stories were produced merely from the imagination and, with this assumption, I had written my earliest poems and stories. But after meeting Prof. Kharat, I could see that it is *reality*, the reality which was shunned by literature in India, that must transcend the imagination, and there lay the birth of Dalit literature. 'We made all those people who were despised by society the protagonists of our stories,' he told me one evening at his home, recalling his meetings with Baburao Bagul, Namdeo Dhasal, Raja Dhale, Keshav Meshram, his friendship with Yashwant Manohar and all those who had made Dalit literature a reality with their sweat, blood and sacrifices. He was telling me what lies at the heart of Dalit literature: a man, abandoned by society, who has never been the subject of literature. With him, I was being educated in the subject of people and how to see their stories, and how to see them *in* stories. While having discussions with him, I began to see some beauty in my life. I discovered that the meanings of my life were different from what English literature had taught me so far. I discovered that I was absent *in* English. These were consequential discoveries that changed my perspectives on English and on reading English literature, forever.

On one evening, Prof. Kharat asked me, 'Have you read Baburao Bagul?' I said no. 'You should read him. Wait! I will give you a copy of his short stories, but you need to return this to me as soon as you are done with it,' he said and stood up and went into his library to fetch the book. He lent me his copy of *Jevha Mi Jaat Chorali* (*When I Hid My Caste*), a path breaking Marathi short story collection by Baburao Bagul. This copy was almost five decades old. It was covered in a newspaper which was slightly tattered. The pages inside it were yellowish and felt thin to my fingers. The book smelled of antiquity. I went home, and I read it that night. Something in me changed forever. Suddenly my life seemed to have become meaningful. *It was not devoid of meaning or hope, my confusion was not baseless*, I told myself. After reading Baburao Bagul, it took me only a few moments to discover the vocabulary for my pain, my dilemma, my confusion and my life. I did not sleep that night. But I felt peaceful; I felt profoundly educated. I think once you find the words to assert your conscience, you no longer remain what you used to be. You become restless because you become conscious. In Bagul's stories, the most evident fact was the existence of an ability to think by those who were rejected by society, and it was this ability of theirs that was central to emancipation. This short story collection was my maiden journey into the territory of the conscience. I reflected: A thinking mind is prone to suffering, and a thinking mind in search of emancipation more so.

*

If Baburao Bagul supplied the vocabulary, the words, to my emotional world, it was Dr Ambedkar who became my light, my map, my guide, on the path of my intellectual pursuits. The year was 2012. The winter in Nagpur was coming to an end. I was slowly shifting my readings from fiction to non-fiction. I remember what Prof. Kharat once advised me: *A fiction writer must also read beyond fiction.* Dr Ambedkar was a default choice in the non-fiction genre. It was not because he was our childhood hero, but because he was the only philosopher, ideologue and thinker to whose writings I had immediate access. As an intellectual and philosopher, he was made available to us by those hundreds of Dalit writers and singers who tirelessly worked towards making his words available to us in the form of their art. If Dalit writers from my community formed the body of literature as per his vision, then Dalit singers kept him alive as a musical consciousness in our hearts. Yet, while growing up, because of my fractured life in the basti, I rarely had an opportunity to *read* him. And when I started reading him, my first impression was: *Dr Ambedkar is real when you read him. And once you read him, his voice echoes in your head. It shatters the infectious peace in your life. Once Dr Ambedkar enters your life, he walks with you till your grave.*

It was an old copy of *Annihilation of Caste (AoC)*, the Marathi version of it, that Prof. Kharat lent me. Reading it in Marathi was like seeing everyone around me in the basti with a history that was not only remarkable in its own ways, but also reading their stories, which they could not share with me, which were erased over time or buried with them. In this country, reading *AoC* was like stepping out of the ignorance constructed by schools, colleges, institutions and all those political, cultural centres that make sure to solidify this ignorance of being. Reading *AoC* for the first time was an overwhelming experience for me. I grew up *seeing* and *hearing* about Dr Ambedkar. It was the first time I was *reading* him. *Reading Dr Ambedkar is freeing yourself from your own cage of being.* Although the impact of *AoC* on my emotional world was colossal as my rage against the outer world grew much stronger, nevertheless, the clarity it offered me about the world in which I had been born and which had shaped me so far completely reoriented my feelings towards people. Now I could see the origin of their ability to hurt me. Hitherto, I had felt myself being in the room filled with nothing but darkness. I felt the objects in it with my hands and listened to them, imagined them, but I could not see them simply because there was no light in there and I had no vision. Dr Ambedkar, through *AoC*, had suddenly lit up that dark room. Now I could see things, as and what they were.

The kind of life I had led or had been made to live so far had made me think that there was no history, no beauty or no meaning in it. But no darkness is devoid of history. Before reading *AoC*, I found my life hopeless. I was wrong. I had known Dr Ambedkar as a photo or a story. I was yet to encounter him as a conscience, as a force, as a flame in the darkness. And once I found it, I was no longer the person I had been. *AoC* laid bare the mental world of caste-society: how it thinks, how it behaves, how it conspires and how it erases the histories of Dalit–Bahujans. In this country, for people, regardless of caste and class, it takes Dr Ambedkar to reach and to be accustomed to *their* truth. In my life, Dr Ambedkar was the beginning of learning to question. He is an unbeatable energy—when you feel it inside, you change forever.

*

As I began reading Dalit literature, it did not take me a long to witness the colossal dilemma from the past that had shaped my father's generation. As I began to see my father as a Mahar man, a Dalit, a Buddhist, I started to learn the roots of his emotional history. In short stories by Dalit writers, I found the source of all that madness, that strength, that self-destructive instinct, that ability to survive and that instinct to defy Brahminical culture, that I had witnessed and with which I grew up in my basti. These stories put *me* and *my father* in my literary imagination. Although it was a self-discovery, it was not at all cheerful. I could not help but imagine this country as guilty whenever I tried to make sense of my father's actions and his silence. I saw this country, this society, as a perpetrator in making him invisible from the national imagination. He was burdened by this weight of being insignificant. This burden is the crossroads of a 'double consciousness' for a Dalit man. That is one of the reasons he tried to be authoritative at home, and he did this precisely because he had no authority outside his home. I suspect this is the dilemma every Dalit man faces. It is inevitable to be hurt by it. To hurt is the repercussion of being hurt: the vicious cycle of emotional violence formed by the caste system. *We all are psychologically terrorized by caste.* My speculation started to be verified by the stories I was reading. Thinking about him, I learnt: *Memory* is what survives. But, the more I imagined about him—his past, his time and his identity—the more I was convinced that survival isn't enough for us. It is imperative for us to translate this survival into a discourse that eventually disrupts the logic of the caste system.

What surprises me about my father is the fact that all this while, he never asserted himself as a Buddhist. Whenever he was drunk and nostalgic about his past as I cursed him for being a failure, he blurted with irrevocable pride in his voice, 'I am the son of a Mahar. I am not a failure.' I fail to understand *why* he said this repeatedly. Why assert the identity that we as a community had left behind and that now lies in the pages of history, which was bitter and unkind to us? What kind of clarity did he seek in being a Mahar, an *untouchable*? It is impossible to avoid streaks of bitterness from the portrait of his life that ultimately made him what he is today. But somewhere I find there is a purpose behind him asserting himself as a Mahar and nothing else. Perhaps he wanted to remain true to his roots no matter how terrible it felt. Perhaps this bitterness was his patrimony. I have never seen as complex a man as a Mahar when it comes to suffering and as innocent and genuine a man as him when it comes to celebrating the idea of life. Perhaps I do not even require any validation for this. When I see my father, having tolerated years of hardship, but still physically strong, like a survivor, I feel: Against the vicious, invisible mind of caste, his body is the only resistance.

*

Does this country have a language to elaborate or comprehend the emotional world of a Dalit person? The answer to this must be in the negative. I think my bitterness, which I sense I inherited from my father, is proof. Because, I suspect, this bitterness was the direct result of being unable to find a language for the complexities of my inner world. This bitterness remained with me for long, until I overcame the fear of reading stories written by Dalit writers. I was reading narratives written by white and Savarna writers in English and desperately trying to find some meaning in it for my life. But you cannot expect a person whose life itself exists in negation of yours to write on and empathize with your life.

*

When Abhay first gave me a copy of *Baluta*, Daya Pawar's autobiography, I read it but invested absolutely no time in reflecting over it. *Baluta* reappeared in my life ten years later when it was translated into English. I was commissioned by Scroll.in to review it. It was 2018. Once again, *Baluta* was in my hands. What had changed this time was neither its cover nor its language nor its story, but me. I had started asserting myself, my identity and my politics. Reading *Baluta* with this realization unravelled many meanings of my being in this society. It also guided me to the root of Meghdoot's strange inferiority complex. I understood then that stories are the science to solve the mysteries of suffering.

For this review of *Baluta*, I also read poems by Daya Pawar. One poem in particular caught my attention. It haunted me. It haunts me still. Reading this poem was like reading the centuries-old emotional history of a Dalit person who always remained honest to this land, this country, but who was always despised and rejected. I thought this poem had been instrumental to Daya Pawar's perspective. I translated it into English and included it in my review:

> Kamble from Mahar Battalion with an amputated leg
> Looks in the darkness with searching eyes
> "Whom did we fight for on the border,
> why did we rot ourselves for the country?"
> The question pierces his heart through,
> with all the agonies of life
> The gun already confiscated from him
> He anxiously searches the bedside.[3]

And then, I began my essay with these lines: 'Some books leave us with a sense of bafflement, a few provide us a sense of clarity, and only a handful shake our conscience. *Baluta* falls into the last category.'

Baluta's words were now permeating into my bloodstream, my conscience. The story of *Baluta* was my story, in the past, of the past. Yet, it was an ongoing story. *Baluta* was all around me; I began to understand the dilemma of a Dalit man (male, specifically). *Baluta* was a diagnosis as well as cure for this dilemma. Now, I knew who I was, in the past and in the present. In the review, I wrote: '[*Baluta*] illustrates the tussle between "being" and "belonging" in the life of a Dalit person.'

My reflection over *Baluta* did not stop with this review. Of the many factors that encouraged me to continuously write in this period, one was the availability of platforms within my reach. Somewhere around April 2019, I pitched a piece to the *Economic and Political Weekly* (*EPW*). Back then, my friend Krupa, who is an accomplished author and editor and someone who has been instrumental in my writing career and my survival *through* writing in Mumbai, was a postscript editor at *EPW*. She liked the idea very much. To write this small piece, I invested a great deal of reflection and interrogated my memories. This means I chose to see my own faults and failures, my greed and my prejudices. I was not *writing* about *Baluta*. *Baluta* was writing *me*. In the *EPW* piece I wrote:

> The book helps us understand the dilemma of a Dalit person in love in a caste society and what it means for a Dalit person to love someone from another caste in a society that fills each of us with hatred, revenge, and anger for each other. *Baluta* would not have become what it is today if it had celebrated victimhood. The book became popular because it problematised the source of victimhood and resurrected the dignity of its protagonist when he transitioned from caste to class consciousness. Yet, he could not fully belong to either. *Baluta* is the clarity of confusion of a Dalit person who is constantly in search of himself in this caste society, especially in and through love. Love is seen only emotionally in our caste society, but never understood intelligently. *Baluta* helps us understand love intelligently.[4]

In writing about a 'Dalit person' in the third person, I wrote about myself. How else could I have made sense of this extravagant darkness of being in a society that rejected me? *Baluta* was a flickering flame in this darkness. Having suffered three break-ups until 2019, having seen three women (one white and two Savarna) leave, giving reasons I couldn't understand, even though they mentioned them loosely, reading this book was like overcoming the hate I had preserved for these three relationships if not for the persons involved. *Baluta* helped me overcome my hate and jealousy. Because now I knew my place, in society, among my ex-lovers. Once you know the reason and the source of why you suffered, you move on.

Baluta freed me from the confusion of being born in a society where one's treatment was pre-decided based on one's caste. Yet, this book scared me with its prophecies. Truth is often scary for the one who is brought up in a society that majorly believes in myths and lies. In the appendix of the second Marathi edition, Daya Pawar wrote something about love in caste-society that continues to haunt me even in this moment. For the *EPW* article, I translated this into English and used it in the article to see if I could make sense of what was happening in my life and with me back then. My words were seeds that I sowed to see if a sapling of love could grow on casteist soil. It is this paragraph:

> Dalit youth experience thrill in loving Savarna women. [In recent times, this phenomenon can be observed among Savarna women too.] While studying black literature, one finds that black men have tremendous attraction for white women. This may be the emptiness of ages. It must be the longing for something which cannot be gained easily. It must also be the sign of seeking revenge, mentally.[5]

If this is true, if the *revenge* element according to Pawar is true, then my suspicion ever since I moved to Mumbai in 2013—that we are all psychologically terrorized in this society—appears more real and more dreadful. If this is true, then it means we are yet to come to terms with our sickness of growing in caste-society. It means our idea of love in this society, especially in inter-caste and inter-religious relationships, is often not spontaneous and certainly not intelligent. How could it be if it has emanated from sadness, emptiness and from the roots from unhealed wounds which we all suffered as soon as we were born here? *Baluta* shattered my understanding of my own being, my own self and of those whom I think *loved* me once.

*

At home, for two-and-a-half years, when I shut myself in a room and desperately read to escape the physical world around me, my father was increasingly disappointed in me. By then I had quit working for five years, and I was yet to create anything which he could call a life. But books made me desire to be someone who one day would write and the society that had shut him down would listen to him, would read him. When I read Dr Ambedkar, I was reassured that my instincts to follow my ambition were not wrong. Dr Ambedkar not only made me see myself but also my father. I could no longer disdain my father. But to witness his daily disappointment made me realize that if I stayed at home any longer, I would never be able to realize my dreams. I would become one of those who had dreams but were defeated by hunger. I applied for a Master's programme at TISS Mumbai. In the summer of 2013, my admission got confirmed. The moment I got this news, I told myself: *I will not come back home until I am a writer.*

To confirm the admission, I needed Rs 4500. I asked my mother but she did not have it. I was running out of courage to insist or persuade her to give me that money. I had hurt her so many times with my frivolous ambitions and by doing things mindlessly. I asked Meghdoot to help me financially. He gave me money, which he called a *soft* loan. It was something he had learnt from his stay in England. When people give you money and do not expect or charge interest, then it is called a soft loan. So I had to return him the same amount of money after two years. I was financially so broke that I did not even have the money for a train ticket. Since the train ticket was just about Rs 400, my mother was able to give it to me. I booked the ticket a month prior to the commencement of the course. When the day of my departure came, my mother somehow managed to give me Rs 450. I did not know if I was going to survive with that amount of money. I did not know how I was going to survive in that city. But I desperately wanted to leave Nagpur. I talked to my mother and took her leave. My father was not home. He was working. I was thinking about him, him being old and still working—what made his body defy the logic of his age? I knew that when he would come home, he would ask about me.

I went to the railway station, alone, like I always had. It was the last week of May 2013, the hottest month in Nagpur. But I was feeling hopeful. Of all things, I was thinking about how to survive in Mumbai to be a writer.

*

I Am 'A Part Apart'

I, intelligently, wanted to love you
Like a blind man wants to view
The sunshine caressing his skin, he can't see
But it's there as long as he's going to be

On my first day at TISS, I had to reconfigure my emotional world. I was not used to speaking my mind. I had struggled my entire life to express my feelings as genuinely as I could and mostly failed. And my introvertedness was mistaken for my being stern and harsh. I was increasingly becoming conscious of my characteristics. Stepping inside the TISS campus was like entering a world of contradictions. The colours, the people, their language, their body language was alien to me. As soon as I got there, I was arrested by two feelings: fascination and inferiority. I was enchanted by the idea of getting lost in this new and strange place. I felt lonely because I sensed an inherent ability of this place to always remind me of who I was. Someone like me was not the norm here. I was an exception. The easy commingling of the two sexes in the public space was something I had never before experienced. When the course began with the arrival of monsoon in June, the place was filled with people across caste, religious and linguistic backgrounds. I neither had the language nor the temperament to be able to connect with them. But as a part of the course, it was *necessary* to be with them and among them. My first struggle here was to move beyond my fear of connecting with people.

The course began with what they called field visits. They were meant to introduce us to the functions of social work in society. During these visits, twice a week for a month, I encountered parts and life of Mumbai that were a world in themselves. These visits were supposed to make us aware of lives that were vulnerable to systemic oppression and how NGOs play a crucial role in 'helping' people fight it. This did not interest me. Was witnessing others' poverty supposed to make me sensitive? Was the injustice they faced supposed to make me aware of the cruelties of society? Was the idea of rehabilitation or welfare of vulnerable people, which was so convincingly introduced, supposed to change my perspective on society? The more I became familiar with the pedagogy here, the more I felt detached from it. The more I got to know the people who were exponents of this pedagogy, the more I became convinced that I would never be able to live what I was being taught here. My poetic mind could not help but see: *Poverty and the vulnerabilities of people are commodities and the means to a business.* I tended to rely on my poetic imagination to understand things. At TISS, there was simply nothing that could help me comprehend the things I was being taught. Soon, I was convinced that I belonged to poetry, not theory. In the time and space when I wrote poems, I was real, I was myself and I was as honest as I could ever be. In this place, where I felt a certain level of inferiority while talking to people, reflecting and writing poems was my assertion that I was able to *think*, unlike most others here. Poems were not only my *belonging*, but also my defence mechanism against my own vulnerabilities.

*

Classes began. There were around twenty-six students in my course. Girls outnumbered boys. In the classroom, privilege was the norm. Their privilege of language, urban upbringing, access to information and literature and their confidence in shouting out their arguments were all symbols of dominance to me. I believe it came from growing up seeing your history in cultural and political spaces that create the idea of nation. When you grow up seeing your community in and as an essential part of movies, literature, histories, stories, even music, you acquire the sense of being an important part of the nation and its discourse. The communities and castes to which these students belonged were an essential part of cinema, literature and politics of this country. Despite them being individuals and having their own uniqueness of being, they knew that they played a dominant part in the national imagination. It was reflected in their words, their eyes, their body language and their cold-blooded ability to look through people who did not fit into their idea of life. My defence was to keep myself away from my classmates as much as I could.

*

Farm Road, which divides the two campuses of TISS, turned mesmerizing and sensual during the monsoon. When the monsoon receded, the season of wet mornings began. In those moist mornings, students, with their various languages and its sounds, seemed to fill colours as they walked from one campus to another to catch their classes. For new students, time was a trick;

and as they become old, time turned into eternity. Afternoons were sluggish. On one such afternoon, in July 2013, as I was walking down Farm Road towards the old campus to go to the library, when my name was called—it was Saira. I was stunned by the fact that a girl was calling me by my name. She was standing across the road, with a smile that often gets lost when a person becomes 'mature'. That was the first time I talked to Saira. Despite us being classmates, I had never spoken with her. For that matter, I had not conversed with anyone from my class outside the classroom. When Saira called me, I went and stood in front of her, too close to be unaffected by her, but too far to understand her. My heart was pounding as she talked. I had not learnt to *converse* with women. I only half listened to her smooth sentences amidst the chirping of birds and boisterous voices of students passing through Farm Road. We exchanged numbers. That very same night, we started texting each other. On text, I was more comfortable. In person, I felt vulnerable and feared being misunderstood by her.

When I had come to Mumbai, among the few books I had brought from home was Rohinton Mistry's *Family Matters*. In Nagpur, by the end of my third year of college, during the hot summer afternoons, I religiously read his novel *A Fine Balance*. In Mistry's prose about Parsi nostalgia, the Bombay of old times and his visceral dislike for the rise of Marathi-speaking people in politics, I found a map to walk through the development of Mumbai, not only as a city but also a story in which culture was an elitist idea. I was unaware of this while in Nagpur. But moving to Mumbai had opened up a new window for me to look at this city, as a story and as a culture. While in Nagpur, Mistry's prose generated curious interest in me about knowing his *Bombay* through his books. So when I had finished reading *A Fine Balance*, I bought a second-hand copy of *Family Matters* from the pavement sellers at Sitabuldi. On thunderous rainy nights, in the

TISS hostel room that I shared with two other Dalit students, reading *Family Matters* was my only solace. It was at this time that my attention shifted from reading to Saira. At night, texting her became almost a ritual that was somehow erasing the sense of being lonely in the city where I had arrived with the dream of becoming a writer. I was slowly unlearning to be reticent. Then one Saturday, she called me over to her flat to have breakfast.

She shared a flat with two friends from Delhi. I walked from my hostel to her flat. Saira was alone. Her hair was untied, her eyes naked—she was not wearing spectacles. 'My friends have gone to attend classes,' she told me. I was learning to look into her stealthy eyes. Surveying the hall furtively, I saw books lying scattered in a corner. 'Can I see them?' I asked her. She nodded enthusiastically and went to make coffee. I began to browse the books, read the blurbs, smell them and distract myself from her. Kashmir was very close to Saira, so were the stories of its people. If I had to predict her ideas from these books, then she seemed to have no idea of my world. But by now, I was well acquainted with North Indian English writers and their idea of the world. I had read their politics and I had read their stories. Neither included my existence.

Saira praised elite English writers, all North Indian. Did she know that books also deceive? I too had not known this until I read Dr Ambedkar. Among these books, the book that I picked up and felt like delving into was a book of poems by Agha Shahid Ali. Reading a few verses gave me a sense that he was a poet who knew his roots and a person who knew how it felt to be *displaced*. I immediately felt a connection. Although I later saw that our worlds were separated by many differences; but his world, Kashmir, enter the public imagination from afar, and mine was still an erased reality in the minds of the people who lived close to it, every day. That is why this clarity, when it came, was too complex to share with her, I felt. This is how caste works: it makes closer reality invisible and distant histories tempting subject in the mind.

'He is very good,' Saira said, referring to Agha Shahid Ali. Then, she spoke about Kashmir for a while. She talked about displacement, violence, abuse of human rights, stories of Kashmiris and their pain. Everything she talked about was part of my world too, but she did not seem to have a clue. *What made a girl from Delhi so interested in the lives of Kashmiris?* I wondered. During her graduation from one of the premier colleges of Delhi, she had interned with an organization from Kashmir. I suspect it was then that she was exposed to the lives of Kashmiris and their victimization. What surprised me was that caste as one of the most cunning forms of exploitation, with which every 'mainland' Indian lives every day, was absent from her discourse of oppression. It was not her fault. Caste is not apparent to the eyes. The current of caste has to be felt as a shock. Caste is a matter of *experiencing*. Feelings are often not visible to the eyes. Privileged people are blind in this sense. And if caste plays a role in your prosperity and access to the system of knowledge and privileges, then you protect it, sometimes with your noise, and sometimes with your silence. Detaching oneself from caste is to be engaged with violence against oneself. And no one wants to violate their own comfort; hence the ignorance about caste-based exploitation around us. In this sense, caste is dangerous because you can *hide* it. Saira and I belonged to different worlds. She belonged to the world of 'haves' and I, I belonged to the world of 'have-nots', at least in a material sense. This gap was essential to our understanding of each other as well as of the world. But this gap was reduced, at least momentarily, when we chose to listen to the voice of our needs, our desires. I believe that at this point, religion or caste becomes a dubious idea. We confront the fact that our needs are genuine as much as our desires to love and to be loved without any prejudices.

She went inside the kitchen while I lay on the sofa cum bed, browsing poems, trying to feel their relevance in my world. I felt Shahid's longing as mine. But I was aware that we belonged to different lands, although they are part of one *nation*. I felt there was an incredible ability in his poems to enchant the heart of a person who may not be a reader of poetry. While I was feeling this, Saira came and lay beside me on the bed. My attention shifted from the poetry to her. The closeness of our bodies was tempting. According to society, it was blasphemous. But in our eyes, it was humane, it was natural; there was only us, being true to our needs, our blameless desires.

Our palms against each other, our fingers entwined, the blood rushing wildly in our bodies, we kissed. A tense silence was our witness. I could feel her pulsating breath and heartbeat against my skin. In that moment, we were ourselves: just humans, with our needs and desires, which were outside the reach of our religious and caste backgrounds. We both equally wanted to consume each other. Clothes came off. Bodies were undressed. 'I have never done it before,' she said. I responded with an awkward smile. 'But let's do it,' she said. The expression on her face was a fusion of curiosity and worry. We went ahead. But penetration was difficult. She felt pain. We tried, but the pain, although not unnatural, overpowered her need or desire to have sex. 'Maybe because it is my first time,' she said apologetically, 'I am sorry.' 'It's okay,' I said, trying my best to make it sound as normal as it was. We lay there, naked, beside each other. What was she thinking? I did not know. But I was thinking about the loneliness that had engulfed me upon arriving in this colossal city, which was now hugely challenged in her presence.

A day or two later, we had sex. It was strenuous but it was an experience that was carved under my skin and that titillated my body and mind. I started seeing that in the domain of desires, we were equal, we were human. But, outside the domain of desires, we remained socially constructed persons assigned with identities— the reasons for our being unfree. She was a Shia Muslim. But this difference melted as soon as we touched or kissed. Did she feel the same way I did? I do not know. We had hardly spoken to each other about our feelings and how we were affecting each other in a relationship. But I reckon that a touch or kiss has the potential to put an end to socially constructed differences or prejudices. Probably that is why conservative families in India are scared of people falling in love freely. They know that if love is uncensored, their lies will be exposed.

Being with Saira, at this point, books became a secondary source of learning for me. This was the beginning for me to learn a great deal from being with people, being affected by them, and often being hurt by them. But neither could they see my hurts nor did I have the language and courage to tell them. Between me and Saira, the most real and genuine interaction was when we made love. In her, I could see that organized religion plays an instrumental role in a person being unfree in social spaces. But it cannot take away the instinct from the heart to love and to be loved by whoever it chooses, to consume each other in the rituals of the body. Whenever there is an opportunity, people savagely defy religion and caste and their existence. Caste and religion melt on lips when kissed, and they are buried when we are inside each other. Those are small but meaningful mutinies of two individuals in their own secret ways.

The more we had sex, the more we felt the need to have it. In the classroom, I remained as wordless as I could. I found myself a misfit among the majority of the students, including Saira. Her access to things, both material and intellectual, was indicative of her privileges. Apart from class and religion, what made us different was our location in society. She had *language* for her history and her being. I had barely scratched the surface of understanding my identity, but I did not have a language to articulate it until then. Hence, my silence was my defiance. The idea of changing social realities, which was at the heart of the pedagogy at TISS, was seemingly not my cup of tea. How can you bring change in caste-society without destroying it? How can you discuss or teach about bringing change without teaching students how to destroy and put an end to caste, rather than producing dull research on it? How can you bring change in society by researching victims and not the oppressors who victimize people? I did not find answers to these questions in my early days at TISS. I got one more reason to hold on to my poetic imagination in order to make sense of the world around me and protect myself from being institutionalized.

*

On several occasions, Saira and I bunked classes and had sex in her flat when her roommates were away, attending classes. Sometimes, I remember, we were engaged in making out until late at night, in the kitchen, while her roommates were in other rooms. I was aware that my attention was getting diverted from books. On the one hand, I felt guilty about it, on the other hand, I was increasingly being exposed to sexual experiences, which introduced me to my vulnerabilities. At the beginning of and during sex, I was fully involved in it. But as soon as I ejaculated, I found myself swallowed up by a curiously bleak emptiness in which I felt completely detached from her. This was new to me. Maybe it was because I was too conscious of my standing, which pushed me to compare myself with her in the social or material realm. Or maybe because it was only in sex when we both were equal. Living and breathing outside those sensual moments, we remained unequal.

I remember her having a smartphone, or using WhatsApp, clicking selfies or consuming fast food (until then I had not been aware of the concept of ordering food from McDonald's or KFC or Domino's), or speaking in urban lingo—all these required buying capacity or privilege of access. My buying capacity was zero; my privilege was nil. This formed in me a sense of me being a liability when we were together. But the materiality was the least hurtful. What was more dangerous was my emotional state while looking at her or her friends or people on campus who exhibited their privileged world, of the past and the present, through their photos.

As far as I remember, I only had one photo, a family photo, a photo in which I was two years old, sitting with my mother and father in their youthful years. No photographs meant no memory. Having photographs meant having memories, a life, one that you could not only proudly exhibit but also assert your history through. In the absence of photos or a smartphone, I had nothing to exhibit or assert. At home, we were not communicative people. It is difficult to transform anything into a memory in the absence of words or photographic evidence. Perhaps that is why I began to believe that stories would be an inevitable part of my life from this moment onwards. It took me seven years to acquire the language for my emotional world and develop an eye with which I began to see myself in connection to the history of my community. When my grandmother died in 2020, in the absence of her photo, I was transported to back to the moment when I used to feel jealous of these elite, Savarna and privileged people from TISS who exhibited their privileged life through photos. Over these years, I have realized that all I have is words. I dug my *historical* self with it, in this article:

Non-dalits may find it unbelievable, but death for dalits is metaphorical. An "untouchable" never existed as a person worthy of respect from society or recognised as a mind. He was simply invisible, except when his labour was extracted, exploited and used for free. Thus it was not very difficult for dalits from a few generations ago to understand how it feels to remain invisible. This reality has not ceased to exist even today, although its forms vary. Not existing for others, not being recognised by others, is a condition of simply not being extant. It is in this sense that death is metaphorical for dalits. Yet, this is not a normal reality. It is an abnormal condition, an ecology, to use a broad term, that has been constructed by brahmins and all other castes who follow them.

This abnormality, too, was first understood by dalits in Maharashtra and dealt with by establishing a body of dalit literature. Those who simply did not exist in the eyes of caste Hindus and brahmins in society have arrived at the centre-stage of stories, histories and memories via dalit literature. Gradually, and surprisingly, their arrival in textual form is being recognised by the world and this community has been reborn in the imagination, both literary and historical, of the world. Text—as history and memory—being the most effective tool to keep our sense for resistance against enslavement of any kind alive, proved to be a resurrection from social death for mahars (Buddhists) and a few other dalit castes in Maharashtra.

Then, suffice to say that as long as the caste system will prevail, physical death for dalits will always remain metaphorical. Their actual death lies in an inability to be in text, or transform into a text as a story, memory and history. But before death, there is life. And here, dalit literature today proclaims their passionate existence, and passion for life.[1]

*

I started spending nights with Saira, in her flat. I would go back to my hostel in the morning and then attend classes. I was forgetting that this hostel was the shelter, besides food, which was my only support for survival for two years in Mumbai. When I was not with Saira at night, I tried reading *Family Matters*. But somehow, I lost interest in the story. I began to explore writings by Black writers, and the first book by a Black writer I bought was Frantz Fanon's *The Wretched of the Earth*. Half-way into reading this book, my world started to go through emotional upheavals, the clarity of which I was desperately seeking at this point. But the biggest hurdle in my way was the *academic* language at TISS, in which I was a *subject* of research, my history was that of victims and my dreams were never recognized. It was becoming a necessity to prove, by using this language in assignments and arguments, that I was learning. Within a couple of months, I had already started resisting the culture here, the culture of contradictions from which I derived my learnings and not from the syllabus.

I did not make friends in the class. At the most, they were acquaintances, some of them sensible. Friendship develops in equal spaces, where your share in 'giving' and 'taking' is equal, or where you are fully accepted with your historical self, where you are accepted with equal respect and the pride with which people perceive themselves, isn't it? Not that there were no students in TISS who did not share my history or past. There were many Dalit students here; they had come after so much struggle, crossing social barriers and acquiring admission purely on the basis of their merit and talent. But I suspected that they were becoming institutionalized. The way they wrote, articulated themselves or started perceiving the world indicated the increasing impact of TISS's pedagogical language on their thought processes. It was not their fault. Institutions are created to institutionalize a person. Be it school, universities or prison.

In India, institutions dominated by Brahminical communities are meant to *Brahminize* a person. What kept me vigilant about this was my engagement with poetry and my growing conviction that it was *through* poetry that I could seek clarity about myself and the world around me. So when students were asked and encouraged to read 'scientific' research papers, I read them quickly just to copy their style of writing and know their methods, but for the clarity of the subject and to assert myself, I always relied on fiction and poetry in Dalit literature.

*

To write an assignment, or to explore the academic world, a laptop was becoming a growing necessity. I could not dare to ask my parents for money to buy a laptop. It was simply beyond their financial capacity. So the only option was an education loan. Many Dalit–Bahujan students who did not have the financial capacity to survive here chose this option. But without any guarantee for substantial employment after the completion of the course, it was a risk. Besides, no one asked whether students would *want* to work in order to repay the loan. To adjust to the demands here, students simply ran out of choices. For example, when I availed the education loan, I knew that it would take years of my life to repay it, which meant I had to work—even if I wanted to study further—*just* to repay the loan. But needs are created and capitalist provisions are there to fulfil those needs. This was a trap, I understood later.

When I got the loan of Rs 84,000 for the laptop and my expenditure for two years, I went with Saira and bought the laptop and books. The remaining money was spent within a couple of months before the end of the first semester. There was no guiding figure to ask the students what they would like to do in the future, and there was simply no mechanism in place to encourage them in their intellectual endeavours. In India, institutes contradict their own philosophies. The problem of Dalit students is that they continue to walk with this dilemma only to realize that many of their dreams, which they once nurtured, are now completely buried in the process of institutionalization. They are *in* it. But they are not an *essential* part of it. They are in the institution to *serve* it in many unknown ways.

It was October 2013. As the semester was coming to an end, many Savarna and privileged students became excited about the idea of going home, having home-cooked food and enjoying time with family. To me, all these things never meant a *home*. I was in TISS, but I defied this space. I was at home, but I defied it too. I felt I simply had no place to go to which I could call a home. I was subconsciously aware of my incapacity for a language which could connect me with people by which I could *feel* at home. Home was never a place for me. It was a space where you are accepted and understood. In the absence of a language to connect with people, I, by this time, simply did not have a home. So when everyone went home, including Saira, I chose to do an internship in Pune, at Manuski—a TBM-affiliated organization that worked on atrocities faced by Dalits.

*

It was here, during the internship, that I first read *Pedagogy of the Oppressed* by Paulo Freire. It blew my mind. I started to imagine people in India in compartments of the *oppressor* and *oppressed*. It was the second book, after *Annihilation of Caste* by Dr Ambedkar, that assigned some meanings to the world around me and offered me clarity about the conspiracies of the world. With this book, I imagined myself too as a part of a structure, a victim of the

institutions where I had been so far and a person whose history has
been erased from his mind by these institutions. I never returned
this book to the library. I carried it with me to Mumbai after my
internship came to an end. Because, in the dark tunnel of life,
Pedagogy of the Oppressed became another lamp to me.

*

Another person from the organization told me about their
forthcoming trip to a few atrocity-ridden districts in Maharashtra.
I did not have a clear idea of what it was about, but it sounded
fascinating. I had never been to this part of Maharashtra. This
was called 'Marathwada', an atrocity-prone region in 'progressive'
Maharashtra. From Solapur to Usmanabad to Latur to Nanded
to Parbhani to Jalna to Aurangabad to Ahmadnagar to Nashik
to Mumbai and to Pune—this was our route. It was the route on
which I mapped the stories of violence and resistance most of us
do not see all our lives.

For around ten days, I was to see the lives of people, of my
community and of other vulnerable communities, such as Pardhis,
fractured by the daily risk of being humiliated, killed or raped at
the hands of local feudal higher-caste people. The people I met,
the stories I heard, the emotions I felt, the narratives of violence
I encountered, all exposed the grand theories to be so pallid and
unconvincing that I felt I had been taught, not only wrongly, but
also heartlessly at school and at TISS. I also saw Dalit-Buddhists
fighting this traditionally brutal society with their vision of a
casteless society. At the heart of their struggle and fight, there was
Dr Ambedkar. No school, no university, no book (except Dalit
literature) had taught me this. They had all hidden this truth from
me. Paulo Freire's 'banking system of education' sounded so real
when I discovered my own ignorance about the nature of caste-

atrocities. Those ten days completely erased the thoughts of Saira from my mind. It was the first time I consciously and so strongly felt the existence and significance of Dr Ambedkar in my life. It was the first time, when I saw the larger section of my community from this region and how they live, I felt I was relatively *privileged* to never have faced the kind of violence they narrated. My alienation from my history ceased at this moment. I could see more clearly now who I had been all this while. I started thinking not only as an individual, but an individual from a community whose history and resistance against caste-society made each of us vulnerable to violence and humiliation, both stark and subtle, at the hands of Savarna castes, Brahminism and feudalism, both in villages and cities. I ceased to be confused about *who I was*. Once you know who you are, you become a threat to those who first distorted and then erased your history, your identity and your roots.

On my return to TISS after the internship in Pune came to an end, I increasingly became convinced that academia in India did not possess the language to understand my life, the life of my community, their emotions, their feelings, their vision and their ideas of resistance while living surrounded by caste and its everyday violence. My fidelity to poetry became even more unshakable. Our lives were too vast and textured to be understood in the dull language of academics. Six years later, I included my experience of witnessing the atrocity-prone districts in one of my short stories, 'The Sense of the Beginning', published in my short story collection, *Flowers on the Grave of Caste*.[2] I could have written a research paper on this, since I knew the location of data and how to interpret it in 'scientific' language. But I chose to write this as a story, because I knew that it was only in fiction that I could be really true and alive as a human being.

*

It was November 2013. I returned to TISS. Saira told me the date of her return. Excited, I told her I would come to see her at the railway station. She said that there was no need for it. Still, I went to Mumbai Central station to receive her. It had been a month since I had last seen her. My introversion did not allow me to express this small yet significant feeling of missing her. When she stepped down from the train, her smile, with which I was familiar, was missing. She spoke, but her words sounded as if they were instructions to distance me from her. I did not understand the changed tone in her voice. We took a taxi to her flat. All through the journey, we were silent as if we were strangers. As we entered her flat, she asked me questions about my internship as if it were a formality. Then, in a calm but weak voice, she said, 'Yogesh, we cannot be together anymore.'

I had not anticipated this sudden loss. It took over my entire being. After she spoke those words, she came close to me as if she wanted to keep the touch of my flesh as a souvenir. She kissed me. My sadness and anger melted on her lips. Lips unlocked, she spoke again, 'This is the last time we will be together like this.' Then she removed her t-shirt. I saw a bruise on her chest. I looked at it and tried to run my fingers over it. She held my hand, stopped me from touching her wound. She suggested we rest for a while, half-naked. She wanted to comfort me. I resisted, not because I did not want to but because I was irrevocably angry and confused by what she had said and what she did after that. This was my second break-up. My second *rejection*. I was least hurt by the rejection, though.

The reason for my anger was different. The problem was not the rejection, but not knowing how to deal with it. I saw in her eyes an attempt to hide her intentions, the reason for her being unkind, which she did not want me to know. I was angry because

I was ignorant of them. I was angry because I had not yet learnt how to deal with loneliness and loss.

I kept seeking answers about this relationship. For years, I kept imagining what could have happened with her because of which she abruptly took this decision. Clarity about the origin of loss helps one overcome hate and anger. Hate is too expensive a burden to carry in our heart for all our life. And once you overcome it, you understand the importance of forgiveness. I believe our strength to survive all odds in life lies in our ability to forgive and, sometimes, forget. It is too difficult to live, carrying the burden of everything you witness. Sometimes you have to forget to hate, sometimes you have to forgive so you can love. Since Saira never disclosed why she broke up with me, I turned to poetry for clarity about this moment. I wrote a poem called 'Forgiveness'[3]:

When they departed
They did not blame
Their Gods—in whose company
They lose their original self—
For that departure.
They did not even curse
Themselves.

I wanted to say that we, humans, are defeated by religions. I wanted to say that we are victims. I wanted to say that we are yet to learn to see how unfree we are becoming, day by day.

*

Mumbai, Me and Dr Ambedkar

I always wanted to be hugged
Hence mistook their needs for love,
Consequently, abandoned, snubbed
On barren land, barren sky above

I avoided Saira in classrooms and on campus. I started to *hate* her. Frustrated, with whatever money remained from the loan, I got drunk for a week. Later, I could not avoid the guilt taking over my mind as a result. I wanted to forget the pain of being alone again. But alcohol did not help. Once again, I found myself with no friends, no language to become a part of a group and no money to bring me to their level.

I also did not feel close to people who shared my caste-background or my life experiences, because long ago I had ceased to belong to their moral world. In it, each person had to behave according to set moral codes associated with Buddhism, and the idea of liberation was reduced to politics and momentary protests. Drinking or smoking were perceived as traits of a person who was out of focus in life. The 'individual' is the focus of Buddhism;

I never found this approach among my people on campus. I chose to live in the utopia of my desires, my ideas and my dream to write and to survive. At this moment, all I had was books. Indian writing in English, be it fiction or nonfiction, seemed to have nothing to offer to me. I felt detached and dissociated from it. I started re-reading *The Annihilation of Caste*. Then I read *Waiting for a Visa*, supposedly the only text Dr Ambedkar wrote about his personal life. As I read Dr Ambedkar depicting his world with intellectual clarity and emotional zeal, I saw him as a profound person and a philosopher. And my interpretation or understanding of his text, especially of *Waiting for a Visa*, led me to find answers in my life, especially with the idea of love, with which I was struggling at the moment. I found Dr Ambedkar's books helping me understand life more than society or politics. I started to *see* life through his words.

Reading *Waiting for a Visa* was unsettling. It was about four experiences of caste-discrimination from his life that had informed his intellectual understanding and emotional clarity. But I read it in my way, to understand the problem of love and my emotional world. In caste-society, I felt, love is not a spontaneous emotion. Hate is. Hate is alluring. Hate is fascinating. It is so powerful an emotion in India because each caste reserves a feeling of revulsion against another. Consequently, a person from one caste rarely feels close to a person from another caste. Hate emanates from the intention of rejection and selfishness. For me—a Dalit, part of a people this land has never allowed to blossom—to develop the emotion of love is to develop an ability to overcome my own instinct of vengeance and take the risk to develop an affinity towards those who might push me into bleaker terrains of life. However, this is also the condition for me to be in this society and be able to speak and write. This is because I cannot write with hate nor with ignorance of the world around me. I feel that only love has the ability to overcome the fear I have of casteist society. Love opens up new avenues of meaning in life that hate closed for us long ago. Love is overcoming the fear of being alone. I learnt this from Dr Ambedkar's life. He not only overcame this fear but transformed it into love that, today, does not let us feel alone.

*

In my eyes, *Waiting for a Visa* reaffirmed my position in society. It was incredible to learn to see the world through the perspective that was true to my history and in which I could feel the agonies of my ancestors, from whom I had inherited this social position. After all, I was not *rootless*. Knowing his roots for a Dalit person means seeing the world in all its conspiracies against him. Suddenly, after reading *Waiting for a Visa*, my understanding of my surroundings became more polemic in a sense that I longer remained what I used to be: an introvert.

The TISS campus was a small world in itself. I was fascinated by it. Outside the campus, the world was different, even contradictory, both in philosophy and practice. Outside the campus, there was Mumbai, which was hidden by the protectively ignorant and elitist world of the campus. I began to see Mumbai in its many hues when I met Jasmine and started to date her. It was her need, more than love: *I was her need.* And I, who feared to be alone in the fascinating vastness of this city, started to learn to act upon my needs and desires, more than my ideas. A month or so after Saira broke up with me, I started spending time browsing Facebook. I came across Jasmine's profile and randomly sent her a friend request because I liked her photos of Mumbai and mistook her profile for some Mumbai-based photography page. A week or so later, we started chatting and then, one day, we decided to meet.

We met at Costa, a cafe in Bandra at Carter Road. This vicinity was evidently elite and crowded with young people. In front of the cafe, there was the Arabian Sea and at its shore, there were rocks and thick mangroves where, I learnt later, people went to make out and have sex. The real sickness of this place was visible in the small children selling balloons, flowers, books and toys at the traffic signal. I reached the cafe early.

Jasmine came when the sun went down. The breeze from the sea was humid but pleasantly soothing. We ordered coffee, and she took out a cigarette to light it up. She offered me one. I took it and lit it for myself. I talked about literature and politics and she talked about photography and literature. She had been a reader since she was a child. Her father had put her into the habit of reading while he tutored children to earn money. Literature was the common thread between us. I shared my readings and interpretations with her. She did too. There were some stories we had both read. We spoke till 10.30 p.m. I did not feel hungry. She guided me on how to catch the last local train from Bandra to Panvel. My stop was Govandi. When I caught the train, I was excited and happy thinking about our meeting. I did not eat that night. The dining hall at TISS was closed, and I did not have money to eat outside. But I did not feel the need to eat either. After that meeting, we met frequently for a few weeks, and the last local to Panvel from Bandra became my regular route to return to the hostel late in the night, often hungry, but mostly consoled.

It was 31 December 2013. We decided to meet in the evening. I started liking going to Bandra, feeling lost in that elite air and walking on the streets with Jasmine, buying books, smoking, drinking, with her showing me the places around. While I did all that, I never felt I was visible to people there. Or maybe it was I who wanted to hide myself from the world. That evening when we met, we went to drink at a pub. It was noisy inside, but it was colourful enough to get mixed into it as another colour and forget who you were. This was Mumbai, a privileged part of it, in which I got dissolved as a colour that did not matter much. Inside the pub, we talked and listened to each other as much as we could. But drinking was something we enjoyed.

Then at night, Jasmine called me to her place in Bandra. She was staying with her Syrian Christian friend from Kerala, along with another girl. All of them were working and staying away from home. Staying away from home was their idea of freedom, I suspected later. We took an auto and reached her place; Jasmine made sure that the landlord did not suspect that a man was entering her place. Surreptitiously, we climbed the stairs. Her friends were out, celebrating the last evening of the year. We smoked and talked. She ordered the food from a nearby eatery called Dukes. The privacy between us was intoxicating. Although we talked, it was difficult to distract ourselves from each other. When an awkward silence arrested us, as we lay in her bedroom, I moved close to her with that familiar pounding heart of mine. The language of her eyes reciprocated my intention. We kissed. Then we made out until late in the night. In the morning, we made love. Throughout the night, we became accustomed to each other's body and intentions. We talked intermittently, which was something I felt was needed in order to confirm our choices. She made coffee afterwards. I drank coffee and smoked. Although my body was tired because of the sexual rituals all through the night, the morning sunlight was stimulating enough to keep me energized. She thought of clicking my photos. She made me pose. I had never before posed for photos. No one had even clicked candid photos of me. That was the first time I was photographed because someone thought that I was *worth* being photographed. That was the first day in my life I saw myself as a subject of a photograph and, hence, worthy of becoming a memory, a fact and someone who had once existed; this photograph was evidence of that. Seeing myself in those photos, an unseen inferiority I had about my body and skin colour vanished. This was happening for the second time. I was discovering myself afresh, as if I had got a new perspective to look at myself, as if I was born anew.

*

Often, we strolled down Colaba causeway, watched movies, visited galleries to see paintings, art shows, ate at Parsi cafes and bought books. As we strolled, I could not avoid a feeling of getting lost in Colaba and South Mumbai's colonial past that was lingering in my imagination. Those roads, those colonial buildings and those posh art galleries fascinated me; I almost felt an instant connection with them. Jasmine knew a bit of this side of Mumbai. Mostly, when we talked about books, it seemed to me that she really had a grasp over the story of the book she discussed. My understanding of books was new in the sense that I had started seeing stories from the location of caste. To convey to her my anti-caste analysis of a book or a story was incredibly difficult. She and her Syrian Christian friend had had access to books and sources of knowledge from an early age and chose to live and work outside the home—to live *freely*. They knew the world, but they were either oblivious to their own caste background or conveniently ignorant or protectively silent about it. Their idea of freedom, material and spiritual, was informed by Western thoughts in the absence of any clarity about their own history and roots. Whenever I asked Jasmine about her caste background, she either diverted the topic or replied, 'I really do not have any idea.' But her not knowing her caste was not my concern at all. In fact, I was yet to understand that such ignorance matters in inter-caste relationships because this ignorance is solely responsible for an upper-caste partner misreading and misunderstanding the behaviour of a lower-caste partner. Caste is an invisible stimulus with which we judge or understand our inter-caste partner—I did not know this back then.

In June 2014, when I shifted the subject of my dissertation from 'A brothel of Nagpur' to 'The Ramabai Nagar Massacre of 1997', I decided to visit Ramabai Nagar, a prominently Dalit–Bahujan locality, located in Ghatkopar East, and asked Jasmine to come along with her camera.

We encountered a huge statue of Dr Ambedkar as we entered Ramabai Nagar. This place was filled with people of many religions and castes. Its streets were busy with hawkers, shops and shoppers. I also saw hoardings of various political parties and groups, even though it was predominantly a Dalit–Bahujan locality. Here, many persons from the same caste were affiliated with various ideologies and political parties and groups. Ramabai Nagar was a fusion of life and philosophy, struggle and survival. This place, as dense with people as it could be, contained a curious charm when it came to transcending the boundaries of caste, religion and language. Hunger, survival and resistance were some of the elements that made the fabric of this locality strong. Ramabai Nagar was a world within Mumbai that was not even present in the dominant literary or cinematic imagination. This world becomes apparent to you only when you connect with the people who made this world possible. I learnt about all this gradually as my conversations with Jayawant Hire (whom I called Jayawant Dada) and Kishor Kardak[1] from Ramabai Nagar developed over the years.

That day, on my first visit, I sought the number of Jayawant Dada from an acquaintance who had been in journalism for a while and knew about this massacre. Jayawant Dada was a thin man, with slightly sunken cheeks and a voice with authority, in which he explained to me not only the history of this massacre but the political history of Maharashtra, the Shiv Sena and many aspects of Ambedkarite politics. He had been a voracious reader from a very young age. He penned a short story collection called *Manus* (Man) in 1989 and started a periodical called *Krantikari Janata* (*Revolutionary People*) in the early 1990s, which was published in Marathi and Urdu simultaneously—the only bilingual periodical of that time. He seemed to have a panoramic view of Ambedkarite politics, politics in Maharashtra and of literature. He was also a man with some incredible tales of oral history that had never reached the pages of books and had therefore remained unknown. Through his words, Mumbai revealed its true face, which had been invisible to me until then. To me, it seemed that he carried the political and cultural history of Dalits and Mumbai at his fingertips. He was a reader of those stories that I was listening to for the first time. These were stories of people I felt I knew, and they too seemed to know me. After meeting Jayawant Dada, I began to see Mumbai through its people.

'You must meet Kishor Kardak also, he will also tell you many things about the massacre,' Jayawant Dada told me. Kishor Kardak too was a resident of Ramabai Nagar. As Jayawant Dada, Jasmine and I headed up to meet him through streets dense with people and life, Jasmine continued to capture pictures. Kishor Kardak was an interesting person. His physique was slim, his moustache thick and his voice thicker. Today he is affiliated with a few groups that work at the grassroots level for people. But he had journeyed across many ideologies when he was young. He took us to meet people who were direct victims of the massacre. I talked to them and Jasmine clicked photos. I listened to their stories of horror and how violence and police brutality had devastated their lives after the massacre. There was a silent rage in their eyes that was impossible for me to understand at that moment. I was strangely detached and unmoved. But their stories, their experiences, their frustrations while waiting for justice and never receiving it and their resistance of seventeen years were entering my mind from the back door, into my subconscious. Kishor helped us understand the politics and nuances behind it. I listened to everything he said, silent as though I were a tree which was being axed but could not speak or cry. The story of the Ramabai Nagar massacre was gradually taking root in my mind.

On 11 July 1997, people from Ramabai Nagar woke up to witness the desecration of Dr Ambedkar's bust. It had been garlanded with shoes and chappals.[2] Dr Ambedkar's bust and statue has been a source of liberation for Dalits and Buddhists across the world. Dalits as a community had been erased, caricatured or vulgarized in the national literary or cinematic imagination. Dr Ambedkar's statue as a symbol plays an instrumental role in rejecting all these Brahminical practices, because it affirms and projects the aspirations of Dalits for intellectual life and the quest for democracy. If this very source of aspiration is desecrated, then it is a direct humiliation of those who witness the liberation that Dr Ambedkar's statue as imagery and symbolism brought in their lives.

In 1997, when the people of Ramabai Nagar witnessed this humiliation, it enraged them. Not that they were not aware of the hate upper castes had reserved for them, but the desecration of Dr Ambedkar's statue meant an attack on the collective consciousness of the community and on all those who strive for democratic society amidst the brutality and sickness of caste. Seeing this desecration, people gathered around the statue and then went to the police station but returned hopeless. As they mobilized on the highway in front of Ramabai Nagar to protest, police vans came within a few minutes. Before people could even sense what was happening, the police opened fire. Shocked by the noise of bullets, people started running back to their homes. Police chased them inside the locality. Eleven people died in the police firing, including a small boy, whose skull was cracked open by a bullet. Twenty-six people were injured. In 2014, even after seventeen years, neither the then police sub-inspector Manohar Kadam, who had ordered the firing, was punished, nor was the person(s) who had desecrated Dr Ambedkar's bust caught.[3]

Several times, I asked Jayawant Dada and Kishor about this, the stories that were entangled within this massacre, the politics behind it and about justice. And each time I was redirected to the reality: If you are a Dalit and demand justice, you'll most likely receive a bullet or further humiliation. Yet, people like Jayawant Dada or Kishor, whose lives revolved around Dr Ambedkar and his vision, tirelessly work, write or speak against injustice everyday. Consider the level of tolerance and persistence a Dalit requires in order to live, survive, resist and aspire for democratic life in such a society. Could people who have internalized victimhood possibly do this? Does this not require sheer courage to seek light amidst the complete darkness around you? But academic institutions in India either ignore such stories of resilience or slyly hide them from public view.

Many times, when I went back to the hostel after meeting Jayawant Dada and Kishor, I couldn't help thinking: *School has failed me.* College had alienated me from my history. And the elite institution in which I was studying had made a victim out of me and always thrust me into a darkness of being. They did not dare to see the light inside me, the light which could be a source of hope for others. A Dalit is rarely recognized as a mind in Brahminical institutions, be it school, college, university or in social space. And that is why his anger is relevant. This anger is rarely, if ever, perceived in a positive light in universities. All they seek in our lives are problems and suffering. All they talk about us is the 'failure' of the anti-caste movement. Not that there have been no failures. But since they have never been a part of our lives, they are utterly blind to anything about us, whether failure or success. Their caste is the blindfold on their eyes. But whatever the reasons they claim about the failure of our movement, I see failures in not being able to produce stories (not of one kind but of many kinds) of each of our generations. One generation is alienated from another in the absence of stories. And in an absence of stories between generations, there grows confusion, political and historical. Black writer Chimamanda Ngozi Adichie, in her TED talk, once famously said: 'The single story creates stereotypes, and the problem with stereotypes is not that they are untrue, but that they are incomplete. They make one story become the only story.'[4] This is what I strongly felt whenever I encountered Savarna narratives about Dalit lives.

Listening to the stories of the Ramabai Nagar massacre for the first time from its victims, Jayawant Dada and Kishor, I thought I was listening to them as an outsider. After all, I went there with the purpose of *researching* that violent episode. But I was wrong. I did not know that pain, whether it is yours or others', when listened to with a purpose of understanding it, becomes a part of you that unravels the enigma of life. Sometimes, it goes into the bloodstream. Sometimes, it becomes a dream we had never anticipated, and it haunts us. And sometimes, it helps you know who you are. That night Jasmine and I went to Colaba, and we drank. Then we went to her flat. I was feeling empty inside. I drank, but my emotions were forming around what I had heard from the victims of the Ramabai Nagar massacre—their silent eyes, their disappointed yet firm faces, their incredible level of patience and the utopian belief in justice that some of them held.

Where was I in everything, as someone who was as vulnerable as them in different times and at different places? Was I ethically eligible to research their stories without fully knowing and asserting who I was? Even after Jasmine and I had made love, I was unable to avoid these thoughts. Thoughts do not have sound, but they protect us from drowning in the ignorant silence of society. I was smoking a cigarette while looking at photographs of John Lennon and other white musicians and actors pasted on the wall in the hall, thinking how my world, though an integral part of this nation, was alien to its imagination. Jasmine did not share her thoughts about the visit; she barely had a discussion about it with me. This was a completely new world to her. She opened her book and started reading, seemingly relaxed after sex and a cigarette. I too lit a cigarette and looked at her. I reached to kiss her and we became intimate. We made love again. After coming, I was exhausted and restless. But I behaved as if I was relaxed.

*

A year after I joined TISS, my entire perspective on Mumbai, its people and their lives had radically changed. The only thing, in textual form, that kept me anchored here and gave me intellectual clarity and emotional courage were Dr Ambedkar and poetry. It was at this point that I felt a necessity to write. Writing became critical, not for survival, but to establish my existence in this vast universe. The subject and language of my poems changed drastically. I could no longer imagine poems unrelated to me and people around me. I ceased to be bothered by not using big and poetic-sounding words. I longer needed to sit and *imagine* poems. Poems became blood, and I, a wound. Poems began to seep through me.

Interestingly, I found Dr Ambedkar more relevant in shaping the course of my poetry than poets. I found *perspective* in his words, without which poetry is incomplete. How can a poet not true to his history be true to the world? I had been writing in English for six years but, until 2014, I had hardly found or felt myself in this language. Encountering the poems of Namdeo Dhasal was also a crucial step. Reading his poetry and his thoughts about literary tradition in caste-society freed me from the dilemma of language. I began to sense that poetry is not discipline. Poetry is madness. And madness is exclusive, it is unique and it must be devastating, either for a poet or its readers. If it is not, then the poet is trapped within language and mistakes the craft of language for poetry. One thing I learnt from Namdeo Dhasal: A poet must avoid the temptation of writing a poem; a poet must let the poem take shape in the background of his madness of being; a poet does not arrive at a poem—a poem arrives at a poet. Poetry is a matter of life, not imagination.

I started writing poems and shared them on Facebook. I let people decide about my poems. I was not convinced by the idea of showing my poems to any critic or editor or any other poet. Many of the poems I wrote between 2014 and 2016 became part of my first poetry collection, *The Bridge of Migration*. Now, my poems were rooted in me; no longer were they outside me. When my first collection was going to be published, I wanted to write a dedication. This is what appeared on paper, in less than thirty seconds:

> I did not know:
> My father, a diligent worker,
> Would speak his love for me.
>
> Today, if I write poems
> He writes through me.

It was a discovery. Because I had proclaimed the roots of my poems to the world.

*

Often, our stories are born and die in our imagination or in our thoughts. They do not become a part of the cultural memory of the society in which we contribute our labour. I did not want this to happen with my life. Maybe this was something so deeply rooted in me that I started finding myself only in words and nowhere else. *Round Table India*, a Dalit–Bahujan platform started by Kuffir Nalgundwar and Anu Ramdas, became my space to find myself in words, to be born in words, with each article I wrote and got published there. I was introduced to *Round Table India* at a point of my life when I was desperately searching for a space that could embrace my words without judgement and publish without making them alien to me in the editing process. This was not easy. Writing was not easy. A thinking mind is prone to suffering, and a thinking mind in search of emancipation is more so. But this time, I knew that to get out of this invisible trap, there was only one solution: to write, to read and write, to read, imagine and write; to do this tirelessly. Writing is not without consequences though. One of the articles I wrote during this time was on the Dalai Lama and his politics, in which I outrightly criticized him for his appeasement of the work and vision of the Rashtriya Swayamsevak Sangh (RSS).[5] I was severely opposed by almost everyone from my class because a Tibetan girl in it found my article offensive. Of course, she knew nothing about caste, and it was apparent that she had no idea about the RSS. Nearly everyone in my class boycotted me. I was firm about what I wrote. I asked them to respond to my article on whatever they found problematic. No reply came; no one wrote.

Maybe their opposition originated from disdain. They did not seem to despise me as long as I did not know who I was. My knowledge of myself and speaking from that position became a danger to them. They knew it—they possessed the instinct of an oppressor, and this was the source of their loathing. And when they could not directly express it, they were deliberately unkind—by ignoring, rejecting and invisibilizing me. Wasn't this an integral characteristic of *untouchability*? I knew this instinctively. It was apparent in their eyes. My defence was to loathe them in return. But I diverted my anger to words. I finally felt that my anger had some meaning.

*

By 2015, I became more accustomed to TISS as a campus. It grew in my mind as a place of contradictions. These contradictions were my lessons. It was possible because I was increasingly becoming more involved with the people, the literary world outside the campus. I travelled—to write and to know more from the people whose idea of Mumbai was absent in TISS, both as a discourse and of life in the city. During this time, I wanted to write an article on Sambhaji Bhagat, the prominent Shahir from Maharashtra whose songs turned out to be a discourse in an anti-Brahminical tradition of music. I had first read about him in *Tehelka* magazine around 2012, back in Nagpur. It was one of my first experiences in reading about such a person in a mainstream English publication. I was in awe of his work. I imagined meeting him if I went to Mumbai in future. Now, I went to meet him at a school a kilometre or two from the Shiwadi local station. He was humble, energetic and informal as a person. There was some kind of naivety in him that endeared him to me. His personality impacted me deeply; I was enchanted by his energy and simplicity and, of course, his songs.

I interviewed him for the article I wanted to write on *Art and Ambedkarism.* This article was published in *Round Table India* a couple of weeks later.

Back then, I was convinced by whatever he told me. But after three or four years, I started to see things differently. When the movie *Court,* directed by a Brahmin director for which Sambhaji Bhagat had composed music and sung a song, was released, I wrote a scathing review of it on *Round Table India.* My review was an angry reaction, but there was a *sense* in it, the sense that Brahminical literary tradition mocked and shunned from public imagination. I heard later that he did not like my take on the movie. But despite all this, people like Sambhaji Bhagat remained instrumental in my understanding of Mumbai, Dr Ambedkar, cultural politics and, subsequently, myself. Sometimes, I felt, we are defined by disagreements with people rather than agreeing with them.

Mumbai grew inside me in this way. I came to know about Sumedh Jadhav, who was a younger brother of Bhagwat Jadhav, a Dalit Panther, who had been killed in the rally at Worli in 1974, when the Shiv Sena had covertly attacked it.[6] I was curious about the Worli attack and the history of the Dalit Panthers. So one day, when I was in Chhatrapati Shivaji Terminus (CST), hunting for second-hand books at pavement booksellers near Flora Fountain, I called him. He asked me to come down to his office. It was located in a colonial-era building, a short walk from there. After we talked for a few minutes, he told me that one person from his office union was going to retire that day. He invited me to come along to the farewell. We crossed the road over to another colonial-era building in which the union office was situated. After the event, Sumedh introduced me to the union leader. He was an old man with fair skin, neat white hair and bluish eyes. Behind him, there was a bust of Lenin and right beside it, there was a small statue of Ganpati. He was a Brahmin. What I was seeing

with my eyes was something Dr Ambedkar had warned about
long ago in his words 'bunch of Brahmin boys' while referring
to Brahmin communists.[7] The words rang very true. This was
also the time I was learning about Marx and communism, and
I understood what Dr Ambedkar had said about communists in
India. The biggest enemies of communism in India were Brahmin
communists, who were also the ruling class. *How can a ruling
class represent the struggle of the oppressed?* I reflected on it, and Dr
Ambedkar's assertion seemed to me irrefutable.

The 'communist' discourse in TISS was no different. There,
human rights and values were discussed in cosy rooms, in which the
liberation of humans from such conditions was imagined through
communist and, surprisingly, Gandhian ideas—without involving
the people who needed this liberation. I could not help but see
that Marx had been mocked and failed by such people. Theories
for the liberation of the 'working classes' were passionately argued
without acknowledging the dual oppression of caste among these
classes. These discussions were held by those who are responsible
for the subjugation of those they wished to liberate. I witnessed
the impotency and inability of such institutions to enact the vision
of Dr Ambedkar.

I was here, but I defied this place. I relied on books and I
was not disappointed. It was my seclusion and distance from all
these groups that enabled me to look at them clearly. But there
was one more reason behind this that became clear to me later
on. Over the years, I travelled to a few premier universities in
India and tried to engage with students there. I suspected that two
things—ignorance and hypocrisy—were the norms that defined
student politics. But I would like to think that before they were
students, they were children, sons and daughters of parents who
had bequeathed their children their caste and, consequently,
the deliberate unkindness that accompanies it. Most people

in this country who have attended school and university end up becoming confused and hypocritical by training. School teaches them something, and they learn something else at home. While school claims to teach students a scientific temperament and democratic outlook (although I have my doubts about it), households teach their children an unscientific temperament and undemocratic outlook by normalizing caste practices. That is why most intellectuals in this country are either hypocrites or ignorant of the life and culture of Dalit–Bahujans. The higher one goes in the caste hierarchy, the higher the level of hypocrisy and ignorance one finds. Breaking the cocoon of caste essentially means exposing yourself to a cruel, insensitive and unkind world. Here, the annihilation of caste is a risk one takes in order to destroy the world within one that was constructed by the home, school, university and various institutions. As I saw, university campuses in India discourage students from taking this risk. TISS was no exception. Most of them deny Dr Ambedkar the legitimate honour he deserves as a home-grown intellectual and theorist. Then, to justify themselves as progressive spaces of knowledge, they embrace and propagate foreign intellectuals, who often falter in their narratives as soon as it comes to understanding caste-society and its vulgar truths.

Ever since I had read Paulo Freire, I started to imagine education as a process to understand your roots. Your perception of the world, which comes from knowing your roots, is a realization, acceptance and assertion of yourself with the history of your ancestors. Whatever little I understood from reading Freire and Dr Ambedkar, I thought that education must lead to agitation in every time and space. When one is being educated, one breaks the monotony of instructions given by institutions. Education ought to de-institutionalize a person, unshackle him. But when I looked around, all I saw were people made into projects of institutionalization. It was apparent from their changed language, their depleted anger, their idea of aesthetics, their sex appeal and, most importantly, from their increasing dependency on the institution's support for further growth in the intellectual domain. I had only two choices. Either do what others were doing, or resist it. I chose the latter. And the problem of resistance is that you are often left alone.

In 2015, I completed my MA course. I had no intention of taking up a job that could bind me further. I knew how dreams are butchered while working to fulfil your needs. I was not sure if people could survive merely by writing. But I wanted to write: This was the only thing clear to me then. I did not sit for campus placements. My thoughts about my family were subconsciously ravaging my ability to imagine my future. My father was too old and tired to work now. My mother, who had been working as a housemaid for almost fifteen years, must have been tired too. How long were they going to work with their weakening bones and tired bodies? These thoughts were pushing me towards the domain of family responsibilities. I could not see myself as a 'family man'. But these responsibilities were real, whether I liked it or not. Suddenly I realized that it had been two years since I had come to Mumbai. I had not gone home even once, trying to find avenues to achieve my dream and keep my pledge.

*

Learning to Write

Have you ever touched fire?
There is a blue light in its heart
I have not touched it, but I aspire to;
I must write about living hurt

You cling on to hate and it eats you, like termites. Hate neither spares the hated nor the hater. And if hate is seen this way, then, it is not difficult to imagine that the 'agitation' should not take place with hate. The subtext in Dr Ambedkar's philosophy is that 'agitation' is the logical understanding of what is wrong with our being and how that 'wrongness' can be rectified. Agitation is deeply personal; society is the site to exhibit it. Agitation is not a seasonal flavour or a flower (like university campuses in India at present). Agitation is having a restlessness for justice and working towards it to the grave. No agitation is fruitful, or for that matter meaningful, if it is not put into action that changes us from being hateful to compassionate— so we stick to the principle of *justice* in love and life. Why is justice so essential in India in connection with love?

If you read Dr Ambedkar and do not feel restlessness in your bones, then you are probably not reading him genuinely. Because reading Dr Ambedkar is arriving at an understanding that the history of caste-society is the history of lovelessness and injustice. In this horrific caste-society, there is no right or wrong side of history. There is only a just and an unjust side to it. Which side do I belong to? Did Dr Ambedkar embrace Buddhism to belong to the absolutely right side of history? I think the answer is no. He knew it. That is why he asked us to strive for the just side of history. Because for us, history was unjust and so was the idea of love in it. Since he was the only philosopher and intellectual in India who advocated the necessity of justice, even in love, he is transformed into a 'love' that today keeps us strong even if we are lonely. But being lonely is not the worst feeling— as his life proves, being abandoned is. The history of caste-society is the history of hateful abandonment, of a few, by many. He was acutely aware of it. That is why he sheltered all of us under his wings.

I jotted this down after I had started to read Dr Ambedkar outside TISS, in my personal time. I wondered why campus life did not allow me to perceive Dr Ambedkar in this way?

A couple of months towards the end of the course, Jasmine had shifted to Farm Road so we could stay close to each other. At her flat, in the open terrace during nights, we drank and had sex. We talked when required. We did not have much conversation. And whatever conversations we had, about books, politics, life or literature, she dismissed my anger when I brought up caste, especially regarding her background.

Soon, I had to vacate the hostel. Jasmine and I started to search for a place near the TISS campus where we both could stay. The problem was that I did not have any source of income and could barely see any possibility of it in the distance.

*

A year ago, I had happened to watch a Marathi film. I had never been a fan of Marathi movies. I found mainstream Marathi movies tasteless and lacking in understanding of social reality. I could never connect to them. By 2014, the world was changing rapidly because of social media. The information that had erstwhile been subject to surveillance, prohibition or was a matter of privilege in terms of access, was being gradually shared by people without many restrictions. On Facebook that year, I witnessed an astonishing discussion around a Marathi film. The film was called *Fandry*. The entire idea of that movie was new to me and to so many people who watched it. I had not witnessed such a story on screen in the history of Marathi cinema. I remember, Jasmine and I went for a matinee show at K Star Mall in Chembur. The movie began with soulful, enchanting music and ended with creating disruptions in the minds of its viewers.

Fandry was an unsettling experience. I shook from inside at the climax. But my body was calm. This movie meant many things to many people. To me, when it ended, it brought to mind the image of my grandfather. He was dark like Jabya (the protagonist of *Fandry*). He was calm and shy like Jabya. He was hardworking and maybe dreamy like Jabya. But in his life, unlike Jabya, the point of revolt was missing. Or perhaps it had been there, but I was unaware of it. No movie had been so powerful to suddenly connect me to my life. *Fandry* turned my imagination towards my roots; it made the people in my life priceless; it introduced to me meanings of people in my life and history. I must have watched hundreds and hundreds of movies in my life. But no movie had made me feel that stories of people like me or my grandfather were significant enough to be made into a movie. All movies had so far alienated me from my history. *Fandry* put an end to this alienation. Cinema reappeared in my life at this point. But with new meanings and purpose.

Six years later, when I met Nagraj Manjule, a poet and the director of *Fandry*, and spent some days with him discussing his poems that I had translated into English, I learnt why certain stories should be told and should be presented by those to whom the story belongs. Because if you do not tell or write or present your story, then your story will become a commodity and never be able to free itself from someone else's imagination, in which you always exist as the *other* and the *outsider*. *Fandry* also pushed me to reconsider my earlier experiences of watching movies. The mere existence of this movie conveyed the irrefutable linkages between imaginary systems (movies being among them) and the history of people—by which myth can be turned into history and memory, and a history and memory can be erased. For example, whenever I had met Jayawant Dada and discussed the Ramabai Nagar massacre and many other stories he told me about the struggle and resistance of Mahar-Buddhists in Mumbai, my mind had directed me to the year 1997. *My history has never been the subject of popular art here*, I thought.

It was in 1997 that I had watched *Border*, a movie about the 1971 Indo–Pak war. *Border* depicted and celebrated the victory of India against Pakistan. This movie was rooted deeply in my mind then. But I remained unaware of the Ramabai Nagar massacre for years to come. Certain stories, of certain people, have always been the part and concern of cinema in India. *Our* stories, which people like me live, were absent in the cinematic space. *Border* was my memory of the year of 1997 and for a while, through it, I was made to feel proud of being Indian. If it was not for my restlessness to follow my dream, to develop an instinct to overcome my confusion, I would have never come to realize that people like me have nothing to be proud of wars fought on borders; that people like me have to fight their own wars *within* the country against their own people, to exist with dignity. As I began to see things in this way, I felt popular movies in India were a deception, because they deceived my memory of being. *Fandry* came as a promise in my life, a promise to exist and to resist in order to exist. And a year later, meeting J.V. Pawar convinced me why I should exist and why I should resist in order to exist.

*

The function of migration in the lives of Dalits is the same as the function of insulin in the body. It works as a catalyst to create intellectual enthusiasm, like insulin helps create energy. Dr Ambedkar saw villages as the deathbed of intellectual growth. Hence, he urged, he aggressively told his people to move from this deathbed to the shores from which they could start a fresh journey in the domain of life. I would like to think this way about the lives of the Dalits who left their villages, once and for all. Cities are not devoid of caste discrimination, but, in the lives of Dalits, cities are catalysts that most likely to produce insulin in the bodies infected with caste. As I look back at the year 2015 when I met J.V. Pawar for the first time, I begin to feel, convincingly, that people like me are not meant for one place. I also begin to see why Dr Ambedkar urged us to move and to search for our place in the world where our dignity is not compromised, where there exist maximum possibilities of justice and love. By migrating from villages to cities, Dr Ambedkar meant migration to a place where one is loved, irrespective of caste, and in the process of love, caste is forgotten like a bad dream.

I would have remained trapped in the confusion about what to do in life had I not left Nagpur. Mumbai was the first step towards my dream, although I was not aware of it then. Vision shapes itself invisibly, the awareness of it follows later when one feels a belonging to the acts that result from the change that is instrumental for developing a vision.

The place where we met J.V. Pawar was the office of the Bharip Bahujan Mahasangh, the political party headed by Prakash Ambedkar, the grandson of Dr Ambedkar. I went there with Abdul, whom George, a friend of mine from Kerala working in Mumbai, introduced to me over a phone. The Nariman Point office was situated in the same premises as the offices of national and regional political parties. It was a busy place with hawkers, food stalls and people dressed in white emerging from and going inside cars with blue-and-red sirens. It was surrounded by tall buildings and breeze from the Arabian Sea. In his mid-seventies, J.V. Pawar was a man whose face was filled with thoughts. Histories lingered at his fingertips, and he told people about them as though they were a part of his own life. His life had been politically intimate and intimately political, I learnt as the years went by. He curiously inquired about Abdul and me and our education. With the same curiosity, he told us about the Dalit Panthers. Listening to the history of the Dalit Panthers from him was like listening to history from a person who had not only written it but who had also been its participant. J.V. Pawar was an exception because he made history on the road and wrote it on the pages. He lived the memories and turned them into a history. As we talked for a couple of hours, he stood up and asked a person from the office to bring the books he had authored, kept in an almirah. He signed them for us and gifted a set of five books to both of us. These were the five volumes he had written about the post-Ambedkarite movement in Maharashtra. I had never heard of them before.

Abdul and I strolled around Nariman Point till night, talked about theories and universities, smoking cigarettes. When we got hungry, we ate kebabs from the roadside. That night, as I reached the room, Jasmine was already there. We prepared food and in the night, we made love, as if it was compulsory. I had forgotten about the books J.V. Pawar had gifted me.

A few days later, Jasmine left for her office in the morning. It was slightly cold; it was unusual weather in Mumbai. In our small room, books occupied most of the space. I suddenly remember the books J.V. Pawar had gifted me. I unzipped the bag. I held all the books in my hands and spent about two hours browsing them one by one. The names, pictures, anecdotes and events mentioned in them appeared to me as if they were part of my life, but they were still new to me because I had never encountered them as history, as facts that were instrumental in shaping the political, social and intellectual culture of my community. How come I did not know them? How come the school, college and university I went to did not mention them? I had no answer to this. I picked up the first volume. It depicted the history (political and social) of the Ambedkarite movement from the period between 1956 and 1961. I did not know that by opening up its first page, I was opening up the first door to enter into the debate, historical and material, of which I am the product.

The first volume was mostly about electoral politics after the death of Dr Ambedkar. It was about how the Republican Party of India (RPI) was envisioned by Dr Ambedkar and, a year later in 1957, established by his associates. It was about how the RPI split, and each leader from different regions in Maharashtra went on to form his own faction of the RPI. The book mentioned several facts behind the factions and approaches of the leaders of our community. It also mentioned victories of the RPI in the electoral domain, its significance in national politics, for a tiny period, which was crucial to change the fabric of politics, consequently the psychological aspects, among the community of Mahar-Buddhists. What triggered me to translate this book from Marathi into English was the realization that the history of my community had never been one-dimensional, that the strength of my community in politics and in the cultural domain had always been undermined or distorted in academics, that we had hardly interrogated the facts that led to the factions in the RPI, probably the first pan-Indian political party of the Dalit community. Reading about the beginning of factions, I drew my interpretations: There was no difference of opinion about ideology among the leaders; there was no dispute over vision that advocated social change as the primary factor to political change; all the leaders possessed the first-hand experience of struggle and hence were in a position to bring possible changes for their community and underprivileged sections of society; the problem, as I saw it, was rooted in the 'ego' of leaders as individuals. Ego overpowered the quest for social and political change. Ego, to be the *only* leader, was at the root of the politics of my community. Over the years, external Brahminical forces from politics merely capitalized on this growing political weather in the community. How can we be broken unless we 'wish' to be broken? As I was done with reading the first volume, I felt an irresistible urge to share this with the world in the English language, in which I felt my world and its politics was completely misunderstood and distorted.

But reading the first volume, I felt I had acquired a kind of clarity that I had always been seeking. With this book, I felt I had acquired a few clues with which, now, I could begin to explore the vision of life. Here, by vision, I mean knowing who you are and doing what you are supposed to do, essentially as a part of the community that has been persecuted by Brahminical norms, which are silent in their working mechanism. Therefore, the emotional world of a Dalit person is as complex as it gets. Nonetheless, it is the very basis of his revolt. But since his world is not verifiable to non-Dalits, he cannot help but feel arrested by loneliness from time to time. A Dalit in caste-society, in search of personhood, always leads a lonely life, if not a secluded one. And the only solution in this loneliness is Dr Ambedkar. He is the bridge between past and present. Dr Ambedkar, even as a memory, rescued many people single-handedly. Yet, not all among us have been able to follow him in the same way. The self-centric politics of our leaders has also shattered the enthusiasm among the people. It has impacted generations to come.

Over the years, it sowed a seed of confusion among the community about their political position and methods of assertion. And if you imagine politics as language, then you must also recognize its strength in making us feel isolated: a situation that is not devoid of people but entails the absence of a language in which to assert the politically shaped self. In the context of the Dalit community, I suspect our 'self' was fragmented into pieces as our politics began to shatter. Hence, we became yet another victim of isolation when we found it overpowering our ability to remain united in the political, social, cultural and even in the personal realm as a force against caste. If caste is a psychological terrorism in this society, then isolation is a political scam. There is no single language in which all anti-caste communities can assert themselves in a unified way. And if there has to be one, then it is Dr Ambedkar's. This is the conclusion I drew from the first volume by J.V. Pawar. I found in it the roots of the confusion that was responsible for the disintegration of the political subconscious among my generation of Dalits. There was another reason I decided to translate this volume. I had experienced that in English academia, this confusion, political and personal, is encouraged among Dalits through trails of academic papers in which our 'self' is studied as a commodity and never as a thinking agent.

Translating this first volume gave me the space to pause and think, to find words with the best possible meaning, to pause again and think not just about how it should be translated but also about the circumstances that birthed the facts written about by J.V. Pawar. Translating is thinking with two minds at the same time. This was a sheer intellectual labour I had never enjoyed before. I felt I *belong* here, the space where I need to think, imagine, codify my thoughts and imagination in words and produce meanings for society, which does not understand my language.

*

A few days later, when I had completed reading the first volume, I told Jasmine about my decision to translate it. I told her I had quit the job. To this, her response was a meek approval. Now, the rent was her burden alone. I felt guilty about it. But I had to be selfish, I told myself. My decision to translate the first volume was the first step towards what I felt I could do all through my life: work with books. I had an inkling of it. But I was not able to convey this clarity to Jasmine. I simply quit the job and started translating the book, without any knowledge of how translation works and what it requires. For the next seven months, each day, I went to the TISS library and worked on translating from morning till evening. A friend of mine shared his lunch with me throughout this time; I simply had no money to spare for food; even to smoke cigarettes, I was dependent on Jasmine. In the evenings, when I returned from the library, I cooked food for both of us. But through the night, my brain was occupied with words. I could no longer avoid not thinking about a word, a sentence, a phrase, an idiom, a figure of speech from the volume and imagining possible

English words and vocabularies for it. Every day, for seven months, three things occupied most of the space in my mind: words, language and meaning. It was my personal declaration of arriving in the domain of a life of the mind.

This was my secret rebellion against the Brahminical English writing in India that had shunned the voice of my history in it. But the problem of English in India is not merely that it has been produced out of the Brahminical imagination or mostly written by Savarna writers. The problem is that it is unable to accurately depict the historical, intellectual and emotional world of Dalit–Bahujan communities. English writing in India lacks clarity about caste oppression. In fact, it mysteriously denies it. The writers who offer a particular image of Indian society to the Western (English-speaking) world are mostly the descendants of those Brahminical or other dominant-caste communities who were the biggest beneficiaries of colonial institutions such as the Indian Civil Service (ICS), the judiciary and other bureaucratic set-ups. They were the first to migrate to Western countries after 1947. After 1947, when the British ceased to be rulers, their positions of power were simply taken up by others from their communities who remained in India. English, therefore, was not only a language of the status quo, but it became a symbol of power and privilege for a long time. And it was mostly Brahmins who remained the undisputed contenders of the power–privilege nexus because of their long-term association with British colonists. When the British left, English became the patrimony of Brahmins.

At TISS, it was discernible in many hues and forms. Savarna students who hailed from urban areas, metro cities and families with a legacy of generations of acquiring higher education had an ease with this language. They spoke English fluently and swiftly. They spoke English with a tone of pride. Of course, there were exceptions to this among Savarnas, but Savarnas were the ones who set the norms for humiliation through language. Although the teachers would shift from English to Hindi in class to facilitate learning for all students, they were far from sensing the dilemma that was always forming in the minds of Dalit–Bahujan students, whose thought process was shaped, informed and defined by their mother tongue. How could Dalit–Bahujan students, whose thoughts were constructed in Marathi, Telugu, Kannada, Tamil, Malayalam, Punjabi, Gujarati etc. produce anything original in the limited time in their given assignments, which were compulsorily supposed to be written in English? *Institutions in India tame the thought process*, I felt.

Translating J.V. Pawar's book transported me into many dimensions of thinking about language. It occurred to me that loneliness is not merely the absence of people with whom you can talk. Loneliness is the absence of *language* through which you can share your anguish with others. Loneliness is the inability to articulate and assert yourself in the world. I think people can live alone but not without a language for their loneliness. This was so evident while I was in TISS. A few years later, while I was reading a book of prose poetry by Claudia Rankine, I came across a few lines by Jill Stauffer in it about loneliness which read, 'Ethical loneliness is the isolation one feels when one, as a violated person or as one member of a persecuted group, has been abandoned by humanity, or by those who have power over one's life possibilities.'[1] What is ethics in India if it's not in relation to caste? Ethics is caste is behaviour. This became clear when I started to contribute articles in *Round Table India* and asserting myself as a Dalit, with a history of being a survivor and a fighter.

The more I wrote and portrayed myself as a fighter in history, the more I was seen as a *threat* by most of the Savarnas around me. A rebel is a threat for the oppressor. When you cease to speak the language (as perspective) of the oppressor, you often face their scorn. The most potent weapon they have is their language—

they either mock you or erase you by their silence about your assertion. In their mockery or their silence lie the roots of ethical loneliness. A Dalit becomes instinctively aware of it as soon as he asserts his position against caste. So, after all, I was not wrong in my abstractions about language, loneliness and an environment dominated by Brahminical castes. And whatever decisions I had taken in my life related to writing and books proved fertile because I was finally able to see life in its many forms and possibilities.

In 2016, however, as I began to get fully clear about what to do in life, something was troubling me, subconsciously. It was subconscious because I was suppressing any thought of it. Sometimes, you suppress the thought of responsibility for family because you know that it has the potential to overpower your energy, which you intend to invest in your dream. Therefore, at this stage, the thought of my family was completely absent from my conscious mind. Not for once I thought that they *needed* me. I had turned thirty-one. I had been practically unemployed for nearly nine years. I had no savings. An education loan was due for repayment. I was yet to consider my responsibility towards my family, which people like me could not and were not supposed to avoid. I was being selfish, as always. In fact, even more so this time, because I developed the sense that books were the only act of 'labour' that I could honestly and persistently do in my life. I had never felt this about anything else in my life. I needed to protect this sense at any cost. I had been told or persuaded to do many things in life, and I had failed in them. No one had told me to translate this volume. My heart and my mind, as if in perfect fusion of dreams and reasons, had told me to do this. I simply followed them. It was my transgression of the beliefs about career and life which had been taught to me by school, society, family and institutions.

*

An evening in 2016, I finished translating the book. It was a rare feeling. I had the sense that this feeling was never going to fade. Maybe because it came from intellectual labour, which I undertook without anticipating any reward or compensation. But I would like to think that it stemmed from a historical need to pursue a life of the mind which was denied to my ancestors. I thought: *If oppression is built on producing stories and myths that justify the Brahminical idea of life that makes people illogical, irrational and incapable of love, then resistance should be the act of producing stories that would encourage people to think of life logically, rationally and enable them to love a person, intelligently, freely, without any caste prejudice.* Dr Ambedkar was not only right, but he was a meticulous visionary when he said that for untouchables, the purpose of struggle is to resurrect their *human* personality. This particular sentence of his was engraved in my subconscious the moment I first read it. If you are erased and kept hidden as a mind, then entering into the public imagination as a thinking agent, with feelings and emotions as significant as any other human on the earth, is a revolution in the truest sense. This was Dr Ambedkar's idea of revolution. He was sceptical about the revolutionary ideologies that propagate dethroning oppressors and taking over their place. What is the guarantee that the oppressed would not develop the instincts that come with the power-position of oppressors? Dr Ambedkar was more concerned about the development of conscience (an anti-caste way of life) across hierarchies.

To him, a particular set of humans (oppressors) was not the problem in the way of revolution as much as their *ideas* of life through which they oppressed people. For him, it was not the oppressed but the oppressor who was fundamentally dehumanized. Hence, his conversion to Buddhism (a way of life in which a human being is the focus of everything and a subject of historical and material interactions) seemed to carry greater vision than any other existing revolutionary ideologies. Dr Ambedkar was thinking about humanity *after* any kind of revolution. My engagement with books as labour and continuing dialogue with J.V. Pawar gave me many hints along these lines. This permanently changed my approach to and subject of writing. I started writing and translating, not only as an individual, but as an individual who is the sum of his history and people. I started writing with a *purpose*. It made me believe in my engagement with books. I developed the sense that it was through producing stories of my people, who, despite their history of being exploited, had poured their efforts to create the idea of a life based on equality, liberty and fraternity. Without stories of justice, stories of beauty do not make sense in India. *The idea of justice precedes the idea of beauty in literature*, I told myself. Elsewhere I jotted down: *Dr Ambedkar is our conscience in our struggle for emancipation because conscience outlives the purpose of revolution.*

*

I sent the translation of the first volume to J.V. Pawar. He read that and made a few required changes. Throughout the process of translation, from time to time, he explained to me the history behind a particular word and the contexts in which it was written. The whole process of translation disciplined me in my intellectual quest. It also impacted the ways in which I was going to write. The role of impulsion while writing was replaced by contemplation. It also made me see people in the light of hope. While I could feel all these changes in me, I was looking forward to publishing the translation once Jasmine had finished editing it. But I had no idea and knowledge of how to get a book published.

During my several visits to J.V. Pawar in his office at Nariman Point, I met Pravin, who was working as a personal assistant to an MLA. Pravin was a Dalit person, educated, politically smart and a visionary. Out of many projects he was engaged with, one was to help people with physical ailments from villages. While they were recommended advanced medical treatment, which was available in cities, villagers risked financial ruin by seeking it. Pravin was involved in helping them avail aid provided by the government. He helped them find hospitals and affordable treatment. Pravin was the first person who showed interest in helping me publish the translation. I also talked to several other people about how to get the book published. I asked a few well-off scholars for a contribution of Rs 500, but they disappointed me. The people associated with Dr Ambedkar's movement were the first to understand the importance of publishing knowledge. The members of the Ambedkar Association of North America (AANA), whom I had met through Facebook, were the people, after Pravin, who helped me collect around Rs 50,000 for printing the translation. It was my first lesson of the sociology of the anti-caste movement. I learnt: *When your goal is bigger, your personal likes and dislikes do not matter; you need to move beyond disappointments, hurt, discomfort and most essentially, your ego; if your work has social relevance, then there are always people, no matter how few, who are your allies.*

*

Next, I began searching the process of printing and publication on the internet. I started asking people around. One day I went to CST to visit People's Book House, a bookstore affiliated with the Communist Party and run by Brahmin communists. Most of their books were in Marathi. They had their own printing press; I had seen this mentioned in one of their books, which I had read earlier. So I inquired at the bookstore if they printed books by other publications. By this time, following the information available on the internet, I had already registered a publishing house by the name 'Panther's Paw Publication'. I created an email id of the publishing house and through it, applied for ISBNs as a publisher. Little did I know that this was my initiation into publishing. To register the firm, I had to visit my home and make a certificate, so I could open a current account, which is required for any transaction. When I opened the account for Panther's Paw Publication, I deposited all the money I had gathered for printing the book. Beyond these trivial formalities, I knew nothing about the business of publishing.

When the person at the People's Book House told me that they printed books by other publishers too, I felt relieved. Now, I had the publication's account to transact from, I had money to print and I had the manuscript. The very next day, I visited the printing press in Prabhadevi, Dadar, New Age Printing Press. I met Charul Joshi there who was a Brahmin and a communist. He was an old man with apparent youthful energy when it came to discussing ideas and ideologies. Whenever I visited the press, we drank tea and smoked cigarettes. He helped me to know more about printing and explained the processes inside the press. For a month, almost every day, I visited the press and closely observed the process of cover design and inner pages design. I began to learn about the various dimensions of a book, types of pages, their quality and prices. I was learning something that I felt I had always wanted to. The book was taking shape. It was like starting a journey on the path you had longed for all your life. Finally, I felt, I was there, I was walking on the path I had chosen.

Almost a month later, the book was in my hand. *Ambedkarite Movement after Ambedkar* by J.V. Pawar was the first book published by Panther's Paw Publication. It was the summer of 2016 in Mumbai. As I held the book in my hand, I almost choked with some strange emotions. Words stuck in my throat. I remained silent because I knew there were people around me. I browsed the pages of the book. They smelled like petrichor, as if they had hit the barren and dry soil of my heart, like raindrops. They were evidence of my survival and being alive. The words in it felt like black pearls to my eyes. I did not know why, but the image of my father's hands, which I saw as a child—blackened with grease and oil, coated with petrol smell and covered by wounds and cuts, marks of hard labour—appeared before me. *Has the blackness of labour of my father's hands turned into these black words?*, I thought. From black hands to black words, it was a story of two generations. I knew that these words are going to be here even after I am gone, unlike stories of my earlier generations buried in the brutal silence of history. I did not need to be told how priceless these words were.

They were not only the products of a labour of love, but also of a vision and politics. The words in it were no less than my assertion against society, which had historically barred me from entering into the pages of a book, with my feelings and emotions, with my story and history, as a heart capable of feeling, and as a mind capable of thinking. I immediately called J.V. Pawar and told him that the book had been printed. He congratulated and appreciated me. I told myself, *One of the founding members of the Dalit Panthers has appreciated me for my labour, for my work.* It was the first appreciation I had received for my intellectual labour. It is still unparalleled as a recognition, because it came from a person who had dedicated his life to Dr Ambedkar's movement.

This was a defining moment for me. The problem of the Dalit movement isn't merely ideological or philosophical or political. The problem is the 'communicative void' between two generations, and of trust. I too was not immune to this problem. When I looked around in my basti and when I stepped outside it, I observed this. Trees can often grow without much nurturing or protection. But I think people cannot. One generation needs to protect and nurture the next generation if its vision of life (especially if that is anti-oppression in nature) needs to be kept alive. This is possible only when one generation bequeaths its stories and histories to its descendants. I had been lost because I simply had no clue about the problems of my father's generation. We had stories of exception (success and assertion) but we did not have stories of failures and desertion, hence we were not able to locate the roots of the problems and confusion among our current generation. This was where the danger of a 'single story' lay. I neither received guidance nor vision from my father—his entire life was consumed by the need to survive. And I would like to believe that I am not the only one who grew up in this way. I grew up, like a tree, without any nurturing or protection in this sense.

When I began to engage with J.V. Pawar, I received a gift of many stories from him. He told me about the moments which had defined his generation. He shared many anecdotes with me which were fundamental to the issues within the Dalit movement. Every story he shared helped build my vision. With him, I learnt to see the locations and roots of the problems of my father's generation. Sharing stories is as essential an act as fighting a battle for our rights on the road. This is because a story fills the gap in our consciousness that is created by the absence of memories of our past; this is also how we liberate ourselves. J.V. Pawar also trusted me with the work I imagined to do with his books and literature. This trust was the most crucial factor that fulfilled the strange emptiness inside me. I think this was the patrimony I had always looked for. But my patrimony had been hysteria, paranoia, inability to speak my needs and express my emotions. I did not understand this for years until I sat down to write this book.

*

When *Ambedkarite Movement after Ambedkar* was published, I thought of doing a formal launch. I told this to J.V. Pawar. We fixed the venue, which was his party office, the place where I had first met him. The book was inaugurated by Bhimrao Yashwant Ambedkar (grandson of Dr Ambedkar), J.V. Pawar, Pravin, Ramesh Shinde (a bibliophile of Dalit literature) and Avinash Dolas (a noted writer, and in whom I have imagined a Gramscian organic intellectual). These were people whose contribution to the Dalit movement was invaluable. It was my decision to follow the path of books that had provided me a space among them. No, I am not suggesting that this was my achievement. This is the event that made me feel responsible for what I had done and what I would be doing in future. After all, I had always hated the idea of *responsibility* of any sort. But with a book came responsibility, as it is social and political more than anything else. The book we choose to publish can demolish prejudices as well as strengthen them. A book can educate a generation; it can destroy one too. I learnt this over the years as a publisher. So, that book launch was the event that expanded the boundaries of my self-esteem and reduced the extent of my ego.

After the book launch, came 6 December. It was the Mahaparinirva Diwas (death anniversary) of Dr Ambedkar. In Mumbai, this is the day when the works and memories of Dr Ambedkar turn into a collective spirit for people to reflect on their past and construct the future as per his vision. Chaityabhoomi in Dadar, the place where Dr Ambedkar was cremated in 1956, becomes a place of celebration of knowledge on 6 December every year. At Chaityabhoomi, people interact with each other through books by buying them, reading them and carrying them for their children. Songs of anti-caste *shahirs* (balladeers) is another element that captures the spirit of this place. This vicinity, filled with books and songs, appears to be the miniature version of

'Prabuddha Bhrarat' envisioned by Dr Ambedkar, or *Begumpura* of poet-saint Ravidas, because in here, the masses live, at least for three days, with the vision of a casteless society.

'Those were the days when Raja Dhale and I used to set up our book-stalls at the shore of Chaityabhoomi. In those days, there was no proper arrangement to set up pandal and electricity for the stalls. So we used to place tarpaulin on the sand and put books there. If the sea wave would come rushing towards the stalls, we would lift our books with the tarpaulin and run towards dry areas. Once the wave receded, we set up the stall again on the sand near Chaityabhoomi,' J.V. Pawar told me one day, when I asked him about his memories of the event.

Even back then, J.V. Pawar and Raja Dhale were almost a phenomenon in literature as writers and poets and in the Dalit movement as leaders of the Dalit Panthers. Along with Namdeo Dhasal, they too were household names. But their modesty and genuine love for books and knowledge were reflected through their small acts. When J.V. Pawar shared this particular memory with me, something in me changed forever. I had grown up as an introvert and, for me, interacting with people in public places had always been a strenuous task. Yet, now, I had published a book, and it needed to be shared with the people. Being a part of the Dalit movement means getting engaged, eternally, with one of its many aspects. I chose books. It meant that from time to time, I would have to move beyond my introversion and engage with people.

After the formal launch of *Ambedkarite Movement after Ambedkar,* I sold this book at J.V. Pawar's stall at Chaityabhoomi and got it placed it at other stalls as well. For three days, I roamed around shops and saw how the book was being received by the people. It is a liberating feeling when your labour is given attention, no matter how little, and bears the fruit of revenue, no matter how small it is. Sharing and selling your labour, freely and directly, is an emancipatory feeling. For me, it was indeed liberating, because I knew how it feels to work only for survival, in the absence of freedom of choice and against the will. *Ambedkarite Movement after Ambedkar* was my first intellectual as well as honest work, which I did with all my energy, determination, willingness and without any expectation. Yet, it made me realize my worth and potential.

Dr Ambedkar said that the value of a man is self-evident. A man, by the virtue of being a human, is equally valuable across the face of the earth. Yet, religion, race, caste etc. make him see others differently and judge them inferior and unworthy in comparison. But once your labour starts affecting the lives of people, in a way, they begin to imagine love and justice as inevitable parts of human life, then you break the chains of the complexes that forced you to see yourself as *inferior* or *superior*. You are no more inferior to anyone and you cease to expect to be superior. Selling *Ambedkarite Movement after Ambedkar* at Chaityabhoomi in 2016, from 5 to 7 December, was the moment which helped me put an end to perceptions in which I often imagined myself in the darkness of life. For the first time, I had begun a journey under the sunlight. A book rescues a person exactly where people fail.

*

It had been more than six months since I had been unable to contribute my share of rent. The discomfort and trouble it was causing Jasmine was apparent on her face. Yet, her face tried to skilfully veil it. Her silence was cunning; it concealed what I did not know and what she never told me. And I was always troubled by words. Our togetherness was a perfect case of living in illusion. Only pain has the potential to break it and wake you up from it. The pain was waiting.

After *Ambedkarite Movement after Ambedkar,* I thought of compiling my poems in a book. The very thought of publishing my poems as a book form was thrilling. I developed a sense that once my words made an appearance in public in the form of poems, my emotional world, which I kept hidden from society to protect it, was going to be revealed to them. For a Dalit person, who comes to realize the existence of caste as abnormal and what it has made out of him, it is a risk to expose his emotional world to society because then he becomes vulnerable to the reactions of people for whom caste is normal. When a Dalit person exposes the abnormality of caste through his stories, society scornfully rejects him, often through its silence. But for him, beyond this vulnerability and rejection, there lies a space in which he uncompromisingly becomes what he wants to be.

For three years now, I had been writing poems and posting them on Facebook. I wrote poems from the location of discomfort, trouble or pain. I cannot recall writing a poem when I was happy. As I started gathering my poems in a single file, it spontaneously led me to write some new poems. I requested Kuffir to write an introduction to the collection. He accepted my request. Kuffir's introduction helped me see my poems in a new light.

Kuffir is an illustrious translator of Telugu poetry in English. His translations are lyrical and, as a writer, he fiercely dismantles the perceptions in which people see Brahminical oppression as *normal.* For me, his introduction was no less than an award to my poems. It sounded real and genuine. In the beginning of 2017, *The Bridge of Migration,* my first poetry collection and my first book as a writer, got published.

After I was convinced that there was going to be no income from books in the immediate future and realizing that my engagement with books was becoming more sincere as a publisher, I decided to apply for a PhD. I wanted to stay in Mumbai for as long as I could. To get an admission to a PhD programme at TISS meant a guarantee of an accommodation and food in Mumbai, for five years, without much expenditure. Going back home simply meant getting lost in the darkness again. There was a Post-Matric-Scholarship, for Schedule Caste students, which was meant to take care of the minimum expenditure of their higher education. My hostel fee and food expenditure were to be taken care of by TISS. So, I sought admission in June 2016. The next month, I was allotted a hostel room and I told Jasmine that I was shifting there. She did not like it. She wept the day after I announced my decision. Back then, I found something attractive in her fragility, in her tears. To me, her tears symbolized her affection and love for me, to be with me. But tears are often sly, even if they exist for the right reasons. Sometimes, tears make the vulnerable person more vulnerable: I failed to imagine myself in this way, and I paid for it.

The distance from my hostel to the room was not more than four hundred meters. It was literally a five-minute walk. It was a practical decision to shift to the hostel because I knew I was not in a position to pay rent. It was going to save her money. But Jasmine did not look at it in this way. She saw more worth in living and sleeping together in one room, despite it being a financial burden on her. Over the year and a half, we had filled our room with memories of living together, cooking together, drinking, watching movies on the laptop, smoking cigarettes etc. We had laughed in it. Smiled within those four walls. We had made love under its roof. We had read books sitting next to each other. We became aware of each other's bodies in it. When we began to live in that room, it was a small place with four walls and a roof. But after a year and a half, it had become a place in which we had accumulated a little bit of life which we could call ours. She clung onto it. I wanted to move because I wanted to focus on my work, without worrying about any financial burden. As I have said earlier, I became selfish when it came to books, and I was no different at this point. I shifted. Jasmine moved in with another girl upstairs in the same building. But we were there for each other, every day. We met every day, once she came from the office, and ate dinner. If her roommate was not there, Jasmine sneaked me in and we watched movies and made love. It was frantic but it was good.

Jasmine's parents lived in a coastal town of Uran, which is a part of Navi Mumbai. Her brother was getting married, so she went to her parents' house to attend wedding ceremonies. She invited me and one of our mutual friends. We rode on a bike for an hour or so to reach her house. It was evening. And in that small town, the evening felt like an eternity because there were less people and more peace around, except on the road. As we went to her house, Jasmine directed us to the terrace. Men were drinking there. As we were climbing the stairs, she introduced me to her brother. However, she avoided introducing me to her parents. I was at her house, but I felt alien there. After a while, we ate and left Jasmine's home.

Jasmine returned to her room after a week. She asked me to come there. She talked to me about our marriage. It was unexpected for me. I was simply not ready for marriage. I avoided the topic. Then she told me that she was leaving for her parents' place and would return in a day or two and look for a less expensive room for both of us near TISS. She asked me to collect whatever things I had left in her room. I had left nothing but books and memories. I collected the books. She went. I was hoping to meet her in a couple of days. I had to wait for three months to hear from her. After those three months, when she responded to one of my innumerable attempts to contact her, she said that it was not possible for her to be with me anymore.

I had not expected her to break-up with me. If you live with a person for three-and-a-half years and are suddenly asked to separate yourself from them, you feel abandoned. But the first thing I felt was baffled. Not that it was the first time I had been asked to separate myself from a person with whom I had struggled to find my place in society, in whom I had invested feelings and emotions and with whom I was touched by the feeling of love and being loved. I was baffled because I did not know the reason behind the separation. As I've said earlier, loneliness is not the condition of being alone but not possessing a language for your being alone. This bafflement was the beginning of my journey into the dark cave of loneliness. Before I could touch the beam of light at the other end, I had to walk through roads of madness against morality.

*

Sometime earlier, in 2017, Jasmine had told me about her history of being sexually harassed, because of which she suffered from anxiety attacks. She was on medication. But she told me this after three-and-a-half years of our relationship. She told me this over a phone call after our break-up. I asked myself why she kept silent about it for so long. But then, I also had an inkling that there are many things we keep buried in our mind and cannot dig out because we are scared of being haunted by the ghosts of the past. Nevertheless, the pain of silence crushes both—the one who possesses it and the one who can sense it. This silence was the violence I discovered when she broke up with me. I had found her to be a person who was not clear about her history. When I tried to discuss the location of her caste, she gave me ambiguous replies. I clearly remember that one day I had told her that it was because of her not asserting her identity in the social realm that she seemed to be confused despite all her reading of books from across the world. To this, she first dismissed my argument and then she vehemently asked me not to speak about the role of her caste in her being the *person* she was. She was one of those people who know the world through books but are ignorant of the stories of people living next to them. Her silence when she had lived in my home in Nagpur was proof of this. To be able to speak in my world is to be able to discover who you are; precisely what is your position in the world and most importantly what you see yourself as.

A Dalit, a person against caste in all areas of life, is hardly understood in society because the language in which he asserts himself is rejected, despised and mocked. But this very language, I presumed, was the key to the discovery of my roots. I needed no reason to feel that words cleanse the dust of ignorance from our mind and heart. That is why I had made a pact with words since I moved to Mumbai. Jasmine seemed to have understood nothing of it. Her abrupt disappearance from my life revealed this. I suspected her disappearance was an act of being hurt, a subconscious function of the brain in which one's hurt is relieved when it is passed on to someone else.

*

There is a poem in *The Bridge of Migration* that I called 'Defining Love'. I was with Jasmine when I wrote it. I did not write this poem keeping her in mind because I was *with* her. I thought about two women from the past. But what I did not know was that I wrote this poem from the location of a person who is untouched and misunderstood in all spheres of life, and when that person is abruptly abandoned in the middle of the journey of togetherness. As I look back on the past, I feel that I did not write this poem as a person, as an individual with exclusive circumstances. I wrote this poem as a consciousness which is the collective of my caste

and its history, its conflicts with society, its struggle against being
in this society.

> Every time
> when you left me
> you plucked me out
> like a flower
> of your choice
> and took me away
> with you
>
> But whenever
> you were with me
> I ate you
> presuming fresh bread
> prepared by my mother
> that nurtured me
> in all the odds of life

The unusual images and metaphors in it are me and my community.
The very moment I was asked to separate, I felt abandoned. But
I saw it as another beginning in life and not an end. What was
the source of my thoughts, my perception? Why did I write what
I wrote? Why did I become a *flower* in her hand and she *bread*
prepared by my mother for me? The English poetry which I have
read from India had failed to teach me to see separation beyond
grief. In my poem, even in grief, I was conscious of my roots: my
mother. I know the struggle of my mother, her being a woman
and a Dalit. But I mostly kept it a secret from my words. Yet the
struggle of my mother turned into a metaphor of resistance as
I fought against abandonment. Seeing her arrival in my poems

without being aware of it led me to believe that the love of those women was not as genuine as our struggle against hunger.

When Jasmine broke up with me, my only weapon to fight it was poetry. The battle against loneliness is the most gruesome battle one can fight because the enemy cannot be seen. Our battle against loneliness is the battle of language against silence.

*

Against the Madness of Morality

With the uncompromising legacy of blue
against the darkness I intend to fight,
my life is not a parable but a clue
where love did not bloom but it might

Even though Jasmine broke up with me and I was sad, my engagement with poems remained uninterrupted. Poetry became my everyday labour in order to survive, resist and exist. In 2014, I had discovered the work of the inimitable Marathi poet Loknath Yashwant, a Dalit and himself a remarkable translator. I read his poems in Marathi first. Then, I found English translations of his poems done by Dr K. Jamanadas, almost a decade and a half ago. Finding this English translation nurtured my confidence further in writing about my inner self in English. Dr Jamanadas's translation was flawless and so lucid that it appeared as if poems had been originally written in English.

The sound of English while reading the translations was the sound of my life. I discovered two reasons to be hopeful and happy at this point: One was the poetry of Loknath Yashwant, who had developed a distinct style in which he dealt with subjects related to the anti-caste discourse intellectually rather than emotionally, and another was the beauty of translation (despite its minimal shortcomings). Beauty, because my world, which erstwhile had dark connotations in the English language, had now arrived in it with its originality, ability to think, reason and love. I decided to publish the English translation of Yashwant's poetry for which, besides Dr K. Jamanadas's brilliant translation, I translated some ten more poems. In 2018, these poems were published in an anthology called *Broken Man: In Search of Homeland*[1]—this was my third book as a publisher. There was a poem in it, which I translated, that explained to me the enigma of being, as a Dalit, in caste-society. It reads:

> Caste is like the flow of electricity
> The wires are visible
> But not the current.

I was the one who, from time to time, had been shocked by the current of caste; yet I had not known its source.

*

I found myself back in the hostel, with the few things that Jasmine and I had shared in our tiny room: books, bedsheets, postcards, pens, diaries etc. These were memories I had to let go of. This was the beginning of my battle against memories. As I became increasingly involved in writing poems, translating them, searching for manuscripts and imagining publishing them in the form of books, some things were bothering me inside. But I was least aware of it. *Home* was always in my mind, subconsciously. *One day I will have to take care of my ageing parents and I will have to be with them; they have no one but me; what will happen to my dream then; will I ever be able to write without worry and without feeling burdened by the thought of survival?* I thought this to myself many times and forgot it right after. I put aside the thought of my parents because I wanted to focus on poetry, writing and books. I was always worried thinking of the tussle between my responsibility and my dream, and it made me incessantly angry. I was never able to tell this to the women I was with. They mistook anger as my dominant temperament. They did not realize that it was important for me to exist, to survive and to explore my place in the society that had deliberately erased me.

I was thirty-two and, according to my parents, I should have had a *normal* life by then, with a wife, children and a *proper* job. But a recluse can hardly fit into the world of rules and demands. And when such a person is caught in the war between responsibility and dream, then either he should develop the strength to fulfil the demands of both or surrender to one of them. I neither had that strength nor did I want to surrender. This was close to my father's situation, which I discovered years later when the Covid-19 pandemic pushed me to move back to Nagpur for an indefinite period. While following one's dream, the only respite is forgetting one's responsibilities. Sometimes, I think forgetfulness in the life of a Dalit person works like an ointment on wounds and provides him the scope to explore his life further. A person who is socially most despised is the mind with the most potential when it comes to broadening the dimensions of mental liberation in society. Flowers of hope sprout from the seed of grief. In this process, an 'act' is the predecessor of the 'meaning' of life. Learning is an unplanned event. Its documentation is knowledge. And its sensible use in life is called wisdom. The periods of my being abandoned by women were the periods of my learning the most crucial lessons of life. I did not know this until I started to write this book.

Writing is creating a meaning that has never existed; in my case, writing is creating a meaning which has been erased, mocked and forgotten. Writing became my 'act' to create meaning for myself and the life I was/would be living. I knew that people would read what I wrote, and that would become their idea of me in their mind and heart. I decided that I would make people see me beyond my grief, wound, identity and history of exploitation; I will make people see me as a dreamer whose idea of life is not tarnished by his pain but which is rooted in the feeling of love, justice and compassion and for whom Dr Ambedkar is not an ideology but a conscience. Ideologies are subject to time and conditions; conscience is an essential part of human evolution. So, I knew that I was learning because I was in a tussle with the world around me. Society continued to reinforce my identity. My resistance was to forget it so I could explore new and fresh meanings for myself. It is exactly at this point that I felt my memories were weighing down on me, and in order to get rid of their weight, I began to smoke marijuana.

*

Jasmine's sudden disappearance and her silence for the next three months grew in my mind as a haunting mystery. I desperately sought answers from her, but her reply was silence. The silence was so powerful that I felt suffocated by it. I felt unwanted and discarded. George was the only person who knew me and Jasmine as a couple and with whom we had hung out and spent time. I had known George for more than four years now. So when Jasmine's silence became unbearable and I was looking for clarity, I called George and told him what had happened. He called me to his place in Chandivali, near Powai, where he was living in a small rented flat. I reached his place by afternoon, alcohol in

hand. George was someone who could understand the situation
in its many aspects. He was intelligent and a reader. His ability
to situate insights from books in people's lives was impressive.
He was interested in people as well as the ideologies they believed
in. But there was something else in him which was very real—his
mischievousness. He was unlike many scholars or intellectuals I
had met. He liked to laugh and make fun. I found intellectuals
pretentious. He was opposite to that. He was the only person
with whom I remained in touch throughout my time in Mumbai.
So that day, when I went to his place, we drank and talked. He
listened to me and then he spoke. He spoke about how weird
Jasmine was as a person, especially when she was with me, and
how annoying was her persistence to not leave me alone to have
my own time. I had never seen Jasmine in this way. And now I
had no reason to not believe what George was saying. Besides,
Jasmine had had a secret which she had kept hidden from me.
Basically I had never studied her behaviour or judged her. Was I
wrong? I did not know. But now, I felt betrayed.

George and I drank till it was night. We got hungry and went
to have dinner at a nearby place. We drank there too. Unable to
finish our food, we got the leftover packed. On our way back,
George climbed up on a milk van that was slowly passing by us,
living up to his mischievous nature. As the van moved ahead,
he shouted my name, laughing and urging me to climb on the
running van. I ran towards it but was unable to climb it as I had
the food parcel in my hand, and I was drunk. He went with the
van till it reached his place and jumped off. I ran towards him,
laughing, forgetting my sadness. Back in his room, we talked for
a while and then he asked me if we could drink more. It was past
midnight. He said he knew a bar which was open all the time.
We took an auto and reached Chakala. Mumbai was dangerously
beautiful that night. The bar was more like a labyrinth with floors.

It was shady, with minimal lighting, filled with smoke and people with drunken faces; the noise was intoxicating, as was the feeling of getting lost into that night. We drank there and returned in a couple of hours. In the last three months, it was the first day I had spent not feeling lonely. It was the day I had laughed, and it felt like I hadn't laughed in an eternity.

*

The life of Dalits (ex-untouchables) 'is the life of insecurity',[2] Dr Ambedkar had once said. But this insecurity is not seen. It is felt. Only a Dalit can feel it, especially in elite and Savarna dominated spaces like TISS. It may have various reasons. But it is there. Language plays a crucial role here. Here, by language, I do not mean script or what we learn in school and various institutions. I mean *life*. The life of a Dalit is one in pursuit of resurrecting his emotional world and his personhood in language. And until he finds it, his life is subject to loneliness. My life was no exception.

One day, on an idle afternoon, I was walking on Farm Road. I bumped into a few of my classmates. They asked me if I would join them to smoke a 'joint'. Until then, I had never smoked marijuana. I felt the sudden urge to lose myself in an unknown drug. The smell of marijuana was intense and distinct; its smoke was thick. Each of us had a couple of drags and then passed it to the next person in the group. Then they rolled another joint. We repeated the process. By the time we were done and I stood up, I felt remarkably light, unworried and fresh, as if someone had erased the troublesome memories from the pages of my mind. While walking back to the hostel, the sound and sights that I had hated earlier now appeared bearable. I felt less troubled and closer to my *self*. I ceased to feel the sense of time. I was thinking; I was imagining. My feelings and imagination were as real to me as my needs and desires. I felt I had acquired the strength to bear what was unbearable around me. I entered my room and crashed into my bed. The swiftly spinning fan over my head seemed to be at an unreachable height. I felt someone had lifted me in the air. Then, I puked. In a few minutes, I felt light again. I slept, without any dream, good or bad. I slept like this after a long time.

The year 2017 had come to an end. Consumption of marijuana became a regular part of my life. I liked the feeling of losing my sense of time. When high, it became possible for me to be around people of wide social and ideological differences. I began to smoke with people across caste, linguistic and religious backgrounds. When you want to get high, all differences crumble, at least for a few moments. Marijuana smokers, it appeared to me, were always in pursuit of detaching themselves from the world, present and material. What they could not see while in pursuit of getting high was that they could never dissociate themselves from the life of demands and needs. But marijuana, as it floats in the bloodstream, makes it possible to *feel* free in thinking and in the act of imagination. I wanted this feeling to last long, because I felt shackled by memories. There was only one challenge for me when I was high—I had to remain mindful of my real life, the need to earn to survive, to send money home, and never forget that I had books to work on and publish; and, most importantly, that I had to write. I was afraid I would lose my connection with my vision behind books. This fear kept me in touch with my life of needs and demands, a life of vision and resistance.

I smoked marijuana with many people. But I liked the company of Faisal. He hailed from Kerala. He was unlike those Malayalis who refused to accept the issue of casteism in Kerala, despite being the state with the highest ratio of education. I liked him because with him I felt no stress of being understood; we both always seemed to have been in an escape mode from the world around us; marijuana became our vehicle. For about a year and half, we used to smoke together, sometimes only the two of us, but mostly with a group of various people. The 'brotherhood' between smokers, as I discovered, was based on the need to float freely in imagination and to feel detached from the immediate demands of material life. Faisal and I also used to drink, almost daily. At night, I sometimes crashed in his hostel room, which was situated off the main campus. Then, as we woke up, we rolled a joint and started our day with it. Starting a day with a joint, that too of Mumbai's spiked marijuana, meant a guarantee of spending a day in vagrancy. Because, as we reached the campus, there were always people or individuals who wanted to smoke up. So we smoked with them, sometimes in their rooms or in their flats outside the campus or just outside the campus, hiding behind bushes and trees. At night, we drank cheap liquor. Our days were spent being high and drunk. We smoked until we got tired late at night; there was no particular time to eat; I learnt to bear the pangs of hunger. I was always lost in my thoughts, or in the books that I always kept in my bag. But the fear of getting alienated from my vision, of and about books, always arrested my mind before I went to sleep. I was struggling to protect my feelings and meet the demands of life. For me, pleasure was never devoid of fear of getting lost into it.

It was also at this time that my vision about books and stories started to grow inside me, uncontrollable like a fire in the forest. Around April 2017, I received an email from Krupa Ge, an editor and a writer from Chennai who later went on to author a remarkable book called *Rivers Remember* about the Chennai floods and how it affected peoples' lives across social locations. By this time, I had published three books from Panther's Paw Publication. But I was not so focused on selling them. I simply did not know avenues to explore the sale of books other than Amazon and one bookshop in Mumbai. I kept posting about them on Facebook, but only a few people who knew me bought them. The email I received from Krupa disrupted my procrastination about books and writing. She requested me to submit an unpublished poem of mine for her series called *Bards of Resistance,* which she was curating for *Firstpost.* She also mentioned the remuneration I would be receiving for it. In the next couple of days, I wrote a poem, thinking about my mother and father. I emailed that to her. It got published in a week or two, with an intense illustration which I think matched with the stream of consciousness from which this poem had sprouted. This poem was about labour and love. I imagined that I, as a consciousness, was formed by the presence of labour and absence of love. A couple of weeks later, Krupa sent me the remuneration for that poem. It was Rs 6000. Seeing the amount I was paid for a single poem, the first thought that came across my mind and I uttered to myself was: *I have never seen a Dalit poet being paid for his poems. A poem for a Dalit poet is a matter of living life. No one pays a Dalit poet for that.*

I had always been convinced about the sentimental value of words. Now, I discovered they had fiscal value too. What did that mean for a Dalit person? This small yet massively significant event in my life transported me back to the moment in the past when I began to work and labour in factories and, in return, received wages which would be below the level of dignity in any other part of the world. In the life of a Dalit person, fair wages for his labour, intellectual and otherwise, matter the most. Because it's a dignified recognition for his labour as a human. It was indeed a poetic moment in my life, as it made me think about the possibilities of surviving on writing, getting paid for the labour of the mind, but most importantly, getting paid for doing the only thing I could do with all my heart in it, with all my honesty and potential: writing. I captured this moment in a poem:[3]

Once, working in factories
for 8 hours
for enduring curses
for facing humiliation
I used to get 30 rupees a day

Now for a poem
of some 100 words
written in 2 minutes
I get 6000 rupees
for a short story, 10000 rupees;
much has gone
under the bridge of life

In between what happened
is not the story nor history,
it is a painful symmetry
of my poetry

In 2017, I had written a poem whose political subconscious was rooted in the vision of Dr Ambedkar, for which I had received more money than I could have ever expected. But it is not the size of the remuneration that is significant here. It is the recognition for intellectual labour that matters the most. I had toiled at factories, worked at construction sites, painted walls at people's homes for money, and I had witnessed the discriminatory gap between the extent of labour of my people and the wages they received. With these wages, a Dalit person seldom fulfils his needs, and would certainly never be able to support his dreams.

His dreams are often killed by the unavailability of the space to *think* for himself. I have seen brilliant Dalit writers and heard stories from those of earlier generations who—despite their words, with which they raised the level of conscience of society— were hardly given due recognition in term of royalties and money. Receiving remuneration for a poem—my intellectual labour, the only work in which my emotions, feelings and consciousness were fully present and undistracted—was a meaningful event in my life. With this, I began to dream to write and earn and survive and assert.

In 2016, when I enrolled for my MPhil-PhD, TISS stopped what they called the non-NET (National Eligibility Test) fellowship, a meagre sum of Rs 3000–5000 that they used to give to those research students who did not have any kind of substantial scholarship or fellowship. By the next year, when Jasmine suddenly announced our break-up, I was financially broke. The only consolation I received was from what I had read during this time, especially from the poetry of Nagraj Manjule. His poems intelligently described to me the dilemma of a Dalit man in love with a Savarna women. In his poems, one could find longing of a Dalit man for a lover as a historical desire. I sensed a certain amount of emotional maturity within me as I read these poems whenever I was alone. Reading his poems was like someone had held me back from falling into the deep chasm of sadness. The sale of the three books that I had published by this time was depressing. I held no hope with the sale of books, maybe because I was yet to see them as my intellectual labour with a financial value. Most people expect books in the form of a gift or free of cost from Dalit writers who self-publish their books; I have become accustomed to this practice for years now.

What rejuvenated me the most after my poem got published in *Firstpost* was the possibility of getting published across various platforms, and perhaps even earn out of it. Online English platforms had so far been undisputedly dominated by Savarna writers. This was a fact of which I was aware ever since I joined TISS for my MA. Every reminder of this fact made me angry and also hopeless about getting my writing published there. I started seeing things as black and white, and I was in denial of the fact that there were many colours in human life. I became bitter, thinking about the impossibility of getting published in so-called mainstream platforms. No, I was not seeking any recognition from mainstream platforms. In fact, what I was writing was neither aesthetically appealing to Brahmin–Savarna writers or editors, nor did I intend to write as per their demand in order to become popular. But I desperately wanted my writings to be read widely.

So I took a chance. I emailed Krupa and asked her if she could connect me with someone from *Firstpost* so I could approach them and see if there was an opportunity to write paid articles. Krupa connected me with Rohini, a feature editor at *Firstpost* who handled art- and literature-related writings. In the first email, Rohini asked me if I could do a series of ten articles on Dalit writers. I received this email at a time when I was becoming anxious to write and financially struggling. The idea of a series of columns was intellectually stimulating. My first article got published in *Firstpost* in October 2017. After almost a decade, I earned for the first time by doing what I really love to do. Over the next two and a half years, I contributed sixty-six articles in *Firstpost* alone. By writing them, for which I also had to read on various subjects and from different points of view, I earned Rs 4,62,000. This is how I managed to survive in TISS from 2017 to 2020 and was also able to contribute financially to my family. Here, by 'survival' I mean living a life of dignity, which is hardly possible without the money you earn with your sweat and blood and intellect; this feeling is omnipotent in the life of a person who has been carrying the generational burden of being an *untouchable* on his shoulders for centuries. Over a decade, I had seen and met a few brilliant Dalit writers and activists who were lost into the darkness of time because they simply did not receive deserving wages for their intellectualism and writings. I did not want to become *them*, or be *like* them. I dared to stand on my feet, financially, by writing alone. I worked towards it. I had observed that the Dalit community looks at the affairs of their literature in an idealistic way. They simply skip the 'financial worth' part of it. In most cases, the decline of dignity starts with financial dependence. If you are a part of the Dalit movement, you can feel this in your veins.

*

It was January 2016. A friend called and told me about the 'suicide' of Rohith Vemula. I had never heard this name before. He asked me what I thought about it. I said, 'Nothing.' I changed the subject and ended the call. After that day, for quite some time, the name Rohith Vemula was all over the news and social media, and it became the subject of protests across universities in India. Rohith was not the first Dalit student who had asserted himself as an Ambedkarite to have been institutionally murdered. There were many Dalit students who had never declared themselves as Ambedkarites but had been murdered institutionally as well in elite universities in India. The list is long. Seldom had they been killed for their assertion. Often, they were killed merely for their existence, which the institution sees in their caste, and only in their caste. Over the years, from time to time, the thought of institutional murders (society likes to call it '*suicide*') of Dalit students had crossed my mind. And I began to understand that the 'real' problem is not institutional killings because institutions in India are designed to degrade the emotional and intellectual world of a Dalit person. The problem is not knowing how to survive *despite* all the bitterness universities have to offer to Dalit students.

A Dalit knows instinctively that the society in which he is born and now has to live is the society which mostly has bitterness to offer him rather than love or acceptance. But he breathes in it, everyday, resisting and surviving in his own way. But as soon as he steps into universities in India, overwhelmingly dominated by Brahmins and Savarnas, carrying a dream with him to rise in an intellectual field, he is forced to alienate himself from his emotional and intellectual world and its language. Those who resist this alienation suffer the most. Those who succumb to institutional discrimination seemingly forget the fact that there is no difference between Indian society and these universities. The culmination of institutional discrimination into the murder of a Dalit student takes places as soon as he distinguishes between caste-society and universities. He anticipates universities to be a site of progress and promise, but always finds himself disappointed. He forgets to remain hopeful in all difficult situations because, while in universities, he forgets that he was born in the brutality of caste. For a Dalit, the ability to hold on to hope in all brutal situations converts itself into a strength to be harsh in such circumstances, because he instinctively knows that this is the only way to survive, everyday, in caste-society. I began to see the suicide of Dalit students in Brahminical universities not only as structural murders but also as an inability of the students to retrieve their dashed hopes and transform them into harshness—a weapon they need from time to time while walking and breathing in Brahminical spaces.

Viktor E. Frankl, founder of logotherapy, philosopher, psychiatrist and a Holocaust survivor who wrote *Man's Search for Meaning*—a book that is no less than a profound commentary on a human mind on the verge of being exterminated for his identity—said, 'Between stimulus and response there is a space. In that space is our power to choose our response. In our response lies our growth and our freedom.'[4] Let me tell you the truth which every Dalit student feels inside his bones as he steps inside the universities in India for the first time. It is the horror of the Savarna gaze. Some of us survive these Brahminical universities not because we know what to do, but precisely because we know what *not* to do here. And each Dalit who fights and survives these places is an anti-caste fighter. But a few among us succumb to discrimination because they are specifically targeted. They are singled out. They are made into an example of being *unfit* in Brahminical universities. It is the most excruciating moment in the life of a Dalit student because he had hardly expected this and partly because he entered into this place with hope and a few small dreams. The moment he is labelled for speaking his truth or his academic performance, a Dalit student experiences the murder of his dreams and extreme alienation. No one, except himself, has the language to console him and make him feel the truth that these universities are not the end of life. Yet, all he feels in the moment is anguish. He finds himself alone and abandoned. The absence of any hope amidst the environment (university campus) which he had once perceived as the most hopeful, often leads him to find a solution from the excruciating pain in this thought: Cease to exist to stop feeling pain. He can no more see freedom in being alive, but in an act of 'ceasing to exist' *for* himself. He forgets that he had *never* existed as a mind for caste-society; caste-society always wanted him to be dead even when he was alive. His freedom was rooted in his *survival*.

Loneliness is not felt in isolation. It is felt amidst people. For a Dalit person, feeling lonely in places dominated by the dominant castes is a struggle of life against death. Some among us lose the struggle. Rohith's institutional murder made me reflect on the idea of death in caste-society in a social sense. The time I had spent with TBM had introduced to me the idea of death in a purely spiritual sense. Almost a decade later, my thoughts about life and its various aspects, including death, had radically changed. The life of a Dalit person in caste-society is an invisible life. Consequently, then, his death too does not hold meaning in it. For a Dalit person, death is a state in which a consciousness ceases to influence people through its words, its actions, both from the past and in the present. In such an emotionally intricate situation, the mere survival of a Dalit person becomes an act of resistance because his very existence is constantly erased in the public imagination. By asserting his presence, a Dalit person rewrites himself on the face of the earth.

As I learnt to read and understand the emotional history of 'untouchables', especially while reading the life of Dr Ambedkar and his works, it became easy for me to imagine what could be *my* resistance. I became more conscious of the fact that the alienation of a Dalit person from the language of his emotions and suffering leads him to the shore where he finds himself abandoned. I needed to protect myself from this. Silence became my weapon; thinking for myself and only for myself became my resistance. But I was also aware of the fact that we Dalits, as a community across territorial and linguistic backgrounds, suffer collectively. The experience of *untouchability* is exclusive to us. Hence we cannot be free as individuals unless we become free as a group from the existence of *caste*. Dr Ambedkar had realized this. His writings and vision captured the suffering of the most oppressed and despised man. I read and understood him in this way. I think this is the reason that today his vision is a 'directive principle' for minds resisting caste; it encourages them to face the collective trauma of caste-society and free oneself and others from it.

What could be my rebellion in a society where I was never perceived without my history of being an 'untouchable', where I was non-existent for others? It became crucial for me to believe that it would be to exist in people's minds even after my body would cease to exist. When I look back, I know that no one remembers my grandparents, or no one will ever remember my parents for that matter. They toiled, they worked extremely hard, but their stories (and stories of people like them) are always missing in public memory. I decided to exist in people's minds and hence I began to write with more vigour, as a discipline. It was during this period that I wrote relentlessly, like a peasant toils on the soil, every day, endures the sun and rain so new crops can be cultivated to nourish society. One morning when I woke up, the first thought that formed in my mind was: *I don't want to be a memory. I want to be a discourse in the field of hope.*

While writing articles and poems tirelessly, smoking marijuana until I could no longer feel a sense of time, drinking with whoever was available, floating around mostly with my feelings about the people around me and letting my mind think freely about writing and research without academic frameworks, I submitted my MPhil thesis. Like my MA convocation, I did not attend my MPhil convocation. I had never felt a sense of worth in receiving degrees as much as I had felt it in writing poems or stories—in them, I was real, I was honest and I was *me* without any adulteration of the outside world. It was the summer of 2018.

*

A year ago, I had met Saraswati at TISS. I saw her on campus, frequently passing by like a rapturous breeze of air, with her smile and curly hair. She was from Kerala and belonged to the OBC category. On her face, the charm of life was still intact. I was fascinated. One afternoon when I was high, I messaged her on Facebook. On campus, although sometimes you never speak to each other, word goes around. She knew about me, so I did not find it difficult to talk to her. We decided to meet in the evening. But the same afternoon, she broke her leg. So I asked if I could come and see her. I went to her rented house in Govandi in the evening—our first meeting. Despite her leg being hurt, she was relaxed. We smoked marijuana, laughed and then we drank. She was hardly judgemental and sorted in the matters of life's needs. But as I grew more accustomed to her way of living, I found it was because of her distance from her home that she felt free. Women like her, relatively privileged with access to education, instinctively feel trapped in their homes.

Our friendship began this way. Twice or thrice, when drunk and high, we also kissed and made out. In 2017, the year when I was struggling with my emotions, I mostly spent time with Saraswati and Faisal, smoking and drinking with them, letting myself feel free in the senselessness of time when high, and then reading because I wanted to write because I wanted to earn because I had to send money back home. I was never fully free to escape the pain while indulging myself in any intoxicating substance. I always felt the weight of responsibilities greater than the weight of the earth on my shoulders. In all this, words protected me from getting lost in substance abuse and being crushed under the weight of my responsibilities.

From 2018, every month, I started to send some money home. I equally became engrossed in smoking, drinking, spending time with people and then reading and eventually feeling a sense of worth in writing. But on the other hand, I was simply escaping my responsibilities. A call from my mother, which I got once in a week, kept me connected with the deteriorating situation at home: My father had started drinking at his workplace in the morning itself and had fainted twice as soon as he returned home. He had high diabetes, but he couldn't care less about it. My father began blabbering senseless words when at home. He started cursing his bedridden mother and my mother. My mother wanted me to talk to my father, make him understand things and warn him to behave. I knew something was wrong, that it was not a physical illness but primarily a mental wound. I was not in a position to deal with it. I assured my mother that I would talk to him. But I did not. I avoided talking to him. Marijuana helped me forget the matters I could not handle.

*

On most days, I smoked marijuana with Saraswati in her house in Govandi, during those still afternoons when the moist sun in Mumbai was neither sluggish nor energizing. Life felt sweet and still when high. I actually began to verbalize my feelings and emotions when high. Life appeared to me bearable because there was enough time—I felt as if I was not actually there—to think about life in all its sweetness and hopefulness. Marijuana was changing the course of my imagination about life and people. I learnt to see commonality between us as well as differences. During this time, I smoked marijuana with many people, mostly from Savarna and privileged backgrounds, and I could not help but observe them in relation to their caste and class. Despite all my efforts, the thought of survival and family never left me even when I was high. How different was my life from theirs? Yet, the need to smoke marijuana killed those differences for a moment. I began to see how the evil of human life lies in the desire to be superior and powerful. In need, we all are honest and sublime. I started disliking soberness, because then, I could see the corruption in people which was the contribution of their caste, class and privileges. I became hateful on seeing these attributes. I wanted to go in the opposite direction of hate, which is a willingness to understand and embrace. Hate makes you judgemental, which prevents your growth as a human being.

*

Most often, answers to our problems are not found in ideologies but in our own reflection on our present conditions. At TISS, I started keeping a distance from people who used nothing but words like 'ideology', 'movement', 'justice', 'rights', various 'isms', etc., and never dare to talk about their *lives*. I had never associated myself actively with students who called themselves 'Ambedkarites'. Because in their eyes, I sensed the moral lens which reduced the existence of people to their habits. I never felt with them the possibilities of expanding the imagination of life and the ideology they believed in. As much as I had read and understood Dr Ambedkar, his idea of 'morality' was deeply centred on individual freedom and their choices in relation to the principle of justice in a social sense. Those who called themselves 'Ambedkarites' on campus assumed all Ambedkarites should have the same traits and habits.

Students inclined to the left ideology were more implicit in their actions. In them, there was an instinct, as historical as Brahminism in India, to avoid Dr Ambedkar as much as possible. If one lacked the intellectual dynamism to accept the person beyond his personal choices and habits, the other lacked emotional maturity to understand the problems of caste-life in India. So I was always on the run, to seek the semblance of a connection. And wherever I found a little bit of intellectual stimulation or emotional touch, I anchored myself there from time to time. I continued to be unfit for these *ideologies* on campus and pursued what pleased me and made me feel free—whether it was alcohol, marijuana or being with girls. I continued to walk against the madness of morality. I felt free, I felt myself. I began to develop a sense that if you are not cautious, ideologies become dangerous because they shape your thinking and imagination in a restrictive way. This is the precise reason we fail to imagine life in its freshness, creativity and with endless possibilities of liberation for ourselves.

From 2018 onwards, my articles started getting published in various so-called mainstream and Savarna-dominated platforms such as Scroll.in, Buzzfeed, *EPW*, *Firstpost*, Indian Cultural Forum etc. For me, it meant creating and broadening the scope to reach readers who were not aware of the anti-caste perspective and literary imagination in the English language. In the past, a few Dalit writers had introduced an anti-caste perspective and imagination into English. I was simply adding to what they had started. The act of writing is no less than a revolution in the life of a Dalit person, I began to understand, because for us writing is fighting against ourselves, against society, and against the casteist darkness that is ever-ready to swallow us. Writing is waking up to the light inside us. I started seeing myself not as a product of the history of exploitation or misery, but as a product of the history of resistance and reason, which my ancestors, by writing their stories, shared with the world. At this stage, for me, writing became an act of self-clarification and a process to free myself from literary notions formed in my mind by reading the literature of Brahmin and Savarna writers.

Often when high, the act of reading and writing made me feel so close to *life* that I forgot to judge people around me. This meant I was becoming less and less hateful towards Brahminical people. We do not hate shallow or ignorant people; we just assert our truth, which *educates* them. I was determined to write more widely. I was learning that if our existence does not abnormalize the existence of caste, then we are not a part of the movement of 'annihilation of caste'. A year later, in 2019, when I had begun to write short stories, which later got published in the form of a book called *Flowers on the Grave of Caste*, my frivolousness in life, my confusion, my anxieties and my introversion were finally making sense to me. Because I discovered the effect that the process of writing had on me. I needed no one when I sat down to write. I felt no urge to have sex, smoke up, drink or masturbate. I was no longer hidden from myself while writing. Writing protected me from hurting myself. And I knew why.

The battle of Dalits against caste-society is the battle of reason against unreason, sensitivity against imperviousness, logic against fanaticism, love against hate and scientific temper against dogma. One of the most divisive and insensitive societies in the world, caste-society functions on the principle of idolizing the few (Brahmins) and disdaining the many (Dalit–Bahujans) in the public imagination and in politics, culture and art. If you carry the horrors of untouchability from the past as your inheritance, in your instincts, you can read the disdain in the eyes of Savarnas for you as soon as you assert your identity against the false and sick 'logic' of caste-society. As a matter of the fact, caste-society is the only society wherein 'justice' is served as per the status of one's caste: The higher the caste, the higher the chances of receiving justice and the lower the caste, the lower the chances of receiving it. The idea of justice itself is often distorted to serve caste hierarchies. Dalits, especially in the cases of atrocities against them, often die waiting for justice. So, being a Dalit if you are aware of all these and continuing to assert who you are in your writing, you tend to defy everything that makes you hate yourself. Although I realized it much later, I had fallen irresistibly into alcohol and marijuana for this very reason. When drunk or high, I never hated myself. When I was high, I was so close to myself that

I felt my inner self to be actually the self which has more love in it than hate, which I thought was the dominant part of me. Caste is a psychological drug that kills a sense of humanity in us every day. I felt more humane when high. I smiled, I laughed and I loved. It was with George that I had first discovered the joy of drinking and meditating *together* on life and the people around us.

*

George belonged to a fisherman community. After the implementation of the Mandal Commission Report in 1992, many first-generation learners from OBC castes across India started gaining admission into central universities. This, as George frequently narrated, changed the political fabric of student politics and the discourse of caste in these universities, which were hitherto dominated by Brahmins and Savarnas. Dalit students had formed a numerical minority and had no choice but to keep their focus entirely on education. George was the product of this changing politics in central universities; this was very apparent from the stories he told me of his student days at the English and Foreign Languages University (EFLU) in Hyderabad. George disliked these universities because he perceived them as dens of butchering the imaginations of Dalit–Bahujan students about life. His use of English was prudent. He was the first person who rescued me from being swallowed up by the infatuation of English language. 'The question is not whether we (Dalit–Bahujans) understand English or not; the question is whether English understands us or not,' he once said. His emphasis was more on the *life* we lived rather than the language in which we depicted it. Once out of university, partly because of his involvement in anti-caste student politics on campus, although a brilliant student, he refused to pursue a career in academics. Rather, he chose the banking sector as an investment analyst. But his heart was always in books and the life around us. On weekends, for me, spending time with him was the escape I required from the intellectually and emotionally monotonous and lethargic life at TISS. We boozed and watched movies. Apart from being a judicious reader, George was also a movie buff. He taught me how to watch movies with their rootedness in our lives and how they have been negatively affecting, not to mention caricaturing, the lives of Dalit–Bahujans for decades. He even took me to watch Malayalam movies in the theatre and, through these movies, explained to me the society of which they were the product. He introduced to me to the history, politics and food culture of Kerala, which changed my imagination of southern states forever.

George and I were those first-generation learners who had entered into Brahmin-dominated universities in India and could not help but defy their methods of teaching/learning at a later stage. Yet, this had given a space, contradictory to our lived experiences, in which we could explore the realities behind the making of movies and literature in India. So with George, as I was learning to watch movies in all their subtle ways of sabotaging the idea of life with which the Dalit–Bahujan population lives every day, I could not help but think about the hazardous impact Bollywood movies had had on my father. He had invested a large part of his life into watching these films. Yet, he never knew that the movies he watched were either a mockery of the life of his kind or created notions in his head which made him hate his own life. The cinematic imagination became more normal to him than his life itself. I too was under the influence of such notions until I started to read books. With George, I began to learn to see the casteist notions which movies form in our heads. My father did not get an opportunity to learn to see his own erasure in movies. A man who cannot see his own erasure in the national imagination, through movies or literature, is a man fettered by the times. He is unable to question what he sees or reads because the means—language—by which he can resist his erasure has long ago been either despised or snatched away from him systematically by the politics of his country. In most cases, he becomes a life-long consumer of state ideology, which in India is Brahminism.

Often change is impossible, not because we cease to change, but because we normalize things that are against rationality and reason. This makes us believe that the change we seek is too utopian. Movies that my father watched had never let him develop the idea of the possibility of a different world for himself that I managed to perceive after entering university. I was able to rescue myself from eternally lingering in the history of being a victim. My father is not alone in this mental incarceration. He's one among millions of Dalits.

With George, I also began to understand the many roles the language plays in our lives, one of which is to degrade some and praise others in society. In my observation, many Dalit students who came to TISS were mentally gentrified by the language to which they were introduced here, in which their lives were subjects of poverty, discrimination, humiliation, reservation, welfare, rehabilitation etc. They were taught to see their lives in this so-called academic vocabulary. Dalit students here were made to see their lives objectively, from a distance, and consequently they were made subjects of research. Conversing with George gradually made me aware of language's modus operandi in Brahminical spaces, which make Dalit–Bahujans lose contact with their history of emotions and feelings and the language which they beget. The more I observed the people here, the more my fidelity to poetry became stronger. With, and in, poetry, I stayed connected with my anxieties, my pain and my, ideas which did not have any currency in the academic world of which I was an *unwanted* part.

So I believed my liberation in caste-society was not in acquiring anything material that provides power, but essentially in acquiring a language in which no one could define me but me. And for that, my sensibilities had to be rooted in my past, in the history of my ancestors and our struggle against casteism. This made me imagine that liberation is not a condition without pain but an achievement of a language with which a man understands the root cause of his pain. You do not necessarily feel liberated even if you are happy. But you feel liberated if you possess the language to understand your pain. Ever since I had begun to read in English, even though I was fascinated by it, I had hardly found myself in it. This made me explore my politics as a Dalit person writing in English. I felt I must identify my position in this language; without that, I found it impossible to write anything original in it. One day I wrote:

English
I am a Dalit poet
I am an infiltrator in your house

I accepted English as the language for my thoughts and imagination, but I ceased to see English as the language of my sensibilities. It was 2018.

*

From 2017 onwards, if on one hand I was acquiring the clarity of my position in my writing and of my politics in English, on the other hand I was treading on the brittle path of searching for love. In the matter of love, in caste-society, everyone is hurt at various levels. Almost all of us in India grow up never seeing our parents hugging each other or explicitly exchanging affection. Inheriting such an experience from childhood, we grow up as self-obsessed lovers. We expect recognition and liberation in love. We become reactive when a moment of conflict arises in our love relationships. But we never consider the fact that we all are prisoners of lovelessness, which is the most overlooked characteristic of caste-society. So I relied on my instincts to find answers, to overcome *my* pain. How could I trust others in this?

A month after Jasmine broke up with me, I went to meet George. We watched a movie, then went to a bar and drank for hours. George was supposed to meet a friend that night. I asked him if I could come along. 'She is crazy. Are you sure you want to meet her?' George said, as a mischievous smile spread across his face. We met her near George's house, where she reached early and stood, waiting for us. We were both drunk. And she seemed high. It took us no time to feel comfortable with each other. Her name was Prachi. We headed back to George's place. I lit a cigarette and so did she. While smoking, she suggested that we smoke a joint. I was drunk enough to feel free from the worries of life, yet the desire to find myself newly in the 'high' of marijuana was never-ending. Prachi rolled a joint. We smoked. Our eyes signalled green to a possible excursion into each other's bodies. But we were all hungry. So we went to another bar, where we ate and got drunk. While coming back, Prachi and I kissed. At George's place, we kissed again and made out. There was no scope of being judged among us. It was enough to feel peaceful and accepted, even if it was for a few moments, even with strangers. I did not feel attraction strong enough to be in a relationship with her. But I felt content with her. We smoked up again and made out till early in the morning. I enjoyed her company and the physical intimacy, but I did not feel attached to her. She insisted she had to return home, which was somewhere in Oshiwara, as her parents were expecting her back. I dropped her to her place. Then I went to a nearby station, but the local trains were yet to resume their service.

So I waited, alone, drunk and high, feeling neither pain nor bliss. I wanted to sleep. Her face flashed in front of my eyes. I thought pain sometimes makes us enjoy the smallest of moments that come our way without being judgemental, because we instinctively know that pain might be waiting for us at the next turn. I was learning to focus on what I had rather than what I should have had. I was becoming capable of remaining detached from people.

Prachi was a Brahmin. When I met her, she had multiple partners, both male and female. She was a junior to George at EFLU in Hyderabad. For years, she had been pursuing her studies and was provided for by her family. But she found *freedom* outside the home, by staying away from her family. It was a life of privilege I had only witnessed in movies until then. I always envied it, but I also could not help feeling disdain for it. I could not unsee the roots of this privileged life that stood in contradiction to mine. The greatest thing marijuana did to me was that it made me see people beyond their immediate identities and material realities. Not that it was not possible without getting high, but marijuana provided the channel through which I sailed in my imagination beyond fear and comfort. There was so much scope to discover the *human* in people.

A month later, one day, I thought of Prachi. I asked George for her contact number. He said, 'Are you sure?' He gave me her number. She had already returned to Hyderabad. It was not difficult to start a conversation when I called her. We flirted over the phone. She said that she would like to come to Mumbai again to meet me. A couple of weeks later, early in the morning, she arrived at the TISS main gate. I went to receive her there. We stayed at a friend's house, which was a walkable distance from the TISS campus. She brought me books as a gift. One of the books was a poetry anthology called *The Dream of a Common Language* by Adrienne Rich, whose poems I went on to admire a lot in the coming years. I tripped on this book for months. For five days, we smoked up from day to night, drank ample beer, had sex and talked until we got tired by morning. For those five days, I was floating with the stream of my desires and, surprisingly, I felt unchained. When she went back to Hyderabad, I did not feel alone. She asked me to come and meet her at the university and spend some time with her.

Over the next couple of months, I spent time with a lot of people who wanted to either drink or smoke up. I was also occupied with deadlines for articles for which I started reading and writing in bars. Then one night, I took a bus for Hyderabad and went to meet Prachi. At her university, I stayed with friends of mine. In the campus of rocks and lakes and huge playgrounds and jungle-like landscapes, we smoked up from day to night and in between, we got drunk and had sex. My imagination of people expanded when I got high. I was living the life I felt I had always wanted to live, but, at the same time, there was a fear that I would get dissociated from my dreams. I also felt guilty, but it was this guilt that kept me under its watch.

*

In the meantime, I continued to smoke up with Saraswati. But we ceased to share physical intimacy. It happened because I got attracted to another girl, Alima; she was Muslim and Malayali. It was one of those ludicrous evenings in TISS. I was smoking up in an amphitheatre with friends. I saw Alima sitting alone, smoking a joint. Her large eyes, curly hair and melanin-rich skin enchanted me. I was high, and my feeling was so spontaneous that I could not prevent it from following its course. TISS is a small campus, and smokers here get to meet each other at least once, either out of necessity to smoke or as friends. So one day I happened to meet

Alima with common friends. The next day, I approached her and suggested we smoke a joint. We met in the amphitheatre the next day. We smoked, talked and listened to songs, the romance of which directly flooded my bloodstream along with marijuana smoke. We started dating. We made out, smoked up and got to know each other. It appeared to me that she was serious about us being together. This time the seriousness in a relationship scared me. Our relationship lasted only for a week or so.

One day, when I went to drink with Saraswati, her friend Bharathi also joined us. I did not know Bharathi until then. That afternoon, all three of us got hell drunk. By the time it was dark and the streets in Govandi were flooded with evening traffic, we stepped outside the bar. We walked to Saraswati's place. Saraswati hit the bed. Bharathi was tipsy. She lay over Saraswati and asked me to lie beside them. 'We should all love each other,' Bharathi said in a slurred voice. Bharathi was a Tamil Brahmin and married. But I did not know this until I dissociated myself from her. The next time the three of us got drunk, Saraswati went to her place, and the two of us went to another friend's house, where we kissed and made out. We were both drunk. She insisted on having sex. I refused because there were people in the other room, and also there no condoms. 'I am safe,' she insisted. Instead, I rolled a joint and smoked up with friends. We slept there that night. In the morning, before I woke up, she had already left. After that day, I avoided seeing her. A couple of months later, she came to me while I was walking to my hostel in the new campus and said, 'My feelings for you are genuine.' I did not know what to do with those words. I felt weak in my gut. 'Sorry,' I managed to blurt out and walked to my hostel. I was running away from affection and a romantic relationship, even though it was exactly what I needed.

After this, I met another girl. For a couple of nights, we slept together and made out but did not have sex. I was searching for an eternity in a moment. I was moving from one person to another, and yet I felt empty. I neither felt attached to them, nor was I in a position to avoid them altogether. I sensed my aloneness as my vulnerability, my weakness. At times, I did not have the language with which to console myself. Hence I always searched for people with whom to drink, smoke, eat and pass the time. When I was high and my body demanded rest, I fell asleep like a baby.

Loneliness is formless and shapeless, but it is the heaviest of all earthly things. I was slowly being crushed under it. My habits were destroying my body, but I was least conscious of it. This time, not only books but music came to my rescue.

*

Hurt and Hollowness

Defined by darkness, I longed for the light
waiting at the abandoned shore I stood
I was not touched by love but I might
if I walk in search of motherhood

My time from 2018 to 2020 at TISS was paradoxical in many ways. During this time, my health deteriorated drastically because of the consumption of marijuana, alcohol and cigarettes; I lost 16 kg of weight. Smoking marijuana all the time led me to consume endless cups of tea which, eventually, led to a loss of appetite; I was not aware of it. I grew up seeing alcoholic people all around me from childhood. Some of them were self-destructive, including my father. Yet I had never understood from what sprouts the tendency to self-harm. If look back on my own experience of being addicted for a year or two, then I can only find in it a widely spread vacuum for the meaning in life, being a Dalit man. One either needs love or meaning in life to resist the oppression of society. The Dalit men I had seen being destroyed by addictions of some kind were men either in search of love or meaning in life. They had failed because society had snatched both from them, long ago, even before they were born. My time in TISS from 2018 onwards made me realize this.

But this time spent in TISS was also the time during which I became creative with my writing and persistent and productive in terms of publishing books. It became possible once I got some clarity about my PhD thesis. One day, George and I were drinking in one of those cheap bars in which we used to feel solace and the presence of life. George had mentioned to me the book he was currently reading: *Noise: The Political Economy of Music* by Jacques Attali.[1] He shared his thoughts on the book and also quoted some lines from it. I got fascinated by the way he explained the ideas about music from the book. George, as usual, also included a socioeconomic perspective. While explaining any idea, George had the quality which almost all the professors I knew lacked: imagination. George was my intellectual companion in Mumbai, and when I say 'intellectual companion', I mean *understanding* life rather than judging it. In the noise of that bar, we talked about music, and life appeared to me charming like never before. The most intellectual art is the most emotional one in its nature and form—this was my first impression when I heard George talking about Attali's book. A week or two later, I suddenly remembered this book and I asked George to send it to me. I printed the soft copy and got it spiral-bound. In the next two weeks, as I read the book, it disrupted all my thoughts, views and opinions about what I understood and felt as music. It was like seeing what is what, in its reality, in its depth. Books were a major part of my life by now. They were cementing my conviction about stories, about themselves.

Days Will Come Back, a manuscript of a collection of poems I received one day to be published by Panther's Paw Publication, was one book that cemented my fidelity in books, and specifically poetry.

Neither the lawns nor the flowers
Exist in our courtyards
Like in a King's palace gardens
We can hardly fit a camping bed here
However, our relationship with flowers
Is as old as Harappa and Mohenjo-Daro
That is why we grow roses
In the bottom of broken pots
With an expectation
That days will come back
When we will fulfil our dreams
We will grow the same roses in our backyards
Then lawns will not only exist in palaces
But also, in our courtyards[2]

This poem from the book made a permanent space in my mind. Man's relationship with flowers is as old as the beginning of life itself. The earth does not only beget flowers but also humans. While flowers remained beautiful and harmless as they always have been, humans evolved to bestow meanings to flowers and life around them; but humans also subjugated other humans and continue to do so in the name of identities and categories they invented. Those who were being subjugated have not given up their will and quest to resist and bloom and flourish, no matter how momentary it is. While those who have subjugated other humans long ago ceased to possess the instinct to understand the real purpose of beauty, the subjugated people have not lost it. Oppressed communities, though made to undergo pain (a result of systematic discrimination), do not dissociate themselves from what is beautiful in life, such as music. Despite the pain, they create music, or life, by planting a seed so that a tree can grow or flowers can bloom. This process is in direct connection to the ecology in which humans breathe and live. Even in pain, they don't think of the destruction of life. Rather, they grow flowers in their own space, no matter how small it is, even in broken pots, no matter how fragile they are. Lack of space or lavish pots, the relationship with flowers can't be broken, and the people who were subjugated have never forgotten it. Within a few moments, this poem connected me with history and encircled me in a beautiful tradition we had when we were not reduced to identities and categories. *I am historical and a protector of beauty and justice*, I told myself as soon as I finished reading this poem. Kamal Dev Pall is the poet who had written this historical poem. Rajinder Azad, a friend of mine whom I met on Facebook, had translated this poem from Punjabi into English.

*

From 2008 onwards, poems had become my vehicle to transport myself into the world of meanings that poets bestow on things and the people around them. I began to see and learn about the world through poems. I was seeking the utopia that poems were showing me, and I also realized that, in this sense, poets and philosophers are no different. Poems never appeared to me carrying a vision of an unjust world. Yet, not all the poems I read at the beginning introduced to me the purpose of poetry, subsequently justice. The majority of Indian poets writing in English were utterly engrossed in their Savarna and privileged self, and poems carved out of that were the manifestation of minds that are socially ignorant and aesthetically Brahminical. As I began to write poems, however, I simply copied these poets, in addition to international poets because I had no Dalit poet to follow in English. This crisis came to an end when I started to read Dalit poetry in Marathi and then from other languages. It changed my imagination in English.

I dared to insert my ideas, my references and my history into English. English no longer appeared to me an alien language. I could read myself in it now, no matter how little. When Rajinder Azad emailed me the manuscript of *Days Will Come Back*, I read Dev Pall's poems in a frenzy, as I felt so thrilled and overwhelmed. They assured me that we Dalits could change the imagination of English in India.

In 2015, I came across the poetry of Lal Singh Dil. A Punjabi Dalit poet who was drawn to the Naxalite movement for a while then got disillusioned with it over the question of caste, Dil had converted to Islam. He left a lasting impact on my mind with his poems, searing with dejection but also compassion, love and longing. At times, his poems were mystic yet comprehensible. But I found longing for love a major theme in his poems. In his poems, I finally saw love in the most intellectual way because it was associated with labour and respect for a person. Dil spent his entire life in hardship, but his poems were far from complaining about it or about hatred; rather, he talked about love and spoke against oppression. Gurinder Azad, a friend and poet from Punjab whose article on Dil was instrumental in introducing me to Dil's poems, once told me that Dil was *khalis*. '"Khalis" means pure,' he explained to me.

Kamal Dev Pall's poems became another significant occasion for me to understand the world of Punjab in its intensity and social reality. Their poems made me restless. They removed the blindfold of delusion from my eyes about the prosperity and romanticism associated with Punjab. In their poems, Punjab appeared as a socially tumultuous land, which was once revolutionary, and how that revolutionary zeal had been mutilated by Brahminical forces over the decades. For me to access this reality was not possible without translation of these poems into the language I understood. We, who inherited the past of untouchability, have hardly shared our experiences and imagination through a common language across linguistically diverse regions. Translation in India is a depressing venture. Translation, of text and visuals, have so far helped Brahminical notions to flourish in India. It did not intend to spread an anti-caste consciousness across the linguistic states. While working on *Days Will Come Back* towards production, I increasingly felt that translation makes solidarity constructive between two oppressed communities across states if it becomes a discipline. It made me realize that there are people in other states who speak different languages, carry themselves differently, eat different food but think alike because they inherit what I inherit too: the past of untouchability and visceral rage against casteist notions.

Days Will Come Back was published in 2019. I printed 300 copies. Out of these, I dispatched a hundred copies to Kamal Dev Pall and Rajinder Azad to the USA. It was hardly noticed by readers in India, and except the review I did, no one reviewed it. But while reading these poems, getting them edited, I grew up so much that I began to see love as the most intellectual and revolutionary act in caste-society.

*

According to Attali, only death is silent. Everything else is occupied with noise or happens in the presence of noise: sound, unarranged music, voices which echo in our ears, even in our dreams. And here lies the power of music. It invades our existence where we expect it the least: in our subconscious.

I was high one afternoon, alone in my hostel room. I opened up Attali's book. Propositions and arguments from the book thrust me into my memories of hearing songs from Ambedkarite *Shahiri* and *Bheem Geete*, transmitted from loudspeakers, hung

at the top of the dome of the Buddha Vihara in my basti. Played
at a high volume so the entire basti could hear, these songs were
synonymous with the most important days in the life of Mahars
who had converted to Buddhism in 1956: 14 October—14 April
1891; 6 December 1956—Buddha Jayanti. These were the days
in my basti when our history, struggle and vision was recalled and
celebrated publicly. In all this, our music was our strongest ally,
our only spirit, our enthusiasm which kept us alive amidst the
hopelessness of caste. Music produced by anti-caste singers and
shahirs were the only history we had which was unadulterated
and unappropriated. It was only in the music that we were not
victims. In the music of the shahirs, we were fighters and soldiers
of the sorrowless society, Begumpura; or, in Ambedkar's words,
Prabuddha Bharat.

*

My reading of Attali's book opened for me multiple windows
from which I could imagine music in its various hues and its subtle
politics, which is inevitably responsible for rousing emotions
among people. Music is a training without any institution or
having any concrete space which trains our world of perceptions;
music directs our reactions. Almost all the songs in movies from
Bollywood, which is among the most powerful entities in the
domain of popular culture in India today, direct us to alluring
a woman, winning her over, impressing her, glorifying her or
commodifying her. These songs rarely show the way to a person
to overcome rejection in love in a healthy way. They misread
women entirely. The idea of love in these songs is primarily the
idea of a Brahminical man who intends to *possess* a woman, rather
than seeing her as an equal. Caste, whose purpose is to separate
two persons so they may never establish a bond on a human level,

has given rise to the epidemic of lovelessness. Society, which has been for centuries suffering from the disease of lovelessness, has been made more violent, reactive, sexist and Brahminical by these songs. Each one of us is a victim, though the degree of our victimization might vary.

With each page of Attali's book, I was getting convinced about the violence of Bollywood songs in my life. They had completely erased the necessity and significance of anti-caste songs, the songs which I heard as a child and which were the truest manifestation of my roots. In their absence, my perceptions, especially in the matter of love or relationships, were constructed reactively. The production of Bollywood movies or its songs, or for that matter popular music composed and disseminated by people of dominant castes, had alienated me from the memory of my history. It was sheer violence. Because these songs made us see the world, at least in the context of gender, as pro-caste. Over the years, they had shaped generations in a sexist and casteist way. They proved to be a pathological training for men in India. All those who grew up listening to them and made them an emotional part of their memory are its victims. Because violence is not always a visible or physical assault—it is also a simple act of erasing a person's memory of their history and their roots and replacing it with notions that are antithetical to a person's history.

I felt free as I started to understand that what I listen to is also deeply political.

I proposed a series on Ambedkarite shahirs/singers to Rohini at *Firstpost*. She loved the idea and suggested adding an illustration and a recorded song of each shahir to go with the write-up. The result was a series of fifteen columns on Ambedkarite shahirs from Maharashtra, with beautiful illustrations of their portraits. I did not find a photo of a few shahirs because they seemed to have faded away from public memory. Because of the time and the circumstances in which they lived, performed and contributed, they did not have the luxury of being photographed or documented. There are thousands of Ambedkarite shahirs who contributed to the anti-caste movement. Choosing fifteen among them and writing about them was a task full of dilemmas. So I chose them chronologically and according to their geographical location. It took me four months to complete the series. It also became the premise for my PhD research.

As I went on writing the columns for this series, my ideas about my research and music started getting clearer. On several occasions, I was solely dependent on the songs of shahirs and nothing else because nothing had been written about them in English, and Marathi references to them were inaccessible. The songs became my data to know about them and the time in which they performed. At times, I felt strangely emotional, thinking about the circumstances in which they produced music that strengthened the anti-caste movement in its cultural and intellectual aspects. *Ambedkar* was an enthusiasm these shahirs lived and spread among the people, even in the most depressed and dark situations. At times I sobbed silently listening to these songs, thinking about their simplicity and their profound vision, and imagining that in their absence, it was hardly possible for masses to know and feel Ambedkar. Ambedkarite shahirs are the backbone of the anti-caste consciousness. Text can often falter in delivering its message. But music, which is politically explicit and produced by the oppressed, does not. And the music of Ambedkarite shahirs is more so. Because their music, produced with the intention of annihilation of casteist notions, sprouts from the need to establish humanness, which is defaced by the existence of caste and the people who hold on to it and live by it every day.

At this time, I was surrounded with books, deadlines, marijuana, alcohol, cigarettes and people. There were always people around me with whom I spent time, yet I did not get attached to. My mother's weekly phone calls would remind me: I have a family, a responsibility. I tried to put it out of my mind because now I saw family as a stranger thing, whom I had suspected to have known but in fact did not. I felt depressed, listening about my family. I was scared to become like my father, who was now a drunkard and a diabetic. Soon after this, I visited home for a few days. One day, my father got drunk in the morning while at work. He took a bus back home. It was about 11 a.m. He fainted and collapsed as soon as he stepped off the bus. He was drunk on an empty stomach. The tiffin which my mother had packed for him was untouched. Someone came rushing to my home and called for my mother. My mother ran to him immediately. With the help of my cousin who was coincidentally there, he was taken to the doctor. I was in my room, reading, unaware of this. My mother called me from the doctor's clinic and asked me to come there. I went there, confused, wondering how to deal with it and having no answer. Two or three days later, I returned to Mumbai. I continued to smoke up, and when I was high, I found the world bearable. Despite all the hatred it contained, with all its problems, with all its cruelty, I felt I was capable of loving. I never lost my faith in loving and being loved. My family was far from my thoughts.

*

One night, I was drinking till late. Before I knew why I was doing it, I messaged Devika, asking if she would like to meet the next day. A couple of weeks ago in TISS, there had been some kind of festival in which I had put up my books for sale. She was in-charge of the books section, so I had been in touch with her. The festival came to an end, but her image stuck in my mind. It was not attraction nor infatuation. I messaged her out of need. I was lonely and utterly impatient. I needed someone who could embrace me. But I had been mostly mistaken in choosing people. I just went along with them, like a fallen flower that goes along with the wind, and then gets lost in obscurity and, falling off a cliff, dies a silent death.

Devika came down to the tea stall the next evening. The vicinity was filled with students who were done with their classes and were idling, smoking cigarettes, drinking tea, eating, giggling. I was there, high on marijuana, smoking a cigarette and sipping sugary-sweet tea. I had almost forgotten that we had decided to meet. She reminded me, wondering over my forgetfulness or perhaps my intentions. We chatted there for a while and then we went for a drink as the sun disappeared. Her eyes were inquisitive and grew suspicious. Later, I learnt that her past two relationships had been violent and abusive: first with a Brahmin male (who she said had tried to rape her), second with a Dalit male (who had physically harmed her). She had been in relationships that had turned bitter after a while, a fact that I had underestimated. I was not serious about us. I ignored the fact of her having been hurt in the past. She had also been sexually abused in a school *meant* for Savarna and elite students. Two days later, we went to my friend's house. We drank and ate there. I went with the intention of staying over for the night. She got angry because I had not informed her. Her anger subsided by midnight. We were drunk and unable to sleep. The tension and anxiety was replaced by sexual arousal. We began to kiss and ended up having sex. I did not come because there was too much alcohol in me. We slept peacefully. In the morning, we had sex again and I came. My days and nights attained a wild rhythm. I was mostly seeking pleasure and detachment because I knew that, once I felt attached to someone, hurt would follow. But this time, unintentionally, I followed the hurt.

*

When Devika came to Pune to pursue her Bachelor's degree, her father bought a spacious flat for her to live comfortably in. As the days passed, I learnt from her that all her material needs had been provided for. She was Maratha by caste. The gap between us, of caste and class, was agonizing for me. As opposed to her, I was constantly in need of something and constantly disappointed to see the impossibility of acquiring it. Consumption, acceptance and rejection shape us differently. People who can fulfil their desires through wealth or social position tend to lose the instinct to survive on a minimum; consequently, they do not have the emotional capacity to understand the anger of an oppressed person. Most importantly, they are least concerned with the practice of justice. This is the precise reason, in India, the struggle, attitude and expression of the oppressed is mocked and sabotaged by the dominant castes in all spheres of life. The anger an oppressed person carries in his bones, even in personal matters, is framed as a threat by the oppressor. Viktor Frankl says, 'Love is the only way to grasp another human being in the innermost core of his personality. No one can become fully aware of the very essence of another human being unless he loves him. By his love he is enabled to see the essential traits and features in the beloved person.'[3] Caste is an invisible veil that blurs our vision and prohibits us from seeing the true existence of a person. With Devika, I became conscious of my own emotional vulnerability.

*

A month or two after Devika and I started to see each other, I was invited to read my poems at Sahitya Akademi, Delhi. When I reached Delhi airport, it started raining. Humid breezes followed as the rain abated, and the air turned unbearably hot and stifling. The accommodation had been arranged at India International

Centre (IIC). It was my first step into the literary world about which I had read, and where once I longed to belong. Now, when I was there, I could not help noticing all the elitism around me. I could smell the artificiality of being. Perhaps the people were like that—full of vanity and sophistication. It took me only a few moments to realize that I did not belong to this literary circle. I felt this more prominently in the evening, when I hit the bar at IIC, which was subsidized for guests and members. I drank a lot, only then feeling like I could bear to be surrounded with all the elitism. The next day, I read my poems at a programme arranged at a hall of Sahitya Akademi. Khushi, a friend of mine, also attended the reading. She was proud of her *Pahadi* (Garhwali) origins and was also nostalgic about her home. But she had little clue about her caste origin.

I had known Khushi for a year and more. After Jasmine broke up with me, I was desperately looking for someone with whom I would not feel lonely. One day on Facebook, I met Khushi. She was studying English literature at Delhi University (DU). We instantly became comfortable while chatting, as literature was the common factor between us. I started flirting with her. She responded to it amicably and, at times, cheerfully. When we talked, I felt no hesitation. I felt as if I was being heard. The fulfilment of a small need is often an instrumental force that encourages us to tread against all difficulties in life. We do not survive painful moments because we are 'strong'. We survive them because we learn to see some meaning in them. After Jasmine, I told myself that I would not fall prey again to the hurt of being abandoned. In those excruciatingly difficult moments when I was all by myself, I began to tell myself that I am a writer, that converting pain into a strength is my job; creating meaning out of it is my responsibility. On reflecting, I learnt that writing your story does not always alleviate your pain or offer you clarity. Sometimes, it is necessary as a testimony or a reference, for future generations, of your persistence to find light in the darkness. I told myself that I would write my story, even If I was confused about so many things. My history did not allow me to be silent. So I began to search for *love*. Meanwhile, I continued to write poems and post them on Facebook. This might sound like an uneventful act. But this was my way of creating a map of my feelings, emotions, reactions and perceptions, which eventually guided me towards the path of *existing*. Talking to Khushi over the phone increased my capacity to converse. With her, I felt I was allowed to open up and not be judged.

On the day of the poetry reading at Sahitya Akademi, Khushi reached the venue in the afternoon. She was the same: cheerful, with a poised smile. The reading finished by 8.30 p.m. Me, Khushi and a Brahmin gay friend of mine, who had come to meet me, walked to a bar in Connaught Place. This was my first time stepping into such a loud and fancy bar. In it, there was loud and nerve-wracking music, dim lights that acted as supplements to alcoholic intoxication. The air smelled of alcohol, and the people were lost and had surrendered to the loudness of music and alcoholic romance. The three of us drank a lot of beer. We talked about life and traded gossip. We got drunk. 'So are you still single or seeing someone,' Khushi asked. Her question made me self-conscious. 'I am seeing someone. But I am not happy,' I said. I did not know why I had not stopped at the first sentence. We drank late into the night. All cities appear the same when drunk. Delhi was no different to me when we came out of the bar. My friend dropped me and Khushi at IIC. In the room, that night, as we were still drunk and muzzy, we cuddled each other and lay on the bed, looking at each other. Our bodies were extremely tired because of the alcohol. Half of the memory of that night is faded now. We slept very little. I had a flight to catch in the morning.

So we rushed to the airport. In the next couple of hours, I reached Mumbai. On the way back to my hostel, I asked the cab driver to stop the cab. I opened the door and puked by the roadside. I was still reeking of alcohol. I felt ashamed. I did not know why, and if I should feel so.

*

I was dangerously dehydrated when I reached the hostel. I drank water and hit the bed. I slept for a few hours, with my phone dead; when I woke up, my head was aching badly and my body was running out of energy; I puked again. By now, Devika had messaged and called several times. I met her in the evening, and she suspected something was not right. I did not have courage to tell her what had happened. I said, 'I got drunk last night and puked and I am feeling sick.' The manner in which she asked about my whereabouts, followed by her own assumptions about it, sounded like she wanted me to always behave righteously, according to some unspoken ideal. In her company, I mostly felt I could not explain my situation because I sensed that I would be judged. Even her concern irritated me because of this attitude.

By this time, she had developed a habit to see me in the light of my past. According to her, I was not serious about relationships. We fought almost every day because we were unable to listen and empathize with each other. In the moment of misunderstanding, or misinterpreting each other's words, we forgot to forgive each other. She had all the material comforts at her feet and command. I was always grappling with worries about the future: my career and survival. The place where you are not judged but rather understood for what you are is your home. I never felt at *home* with her. Her concern about me was also her way of monitoring my activities and habits. This scared me. I told her on several occasions that this relationship wouldn't work and we should break-up. She mistook this for my desire to be with someone else, someone new. I was too weak to take any stress from her demands to prove my innocence, fidelity and commitment. After arguing for a day or two, she always insisted on staying in the relationship. I too needed someone. But I was increasingly growing unhappy and unfree. She wanted to *define* my being. *The day I will be defined by others will be the day of my death*—I was not far from sensing this.

I believe that writers live in multiple worlds. Being a Dalit and writing continuously is not only living in multiple worlds in a single moment but also constantly destroying, creating and recreating oneself several times. That is because one's experiences are largely formed within an 'invisibility' of the self in the national discourse; this self has never been a matter of intellectual curiosity in this country. *To defy casteist norms is to make myself intellectually visible and emotionally vibrant in the minds of readers.* This sense was my way of remaining sane amidst the emotionally tumultuous relationship with Devika.

A few days later, Khushi messaged me, recalling how soothing it was for her to feel my fingers running through her hair. I was asleep. Devika read the message. When I woke up, I saw rage written all over her face. I had not told her about this earlier. Now fear arrested my mind. Devika shouted at me, cursed me and angrily said this proved my infidelity. Her anger was justified. I was guilty of not having told her the truth. What I did not anticipate was her anger turning into a destructive intention which, for the rest of our relationship, harmed both of us. Devika continued to yell and accused me of several things, including womanizing. We fought. It was too much for me to handle. I needed some space to think clearly. Even though I was wrong, I knew I did not deserve to be accused of womanizing or other things that she was making up in her mind. I zipped my bag and got dressed. I said I wanted to go to the hostel. Devika accused me of running from the truth. We tussled with each other, mentally, verbally even physically. I finally reached my hostel. I wanted to think and not talk because I knew it would lead to reactive arguments. Devika messaged, called. I felt guilty and scared. She was unstoppable. She sent me more than a hundred messages and called me over a hundred times. This was not normal. This was alarming.

Her anger against me never subsided, yet she kept coming back to me despite there being enough proof that something was strangely unhealthy between us. That something was lovelessness. I saw we both were suffering from it and yet could not know it, could not accept it. I had my reasons for being selfish and staying in a relationship whose mental effects I had undermined and hardly anticipated. But what was hers? Today, the only explanation I have, I find in the sentence of Lemn Sissay which he writes in his remarkably tender and emotionally educating memoir, *My Name Is Why*. He says, 'Hurt people hurt people.' Devika was hurt too, not only now, but from her childhood. Men were the reason for it. Her only mistake was to group all men under a single category. She could never fathom the idea that she, as a Maratha woman, was much more powerful than Dalit men in many ways in caste-society. She never understood my dilemmas and how they shaped me. And I, who lived the life of a recluse, as an introvert during my formative years, had not yet learnt that communication was the key to resolving conflicts in relationships.

I had hardly seen my parents conversing with each other. The labour to survive and feed us consumed all their time and energy. The only time they talked was when they needed something or needed to vent out their anger. I suspect that growing up in such an environment did not teach me the value of communicating our thoughts and feelings and expressing our emotions openly.

I did not know that it is the primary factor which keeps us connected to our partner's mental world. Books came very late in my life. The movies I grew up watching were patriarchal and pathological. Onscreen, these movies never portrayed the value of the communication between two persons in love. Instead, the dialogues were predominantly sexist. They silently affected me. Then, I began my journey with books, and books completely reconstructed me. I had been an introvert for most of my life. But in my early thirties, marijuana opened me up. I discovered that I could talk about my feelings. I felt it as an achievement. I found myself talking sense with Devika mostly when we both were high.

I spent two days in my hostel, avoiding Devika's countless calls and messages. She even threatened me with harming herself. It was traumatizing. Then, in the afternoon, I smoked up with my friends in the hostel. I was high, and a part of me wanted to respond to her. I was thinking if I met her, she would change, she would calm down.

We met two days later. We went to BSE, the bar, which was right next to Maitri Park, where Devika rented a place. She was still angry. I neither had the capacity nor the language in which I could explain to her what had happened and apologize. I did apologize, but it meant very little to her. Over a beer, we argued rather than having a dialogue. An attempt to have a dialogue with her always turned into an argument, and the argument transformed into fury. We drank till night time. From there, we went to her place and rolled a joint. We both smoked up. We got high, and had not eaten enough. We smoked up again. It calmed me down and I began to imagine that her anger would fade away. I think it was around 2 a.m. We had sex. While having sex, it felt as if all this frustration, this anger would disappear and we would be good again. I came. I felt extremely hungry. So I got up and wore my trousers. 'I am going to get some food, what should I get for you,' I asked while wearing my t-shirt. 'You piece of shit, you selfish bastard,' her voice hit my ears, and I turned my eyes towards her. Before I could understand what was happening, she threw a plastic chair at me, then rushed at me and bit me. The bite was so hard that it pierced through the flesh on my chest. The agony was so mind-numbing that I could not feel anything else. To release her hold from my chest, I punched her face. It took me a while to comprehend what had just happened. She cursed me again. Then, we both went to the hospital. Her eye was swollen. The doctor prescribed her some kind of ointment and tablets. My chest was burning with some weird sensations. I put my finger where she had bitten. It was bleeding.

Even a little bit of anger on her face started to scare me after that. I did not respond to her messages or calls for the next few days. To avoid seeing her and feeling confused about my feelings for her, I left Mumbai and went to Nashik to Sumedh's place. Her messages and calls followed me ceaselessly. I felt scared seeing them. She again threatened to harm herself if I did not respond. I wanted to cut all ties with her. I decided not to answer. At Sumedh's house, while he was away working at a factory from morning till night, the only thing that provided me courage and comforted me from the memory of what had happened were words. I had deadlines for articles. So I had to read, make notes, and interpret them along the lines of the subject at hand. In the afternoon, I listened to songs about Ambedkar. They kept me connected with my vision and roots. Though I felt extremely weak in my guts and emotionally vulnerable, words and songs instilled in me the enthusiasm I needed to think beyond the pain of the present.

*

Ever since I turned to books and they increasingly became an everyday part of my life, the distance between me and my father (and my family) increased. I perceived home as a cage and escape from it was the first step towards freeing myself from the burden of misery which was part and parcel of growing up in a Dalit basti. Books had made me realize my own oppression in the larger world. The sense of being imprisoned by some invisible force was growing inside me. That 'invisible force' was caste-society and its burden, its lethal norms, which had shaped my father. The sense of being its prisoner became explicit because I realized that it had the potential to eventually shape me as well, like my father. This realization led to a manifestation of bitterness, in the form of silence, between me and my father. Because I could see the roots of his ruin and that he could not. What angered me the most was the way I could look at his miseries but he could not. In our lives, one generation fails the next because they leave no legacy of talking to each other. By the end of 2018, when my mother phoned me regularly on weekends and told me about my father's paranoid behaviour, I sensed the beginning of his ruin, stemming from the bitterness of silence.

It was at this time that I got involved in a relationship with Devika. From the beginning, we started to scuffle with each other, which only increased, day by day. I increasingly felt misunderstood by her. This was happening when my mind was mostly occupied with searching for answers for my father's madness at home. Devika never saw this as a serious thing. She mistook my silence for avoidance, my unresponsiveness as being unserious about our relationship, my inability to share my emotional suffocation as being a womanizer. The latter was also responsible in pushing me to find solace with other women.

*

Devika's mother, although not very educated, always carried the pride of being from a feudal and dominant Maratha family. She treated Devika and her brother differently. She had grown up in a casteist and patriarchal environment, which she continued to maintain even after marriage to Devika's father. His family was not affluent but, as an educated person, he went on to make his name in the construction business. Caste helps people in an ascending order. And it degrades the person, no matter how talented the person is, in a descending order. Many times, I saw that Devika felt irritated by persistent enquiries from her mother over the phone. 'She is a control freak,' Devika once said about her. Studying in an elite and prestigious institution which advocates social justice, Devika learnt that her mother's behaviour was partly responsible for her feeling unfree and becoming irritable. But what she could not fathom was that her mother's traits were also inherited by her to some extent. A person who is born in an oppressor caste might read about or advocate the practice of social justice but is rarely moved to become a vehicle for it. Because to be a vehicle for social justice means disrupting his own mental and material world.

Coming away from home to study, Devika felt there was at last space for herself. This space had been provided to her and had not been earned. Unlike me, she never had to worry about survival, expenses or material needs or about providing for the family. The struggle to fulfil our basic needs can often govern the core of our being. Devika saw me as a 'man' in an idealistic sense, because she was far away from seeing how deprivation or social discrimination can shape a person. Although she claimed to *understand* my pain and its source, in reality she did not. At the most, it was sympathy; but empathy was never present between us. It was not her fault. She, like so many dominant-caste students, conveniently did not bother to discuss the problems of caste in the public sphere or in classrooms. This made them not only ignorant of their past, but also strangely arrogant, often, while interacting with someone from an oppressed caste. Our difference of caste and class worked as an invisible enemy in our relationship.

From where I come, I have witnessed that cruelty is dangerous yet it is seldom dishonest because it is explicit in our agreement with who we are. Insensitivity is far more dangerous because it stems from disguise, lying, and believing in lies. Caste is dangerous in this way too because it makes the dominant caste people believe, from the beginning, that their roots are associated with 'superior' history. They believe in lies, they raise their children with these lies, their children are the product of these lies. When these children enter universities and encounter these lies for what they are, in the company of Dalit students, they turn paranoid. On the other hand, some among them feel an utmost desire to de-caste themselves, by associating with the struggle of Dalits, being their allies or by being sympathetic towards them. But these seemingly 'sensitive' ones forget that it is nearly impossible unless they *de-construct* their being in a material and spiritual sense, which is informed and formed by their caste privileges. In Indian universities, the dominant-caste students seek their liberation through the *welfare* of the oppressed. To be in love with someone from an oppressed background, an oppressor feels the sense of being upright and 'just', of acting 'sensitively'. But they ignore the fact that to do this is to also bear the psychological repercussions because both of them, one oppressed and another an oppressor, have been shaped by two opposite histories—they don't merely stand in opposition to each other but in utter hatred for each other. The hatred of the oppressed is understandable and can also be justified from time to time, but the hatred of an oppressor is viscerally chronic, a phenomenal sickness, which stems from contempt for humanity or what I call '*human-ness*' in society. We all carry the past in our bones. Only some of us become conscious of it. Devika was conscious of her past, of the history of cruelty of her caste and never in denial of it. She was intelligent. Yet, she had been raised in utter comfort as well as with patriarchal values. This is the reason she was caught between cruelty and insensitivity and the desire to break free from it. The tussle between us was the creation of her confused and equally complex position of being. She hardly had any idea of it. Savarna kids who develop an instinct to de-caste themselves, to liberate themselves, to be an ally of the Dalit movement, do not have narratives of *their own* to interrogate their lies, cruelty, insensitivity and the history of oppression by their ancestors. They want to liberate themselves from caste but have no theory of liberation created by their ancestors or their leaders.

Namdeo Dhasal had once said, 'Knowledge is a peculiar thing. Once it enters your brain, it does not stop working.'[4] He was right. He knew that a person waking up to knowledge that had been historically denied to him was waking up to the light inside him, hitherto veiled by the darkness of social oppression. For an oppressed person, it also meant acknowledging the source of his discrimination. Knowing what is what also kills the comfort that ignorance offers. As I began to read about people from across the world and different cultures, I realized my historical uniqueness, but I also often related to their stories. Subsequently, I told myself that I was not an 'untouchable' because I could *share* their feelings of pain and the instinct to resist oppression.

The meaning of love also changed for me eventually. It was no longer merely about having a romantic affair. By then, I had also read Lal Singh Dil, and he made me see love intelligently rather than only purely emotionally. I started seeing love as a process in which my freedom, considering my history, should expand, and the sense of justice should grow. If in a relationship I could not feel free, mentally, then it no longer fit my idea of love.

With Devika, I walked on the path of my mental vulnerabilities. I stayed on with her, simply out of the hope that, one day, she would understand my weaknesses, my worries for survival, and be my companion in eradicating them. She acted the opposite. I did not exit the relationship despite being aware of my becoming emotionally vulnerable with her, because I felt too weak to be alone and was scared by my insecurities. I felt I no longer had the strength to be with a new person once again.

By reading about love as an idea and a phenomenon in the work of Dalit poets, I was persuaded to see love not only as a romantic–sexual act between two people, but essentially a conscious agreement to emancipate each other from the clutches of an oppressive past. It wasn't difficult for me, then, to conceive that the purpose of loving is to be 'unbecoming', because by the time we start 'loving' each other in caste-society, we have already turned out to be a 'sick' person in many ways. So *loving* in India is political in every sense of the word. It is more so when the histories of two persons, conscious of their past, stand in opposition to each other. By this time, when I was increasingly being misunderstood by Devika—or so I felt—I began to search for an explanation in poetry. I simply lacked the ability to make her understand by talking to her, especially when she analysed each of my words and acts through the lens of doubt, not trust.

*

After I spent a few days in Nashik with Sumedh, I went to Hyderabad and spent a day with Prachi. I wanted to get as far as possible from Devika and the horrible memories of that night. We smoked marijuana and I told her about what had happened. 'Emotional abuse. You are being emotionally abused, Yogesh!' Prachi said when I narrated the whole story. In the evening,

I went to meet Kuffir and stayed in his office overnight. The next day, I took a bus to Nagpur. During this whole month, Devika's messages and calls were unending. Gradually, her anger began to subside. She apologized. She promised to rectify her mistakes and improve. 'I want you back, I want to be with you,' she said. I had no reasons to not believe her. I was still terrified by the memories of the night when we had hurt each other. I was not mentally prepared to see a person I was in love with and who hurt me exactly when I needed to be healed. Still, I decided to go. After spending some ten days at home, I booked a bus ticket for Pune, where we were to meet.

*

Vulnerability was the first thing I felt when I met Devika in Pune after a month. We had lunch near Fergusson College, as she had suggested. Over lunch, I told her about places I had been to and the people I had met in the last month. As soon as I mentioned Prachi's name, the old fury in her eyes returned. It frightened me. Her eyes told me what she thought of me. She started to cry and threateningly accused me for not telling her earlier about meeting Prachi. I had not talked to Devika at all for a month, nor had I wanted to. She had always lived in the past, and the past was eating her from the inside. While she was crying, I got up to leave. 'I may be wrong and I may have been wrong all the while, but now you do not have to follow or be with a wrong person,' I told her once again, as I had countless times before. I walked out on FC Road, confused about her behaviour and feeling the weight of emotional stress in my nerves. The thought of ruination, which old age and life had brought upon my father, dominated my subconscious; I had recently witnessed it at home. I felt a tremendous need to be alone. I went to a bar and ordered a beer. Devika's messages and calls started flooding my phone. Over messages, she accused me of treachery. I did not respond. A few hours passed. Now, her anger melted. She apologized over a message. 'I won't do this again, I trust you,' she wrote. I was drunk by this time. I called her to the bar. Like marijuana, alcohol too made me like people. From there, we went to Bhaje, a village near Pune, famous for its 2000-year-old Buddhist caves. We wanted to feel each other's flesh, sweat and smell and let them enter into our bloodstream. It was almost like injecting cocaine in our blood. It numbed the intensity of our hate, of our anger, and helped exile us to the moment in which we both were a pleasure for each other—pleasure and nothing else. I think this was the only way in which we could trust and embrace each other, without any suspicion or prejudice.

Bhaje was a beautiful place. I had liked it ever since I had first visited it with Carol. Bhaje had grown in my mind like a permanent memory of remnants of the Buddhist past, while Carol as a memory had long ago faded. I liked the cold soil here. The sky above was clean. The Buddhist caves were carved at the top of mountains, a part of the Sahyadri range. A little further from it, there was Lohagarh Fort from Chhatrapati Shivaji's time. It was an ancient town. Bhaje, the village, was surrounded by these mountains, fort and Buddhist caves. People mostly cultivated rice here. What I liked the most in this place was its undecorated appearance and silence, protected by these huge mountains, and the greenery of its soil. I had craved to visit this place again and again to find myself surrounded by the bareness of life. Devika and I reached here by night time. She booked a hotel which had recently come up here, as the number of tourists had increased. Everything which pulled us away from each other seemed to vaporize as we had sex. Then we smoked a joint. After sex, I found myself again being emotionally vulnerable. I think we both knew what was wrong between us and had an instinct that it was almost irreparable. But both, I reckon, were equally weak to accept that and live with it. To a great extent, we never wanted to forget how we hurt each other and never wanted to forgive each other for the same reason. The thought of being rejected for my *caste* by her family was real; it was anchored in my mind as a haunting substance. Yet, love encourages you to face the fear of the unknown.

*

Life is nothing but the space of ceaseless possibilities to follow our dreams. I always believed, quite irrevocably, that the world is made up of two kinds of people. First, those who follow their hunger (or made to follow often), all their lives, they live *in* hunger and *die* in it. Second, those who follow their dreams and surpass the temptation of life while doing so. The former abide by the rules set by those who create the trap of hunger and push people away from their dreams. The latter ones are the ones who go to the extent of insanity and madness to follow their dreams. Ever since I had started to read, and consequently write, I wanted to be the latter. As I was increasingly becoming conscious of this fact, it made me value the significance of time and, to say it more profoundly, life. It is exactly at this point that I became very conscious of my being a publisher. On one hand, if I was struggling emotionally in my relationship with Devika, on the other hand I was becoming clearer about my dream. I had chosen books, and now books were showing me the way.

By early 2019, I had published *Days Will Come Back*. It is a poetry collection from which not only did I learn a lot, but the book also taught me that no matter what the subject of a poem, it can be written with empathy and beauty, and most importantly with uncompromising intelligence about life and reality. I arranged a small event to launch this book. The poet and translator were both in the USA. Because of the rain, only a few people turned up at the venue, which was a small art gallery situated near Flora Fountain. Among the audience, Dipti Nagpaul, then a journalist with the *Indian Express*, was also there. After the event, Dipti introduced herself and took my contact number. She said that she would like to do a story on the book.

Finally, when the story came out a few months later, it was not about the book but about the work of Panther's Paw Publication and its vision. It was the first major event in my life as a publisher, because it brought me in front of the eyes of the people across the nation when I myself was not confident about my role as a publisher. The story was published on 3 November 2019, in *Eye,* the literary supplement of the paper, which I had been dedicatedly reading since graduation for its content about books, authors and stories. Now, my story was a part of it, *in* it. It was an emotional moment. Not because it was the first media recognition I had received for my efforts, but because my story had become a part of the national imagination. Only I knew what it had taken for me to reach people's minds with my thoughts and vision. I began to foresee living my dream to new dimensions. Suddenly, I felt all my previous life had ended, and I was beginning anew. In the next two months, I published three books: *Flowers on the Grave of Caste* (my short story collection), *We the Rejected People of India* (poetry collection by Sunil Abhiman Awachar, which I translated from Marathi into English) and *Savitribai Phule and I* (a story about the fictional diary of Savitribai Phule, written by Sangeeta Mulay).[5] I lost the sense of time while working on the production of these books. And my engagement with these books also saved me from being swallowed up by the emotional madness that I felt, when Devika and I quarrelled, and when these quarrels, this madness, were normalized between us.

*

Devika and I got back together after a month. I realized that the unending arguments between us and her obsession with my 'infidelity' were due to her inability to invest her energy, emotional and intellectual, in her 'dream', which could have been anything. I started advising her, sometimes quite patronizingly, to apply for higher education, since it would expose her to wider perspectives. She was intelligent. But she was not a reader. I believe that books are a necessity for our emotional education. In inter-caste love stories, empathy is the key, as it makes us see the beloved along with his history. What I have gathered from my memories of the years that I spent with Devika is that her claims to understanding the history of Dalits stemmed from her sympathy, which a Dalit rarely wants, especially from his beloved. So I asked her to read stories, which she hardly ever did, at least before my eyes. So, I do not know why she listened to my suggestion and registered for the IELTS—an English test necessary to apply for European universities—but its result was going to be productive in her life.

I started spending most of my time with Devika and working on books from her place. Right after she completed her MA from TISS in 2018, she got a job in Mumbai, and we started living together. A month or two before the night in which we fought, she had quit the job. Now, she was focusing on the IELTS examination and applying to German universities for another MA. She never had to worry about funding and money. On the contrary, my aspirations never passed the scrutiny of my worries because often, I was not in a position to act upon what I wanted to do. This shaped me differently.

When Devika and I fought, I began to sense that words would be incapable of resolving the quarrel; only silence would make some sense. So, I tried to stay away from her and needed to be alone for a while. She threatened me by saying she would harm herself, and on a few occasions, she scratched her hands and banged her head against the wall and sent me pictures of it, as well as recordings of her berserk voice. I simply did not have answers for her endless doubts and questions. She also got paranoid on a couple of occasions and accused me of having affairs with girls with whom I had never spoken. She held those girls responsible for spoiling her life. She was making up things in her mind, where she was harmed by people who had no contact with her or me. I had committed a mistake in the past but I moved past it, otherwise I could not have survived memories that were so unkind to me. She held onto the memory of my mistake, of my past. Something was terribly wrong with her. She was deeply hurt, and the root of her hurt lay in her past. But Savarnas have rarely ever accepted and consequently exposed in the public discourse what is wrong with a casteist upbringing. Devika was no different. Being together with her for a year or so, I witnessed my first panic attack.

*

I went home for a few days in 2019. I had ceased to feel any affection for Nagpur, the city in which I was born and raised; it was now more like a despised or an invisible entity. At home, I began to observe the invisible sickness that was taking root in my father's mind as his mother's health increasingly deteriorated. My mother tolerated my father's alcoholism and took care of his mother as well. The sheer strength which my mother maintained all this while was beyond my comprehension—I lacked the ability to commit myself so totally to the responsibility of others. All this further increased the degree of my detachment from home.

I returned to Mumbai. Devika had gone to her house in Pune and was returning that night. On campus, I met Saraswati. Her course was over. Most of the students had already gone home. It was April or May. She asked me if I would like to smoke up. As the sun went down, we rolled a joint at the volleyball court in New Campus. We smoked up. The silence turned more intense as if to make me hear my own thoughts. Suddenly, and quite unwelcome, the thought of Devika crossed my mind. Her face, with furious eyes and cold expression, flashed before my eyes. In the next moment, I felt extremely vulnerable. Saraswati wanted to smoke more. But I left, saying it was enough for me. As I reached my room, I heard my heartbeats—my heart was pacing so fast that I could literally count each beat. I had smoked marijuana after a week or so. I felt uneasy and was sweating. A couple of weeks ago, a Dalit student had collapsed in the bathroom and died; some said it was a cardiac arrest. The memory of this unfortunate event was still fresh in my mind. I thought my racing heart was an indication of a heart attack. I called Devika immediately and told her that I was coming over. She had just got back to Maitri Park. As I reached her place, finding it slightly difficult to register things around me, I told her what had happened and she took me out in the open air. We sat there for an hour or so. I slowly relaxed. 'It was nothing, you panicked,' she said. Why would I panic, to this extent? Fear and insecurity were a common part of my life. But they had never affected me to the extent that I started assuming my *end*. Something was wrong. Something had affected me severely. I thought it was triggered by a video footage I had seen a couple of months ago.

One day, in the TISS cyber library, while browsing Facebook, I came across a video. It was CCTV footage. A girl and boy are walking slowly towards the gate of a hospital. A tall and robust-looking man suddenly emerges behind them and is seen following them. In the next few seconds, the robust-looking man hacks at the boy's head, twice, with a butcher knife. The boy is killed on the spot. For a few seconds, I thought of it as a clip from some movie. But then, I began to read the caption, and then news about this brutal incident flooded the internet for the next few days. Those who know the nerves of India know that this incident was not the first of its kind and it was not going to be the last. They know too well that it has been going on for centuries, and it will go on for centuries, to eventually make us witness our end as a society. It was the sickness of caste that helped people in India to develop various kinds of paranoia that, eventually, translate into violence.

Pranay was the name of the boy who was killed on 4 September 2018. He was bright, young and educated as an engineer. He was Dalit, the primary factor for him being murdered. In college, he fell in love with Amrutha (a girl from the Vaishya caste), their love bloomed and they decided to get married. What a beautiful thing it is to choose each other, being in love, and deciding to commit to each other for a lifetime! Such beautiful things are despised and vehemently opposed in caste-society. Loving a person of our choice irrespective of their caste or class, language or background, or colour of their skin, are opposed by Brahminical feudal castes, who also possess power and influence over masses to dictate what is our 'culture'. Amrutha's decision to marry Pranay violated the caste pride of her father, Maruti Rao, who was also a powerful businessman. He hired a hitman to kill Pranay.[6] This is an infamous story today.

India is a society in which the existence of logic, reason and love are mutilated everyday by caste norms which are premised on hatred for Dalits. Devika knew that her parents were never going to accept me with all their heart. I had gathered from her description of them that I must be ready to face their scorn, contempt or, at the very least, their hatred. Hate does not have a sound in caste-society. This soundless hate intends to reject your existence. What does it mean to begin a journey of life with a person whose family has no place for you? This sounds like a paranoid thought, but in India, it doesn't take much time for paranoia to translate into violence that ends up destroying many lives at once. I had developed a fear, thinking about Devika and our relationship.

Paranoia is the most undermined characteristic of caste-society. Everyone seems to be paranoid here all the time. What is the function of caste if not creating fear of each other? On the one hand, Dalits are paranoid, usually for the right reasons, hence they behave self-consciously every breathing moment when facing dominant-caste people. Dominant-caste people, on the other hand, get paranoid thinking about the possible challenge to their delusional superiority and of course, their caste-capital. The paranoia of Brahminical–feudal castes almost always translates into gruesome violence—it isn't just simply a violent act or revenge, but a manifestation of a centuries-old sickness that terrorizes our entire being. Discarding a son or killing a daughter for marrying a lower-caste person, especially a Dalit, Brahminical–feudal caste parents often resort to violence because they are unable to think beyond their delusional caste-pride and are too ignorant and egoistic to see their mental sickness. Love is the biggest threat to caste. Because love resurrects what was killed by caste: the strength to embrace a person without any prejudice. Yet, inter-caste love stories do not exist without their mental challenges, and not to mention daily agony, which destroys something in you forever.

*

As the tension eased between us, I learnt to teach myself to work on books in spite of all of it. Marijuana, though it sounds exaggerated, helped me tolerate the tension because when I was high, I mostly thought of books that I wanted to publish. The idea of my short story collection took shape in these circumstances. Writing is the only presence in my life that encouraged me to love people; otherwise, previously, when I worked out of the brutal need to survive, I felt an irrepressible rage towards people for their casteist behaviours, which they were mostly ignorant of and hardly ever took responsibility for. The thought of writing short stories not only excited me, it also rescued me from the threshold of acute depression. I did not feel the need to *imagine* stories; stories were there in my life, all around me, inside me, struggling to come out. In fact, I knew that the stories I was going to write had probably never existed in the English imagination, neither as stories nor as lives. Caste is the alienation from 'common sense'. I wanted to write stories of common sense, although I did not know this explicitly back then.

I wrote the stories in *Flowers on the Grave of Caste* mostly at Devika's place, when she was at work. I would be still writing in the evening when she returned. I wrote these stories while smoking marijuana, or sometimes when I was drunk or under the spell of extreme tension between me and Devika. I wrote these stories in cheap bars of Govandi, and the people out there felt close to the world of my stories. The stories stayed with me, everything else came and went. Once you attain the vision and perspective, intoxicating substances and mundane conflicts cannot overtake your ability to work. Dalit literature is based on this principle. Once you reach this position, you utilize an intoxicated or troubled state of mind to create your art. What guides you all this while is the insatiable need to create and recreate yourself through words.

One day, my left thumb started aching from the inside. No wound was visible on the skin and there was no scar. In moments of stress, especially when Devika and I argued and she turned uncontrollable, this ache became severe. I told her this, but mostly she accused me of giving an excuse. I called my friend who was a doctor, and he called me to his place. Devika and I reached his place in Thane by the evening. I told him the problem. He suggested that I come with him to his hospital for a check-up in the morning. At his house, I remember, though the reason is difficult to recall, Devika and I fought a lot at night. Then, we had sex and slept. The next morning my friend took us to the hospital and directed me to his colleague. Tests were done. I was terrified by the very thought of being tested in a hospital. Nothing abnormal was detected. Then, the doctor asked me about my habits and lifestyle. He started questioning me: 'Do you smoke?'

'Yes.'

'How many in a day?'

'Thirty or thirty-five.'

He frowned.'Do you drink? How often?'

'Yes. Almost every day.'

His eyes grew intense. 'And? Any other habits?'

'I smoke marijuana.'

'How often?'

'Every day.'

Then he asked me to listen to him carefully. His hands reached the drawer of his table and he took out an object from it, a replica of some body organ, as it seemed to me. He showed me the structure of veins and how blood flows within them. 'Blood doesn't seem to be reaching the end of your thumb. Hence it is aching. This is the most plausible reason. It is because of too much nicotine and alcohol in your body. If you want to live, quit smoking and drinking today,' he said as if he was giving me the most ardent sermon.

His words terrified me because they indicated death—my death. The thought of death was real to me now. I did not smoke, drink or consume marijuana for months to come. Withdrawing from all of them at once had its repercussions. I felt anxiety from time to time. I had mood swings and irritability. My second panic attack came when Devika and I went shopping to Colaba and decided to watch a movie. *Gully Boy* was screening at Regal Cinema. There was a scene in it: Ranveer Singh desperately tries to convince his father about his decision to sing rap and how meaningful and close it is to his heart and life, but his father is staunchly opposed to it. It reminded me of my father and the thought that he would never understand me or my writing. It suddenly arrested me emotionally. I felt my heart racing. I felt anxious, suffocated. I went out and sat in the corridor to get some air. Devika followed me. I folded up my sleeves. 'Breathe, don't worry,' Devika said. I did not find the courage to walk back into the theatre. We took a taxi and went to her place. After a while, we had sex. I found no other way to distract myself from my worries. Sex between us was the only act in which we were receptive to each other and fully embraced by each other.

The spells of panic persisted for a while.

Devika got an admission to a German university. In a month or so, she left Mumbai. A day before she left Mumbai, we fought. So I refused to see her off. She went to Aurangabad to spend some days with her parents. After a week, I started missing her. We decided to meet in Pune, at her house. She went and lived there from time to time, away from her parents and the surveillance of her mother. I went to Pune. This time, sex was intense and quick, as though we both had been longing for it for ages. Until she eventually moved to Germany in October 2019, I frequently visited her in Pune. I spent days with her, in her home, the home bought by her father, where she could exercise the freedom to be with me, her boyfriend. But her freedom was a secret. I was a secret, in her extended life. I was in her house, but never existed for her parents. I was not visible for them, nor for the housemaid who came over there to clean and cook. I existed only for her. How different this was from the time when Devika came to my home in Nagpur, and everyone knew she was there, with me, in my tiny room, in my small home. There was no need to hide. Life was naked in my home and among my people. Despite their own problems, they had never learnt the skill of invisibilizing a person. The memory of being invisibilized pierces the mind like several needles going through it at once. After being in an emotionally draining relationship with her for two years, one day, I wrote:

In inter-caste love stories
the distance between two
is not horizontal, it is vertical
it seems always reachable
but is always un-touchable

If I felt such agony on being invisibilized by a Savarna person with whom I was in love, what about my ancestors who had been entirely invisible to society, for centuries? Because being untouchable also meant they did *not exist*. How come millions of people who are born human, breathe as humans, love as humans and suffer as humans never exist for society as humans? The question unravelled my own fear, which led me to question my own existence. And I asked myself: What does it mean to exist?

*

Before Devika and I eventually cut all ties around October 2020, she told me what her father had said to her at the airport when she was leaving for Germany. 'Don't marry a Dalit,' he said. At the root of this simple suggestion, these few words, there were centuries-old hate, unkindness and tangible cruelty. My ancestors had lived with it, and now it was my time to witness it. Behind this brief sentence of her father, there was centuries-old complexity of

what caste has made out of us. When it comes to establishing
blood ties, Savarna parents rarely trust their children. This simple
distrust subconsciously shapes their children abnormally when it
comes to choosing a life partner. Due to the absence of freedom
of choice in this most important decision, Savarna children are
alienated early on from commonsense in the matter of love and
relationships. Thus, they turn out to be emotionally reactive and
hurtful; some of them also become harmful. Whether the injury
is physical or mental, it affects all those who share life with that
person. When Dr Ambedkar referred to Indian society as a 'sick
society',[7] he primarily meant that each one here is suffering from
the disease called lovelessness. For aeons, lovelessness has spread
like an epidemic here and attacked people's ability to empathize
with others.

Savarnas have produced negligible knowledge about the cruelty
of their ancestors, the ignorance of which, in turn, has made their
generations emotionally puerile. This emotional cruelty affects
everyone from top to bottom. But they spend their lives in denial
of the truth. Devika was also a product of this denial. Although
she frantically recognized it, she never *publicly* denounced the
cruelty of her caste and her ancestors. There are barely any Savarna
academicians or scholars in India who are interested in researching
the oppressive role that their caste or community has played in
history. This is why Dr Ambedkar had remarked that intellectual
honesty has never been the characteristic of caste-society.[8] To
make one's dark history public to rectify the premise of social
interactions also means to jeopardize one's privileges, which are
essentially accumulated out of cruelty and oppression. Within
the visceral reluctance to expose and comprehend the history of
one's caste, whatever that may be, lies the secret of sustenance of
caste, as well as the casteist mode of production, both psychic and
material. Devika repeatedly manifested this fact to me through

her very being. And it is here that I understood that being in love with a Savarna person in caste-society comes at a price.

Yet, love is not without its madness, where one chooses to be selfish rather than pragmatic, emotional rather than logical. The feeling of love is nourished by our instincts rather than interests. And it is also true. If love cannot annihilate caste, then nothing can.

*

Beginning from the Roots

Abandoned by history
in search of shelter I roam,
come, touch me, hug me
be my love, be my home

On 14 March 2020, the story written by Hansda Sowvendra Shekhar, profiling the work of Panther's Paw Publication and about my efforts behind it, was published in *The Hindu*.[1] It was a long read. It was a big moment for me. Sometime back, I had read *The Adivasi Will Not Dance*, the short story collection by Hansda. These stories left me spellbound. Hansda is an effortlessly brilliant writer—I did not take much time to grasp this fact. Hansda writing about me and the publication I was running or trying to manage from my hostel room was indeed a remarkable moment. Of course, I felt praised for what I had been doing, but I equally felt more responsible because I was now open to public scrutiny and also automatically became answerable for my efforts. Ten years ago, when I read the first English novel of my life and did not understand anything and went on reading it several times from start to end, I had never thought that one day I would be a publisher myself. No one dreams of becoming a publisher. Becoming a publisher is an irresistible urge that develops over time. Yet, despite this universal rationale behind becoming a publisher, each publisher has his own, deeply personal purpose. 'Reclaiming human personality' was my purpose.

*

I was with Devika, in Pune, when *The Hindu* story was published. To spend some time with her family and me, she had returned from Germany after completing the first semester. On a slightly cold midnight in February 2020, I went to the airport to receive her. I had mixed feelings, yet I was anticipating a change in the way we would interact with each other, because the time in which we stay away from each other makes all of us long for a hug and warmth which cannot be replaced by anything in the world. Sometimes, our memory of 'good times' overpowers our memory of 'bad times' when in isolation from each other. And if it does not, then it means we have not progressed in the course of our relationship. I saw our relationship in this way. Tension had become a dominant part of my relationship with Devika, but I had no reason to cling to its memory. In order to progress intellectually in my life and emotionally in my writings, it had become essential for me to construct the future instead of digging into the past. This is the reason why I went back to Devika, repeatedly.

And I was right when I saw her at the airport, coming out of the arrival gate. We took a cab to the hotel she had booked. As soon as we reached the hotel, we made love. It was about 4 a.m. We made love again. Then, tired and exhausted, we both took a nap. The sun rose, and we got up to eat. Making love twice in a couple of hours had horribly increased our appetite, and it was apparent from the amount of food we ate in the breakfast at the hotel. Hunger is so human that we all appear the same while dealing with it. To pick her up, her father sent an SUV car from Aurangabad. 'My car is here, you must go now,' Devika said. I went to my hostel and fell asleep as if I hadn't slept for ages. Two weeks later, I met her in Pune, and that was the last time we were together, physically. But it was also true that between us, the mental distance had started to increase long ago. Our physical separation confirmed it in the next few months.

*

'Every new environment,' James Baldwin says, 'particularly if one knows that one must make the effort to accustom oneself to working in it, risks being more than a little traumatic. One finds oneself nervously examining one's new surroundings, searching for the terms of the adjustment.'[2] Baldwin has never appeared to me truer than in my reflection on my time at TISS. Back then, when I was living in the TISS campus as a part of it, at least theoretically, I had no words, or I must say the language, to describe my feelings about this place and what it was making out of me—an emotional wreck. But then, there were books, and I survived through them. I reckon that the essential purpose of reading is to discover our own voice, shaped by many voices around the world. This is how we locate ourselves on the map of history. This is how we relate to each other, empathetically, as humans and most crucially, as we must, intelligently. This is how, and for this precise reason, we educate ourselves in the matter of our emotional and intellectual world. This is how I related to, or to say it more intimately, found myself at home while reading Baldwin. Because, like him, I too was always on the run *from* myself, in order to arrive *at* myself. Only a mind that knows how it feels to belong to the unjust side of history knows what it means to escape the place where its ancestors were enslaved once and which it has to call its *home* now. Such a person never feels at home, anywhere, in the world. The reason for this is his instinctual ability to identify himself with the oppression wherever he goes. When I first stepped inside TISS, I so craved to belong there, to experience myself walking there and to be a *part* of this institution and its academic world—a delusion everyone wants to devour at the beginning. But in reality, I was escaping—from myself, my roots. Seven years later, knowing this was both a discovery and a trauma.

*

By 20 March, the news about COVID-19 virus had started to create panic among people. People were slowly getting nervous, especially those who had left their homes far behind to fulfil their hunger and pursue their aspirations in Mumbai. New words and vocabulary, with their own terror, started making their way into people's lives. The students at the TISS campus were served a notice to vacate the hostels by 23 March. I totally undermined the notice and decided to avoid it. I did not want to go back home. Where was I supposed to go with more than a thousand books? I had around 600 books in my personal collection, and around 1,500 copies of the total of seven titles published by Panther's Paw Publication over the period of four years. But students started disappearing everyday in front of my eyes. My roommates too left for their homes. And within a week, the hostel became so empty that it became ghostly at night. In the hostel, the rooms were deserted, the corridors fell eerily silent, and the few who had stayed until then for some reasons appeared to have been arrested by the fear of the unknown. Shifting back home, to me, meant shifting all my memories of Mumbai with me. I was not prepared for that. I looked at all my books and began to recall those moments, stretched across seven years, which had shaped me and shaped the course of the books I had published—the books which, in turn, shaped me, supported me and held me back from falling down in the chasm of depression and loneliness from time to time. It was not possible to carry these many books with me back home, nor did I want to leave them in the hostel. Of my memories in Mumbai, books occupied the most crucial part, because they had kept me alive when life touched a low. A book is an inanimate object. But only a reader knows that it can spin your life around by 360 degrees and in all the possible dimensions of life.

By 21 March, I began to realize the impossibility of staying in Mumbai. Outside the campus, eateries and restaurants were shut down. The canteen and dining halls on campus too stopped functioning. On Farm Road, a couple of grocery stores were open. I bought some nuts, Maggi and packed food to eat. For two days, I cooked alone, ate alone, smoked a cigarette alone and slept in the complete absence of human sounds. I had never imagined that life would come to a standstill so abruptly, so soon, within two days. People, like always, seemed to have no clue about what course the law and order would take. No one around me, including me, seemed to have any inkling about the severity of the pandemic and how it was going to affect our lives, forever. I thought this would end in a month or so. My prediction was utterly wrong.

I was reluctant to go home but, like millions of people, I too had no choice. Train services had already shut down. I talked to Devika, and she insisted that I go home the next day. She booked a flight ticket for me. It was 22 March. I immediately packed all the books by Panther's Paw Publication. It took about five hours to get them in one place. I had already talked with a friend, at whose place I shifted those books in the evening. I kept all my personal books in my almirah; every inch of it was now filled with books.

The next day, Mumbai appeared more deserted. I had not seen this city like this before. I felt that the people who keep this city running everyday were the only charm Mumbai had ever had, and in their absence, this city appeared meaningless and pale. On my way from TISS to the airport, I sensed the silence of fear. Because I had foolishly predicted that this imposed evacuation would last for a month or so, I carried only three books with me to read, besides two trousers, three t-shirts and a laptop. The books were Frantz Fanon's *Wretched of the Earth*, Lemn Sissay's *My Name Is Why* and Ismail Kadare's *The General of the Dead Army*. In another bag, I packed twenty copies of each title published by Panther's Paw Publication. *What if some people want to read and order a book even in this terrible time?* I thought.

In the next two hours, I was in Nagpur. The news of the pandemic had paralysed the activities of this city as well. This was apparent as soon as I stepped out of the airport and found myself in the absence of public transport. For the last seven years, I had sensed, from time to time, that I had started developing an aversion for this city. I began to dislike the way roads were being restructured and how the greenery, which once made the air bearable here, had started disappearing, with the rise of ugly cement infrastructure. I was born in this city, and it is an essential part of my personality. Yet it had never encouraged me to follow my dreams. In fact, it had somehow developed in me an instinct to escape it.

In my childhood, I used to observe flocks of birds, flying high in the sky above my basti, moving from east to west in the morning and back from west to east in the evening. Observing them, I used to think that everyone, eventually, goes back home. And I decided, once I leave home when I grow up, I wouldn't return. In the routine of the birds, I felt the monotony of life. Over the last twenty years, these birds have disappeared or witnessed decay due to rising pollution—the chances of them having migrated are slim. So, even then, I instinctively began to understand that one needs to migrate from one place to another in order to evolve, because the monotonous acts of any species become responsible for its extinction. Humans evolved because of their imagination more than anything else. So I taught myself that defying everything that endangers my existence is the only method I have to achieve the state of liberation. This may sound pessimistic, but I knew that it was my home, in which my existence as a mind was in danger. But here I was now, at home. My grandmother was bedridden, dying. My father was showing signs of his mental ruin. In my home, one generation was witnessing the decay of another.

*

The nationwide lockdown was declared in India on 23 March. A lot of people did not even know what it meant for them, simply because they used to work tirelessly in spite of whatever disaster, conflict or calamity shook society. For such people, work was synonymous with survival. The news channels, instead of providing factual information, started retching venomous rhetoric and sensationalized the otherwise sensitive problem that concerned all. Instead of awareness about the virus, fear and lies were spread.

I spent a week thinking that it would get 'normal' in a couple of weeks. In the second week, I constantly visited my memories of travelling across districts in Marathwada and Western Maharashtra, in 2013, when I was an intern with Manuski. A memory of visiting a village in Parbhani district was the strongest one. There, all the families of Mahar-Buddhists had been ostracized by the local dominant-caste families. Over a dispute of 'who should fetch water first from the common source of water', these Mahar-

Buddhist families were banned from fetching water or buying groceries from the village. The village was shut for these families.[3] Nearly a decade ago, the dominant-caste people had imposed lockdown in the lives of Mahar-Buddhist families. This is the story of many villages, across this vast nation, and it takes place almost everyday. But for the world, these stories are not verifiable, because they never reached their ears and never concerned their literary imagination.

I was trying to understand if this pandemic would change the way people think about each other or if it would make the lives of Dalits worse and unimaginable. They were the ones who would have to face the contempt of the rest of the society for practising commonsense, which challenges caste practices—casteist thinking had already started mocking scientific practices meant to deal with the virus. The pandemic affected everyone, but it affected Dalits at a scale for which society has no measure. Caste-society, devoid of any conscience, is the society wherein methods of discrimination are subtle and hence cold-blooded. People were dying out of hunger before a virus could claim their lives. In a few days, I began to observe queues, in my basti, where people came to fetch food packets. These food packets were distributed by local activists, individuals or voluntary groups who seemed to have retained a ray of humanity. Those who are ruled connect with each other in the matter of hunger and survival. Those who rule, or want to rule, have long ago forgotten to practise empathy and compassion—an equilibrium of intelligence and emotions that intends to protect the existence of humanity.

*

The world cannot be changed by shifting the location of power. It can only be changed by humanizing each other. The more I looked at my father, the more I was convinced about this. In June 2020, despite the fear of the virus and its spread, my father often went outside, to earn just a little so he could drink. When he returned home, drunk, he would lash out at us about his frustrations. In his words, he was always in the *past*. It was clear he was hurt. He had probably realized that his mental wounds were beyond the scope of healing. This affected him more. Repeatedly, he blamed his mother for ruining his life. The closer his mother moved to death, the more my father seemed to deny this reality. If he had accepted the 'present' in our lives, he would have been empathetic towards his mother. At one point, we are all scared of the idea of dying. But gradually, there comes a point when we understand that dying is an inevitable reality and we will have to face it one day. What makes the difference in our lives is how soon we travel from the point of fearing death to the point of accepting the reality of death. Because once you accept death as an undeniable fact, you start respecting life and see value in it.

The emotional complexity with which my father, a Dalit man, lived throughout his life was the innate characteristic of caste-society. If on the one hand he had little awareness of his oppression as a Dalit man in the outer world where he walked to earn his bread, on the other hand he was conscious of his position as a man at home, the place he had never taken seriously and at which he was never fully present. I grew up seeing this and, in childhood, also bore the brunt of it. The oppression that a Dalit witnesses is not objective but subjectively phenomenal. It is ever happening. His murder is fundamentally bloodless, and his stories do not occupy the mental space of the world. He simply does not exist for the world with his history, which is a unique chapter in the book of oppression. But he is very much alive—often he is sweet and dangerous like a honey bee, and when the time comes, he roars like a lion. But it is the problem of the world that it does not possess the language of his emotions, his feelings and forms of his sufferings.

The problem of and with my father was this: language. The world did not have his language, and he did not search one for himself. He searched for solace, consolation and healing for his wounds in the outside world. But the answers to his dilemmas and his pain were all inside. He was the answer to his own questions, but he never did realize this truth. And that is why I always felt that the dilemma of a Dalit man often takes a deadly route in the absence of language to deal with it. But in my case, the circumstances seemed to be improving. If not for books, I would have been swallowed by my own dilemmas and confusions about my position in the world's imagination. My father's paranoia was caused by the absence of language.

*

In childhood, my father was the only person who occupied my mental space. As a child, I got scared whenever he got late in returning home at night. He had often narrated instances of accidents in his line of work. So, on the nights when he was late, I used to stay awake and imagine him in an accident while driving the trailer-truck. I would feel dreadful because of my assumptions. This time, when I witnessed his paranoid behaviour, I began to wish him dead. He was being eaten up by bitterness, and he could not see it. His condition was mentally affecting all of us. I felt guilty and shameful for thinking as I was. I also felt scared because my thoughts were the manifestations of the disgraceful failure of the generations that preceded me, and consequently, this failure was now mine as well.

On two occasions, I was almost caught up in a physical scuffle with my father. He was drunk and tried to hit my mother; to stop him, I had to use physical force: I pushed him on to his bed. He was so drunk that he could not even stand properly. Seeing him like this, I hated him, and I hated myself for having to see his mental deterioration. I felt weak and was unable to remain calm in this situation. I had grown up seeing this: madness and a life in which violence could take its course anytime. But this time it was different. This time, I began to understand the circumstances that had pushed my father to this condition. Sons engaging in a physical scuffle with their fathers was not new for me. But I now began to understand that there was no hate in it. It was a result of our inability to respond to the situation with dialogue; we had never developed the capacity to engage in dialogue with each other because, in my basti, there was simply no legacy or example of this. If there was anything, then it was the bitter silence between father and son, passed on by one generation to another.

Sometimes, our strength to remember things becomes a curse. Reading books and growing up with them for a decade had taught me the value of forgiveness. The function of memory is to keep us connected with the process of our being and becoming. But the function of forgiveness is to nourish our being in every time and space. I learnt that forgiveness is not a weak act to perform but a necessity in order to create life afresh. My father could not realize the necessity of forgiveness. He held on to his memories, which eventually crushed his ability to move on. Through books, I was learning about his circumstances and how they had shaped him; consequently I was learning about myself. I remember reading Baldwin seven years ago and how he explained the situation of his father. It was no less than wisdom for me, because it was the first time that I was reading in English the words of a son about his father who had faced his share of discrimination for being Black, and how these words intended to look at a father and fatherhood beyond their miseries. In May 2020, as the lockdown was yet to be lifted, there was no way to get my hands on Baldwin's books. So I emailed a friend who was studying in Canada, and he sent me a PDF copy of *Notes of a Native Son*. My youngest sister, who is a lawyer, got it printed from her office. Baldwin has never failed to offer me clues about the *self*, which is shaped by the historical burden of vulnerabilities. He had also never failed to offer me hope, especially when there was a vast darkness of confused thoughts and miseries ready to swallow me up.

In *Notes of a Native Son*, Baldwin talks about his father as wittily as one could, which in turn makes his emotions profoundly relatable to all those whose relationship with their father has been bitter and mostly conflictual. Reading Baldwin became a discovery of many unknown corners within my mind. Baldwin says, 'I imagine that one of the reasons people cling on to their hate so stubbornly is because they sense, once hate is gone, that they will be forced to deal with pain.'[4] So true these words appeared to me when I began to imagine the source of the problem my father had been dealing with for years, for decades. How could a person who is keenly aware of his vulnerabilities in the external world afford to hate a person who is more vulnerable than him? I could barely dare to imagine the time and circumstances in which my father, a Dalit man, earned his bread in a society which, each day, reminded him of his *place* and forced him to carry the *stigma* and burden of it. I could barely dare to imagine the circumstances that led my father to curse his mother, a Dalit woman and therefore doubly vulnerable. In his case, it appeared that he was trying to protect himself from his painful reality—that he was simply invisible in the eyes of his conscience-less nation. But he survived. In the life of a Dalit man—and this has been proven so often in the past—survival is the precondition to resistance. The first generation survives, and survival is its resistance. The next generation thrives, resists and evolves.

*

I believe that, although we all suffer in more or less similar ways, our response to our suffering is quite unique. And in this uniqueness to deal with our sufferings lies the story of our life. After arriving at this realization, I started to sense the shallowness of 'scientific' research and its methods, which I was introduced to at TISS, which eventually intended to make Dalits a *common story*. They simply lacked the wit and emotional stamina to understand the life Dalits live every day and in every time and space. Baldwin brought me much closer to understanding the problem of my father: someone who has survived the brutality of a society that had invented strategies to kill a man without even touching him. It could make him disappear and, if not that, then appear contemptible, in the eyes of society. Narrating his mother's view about his father, Baldwin writes in *Notes of a Native Son*, 'my mother's observation that it was he, after all, who had kept them alive all these years meant nothing [to his children] because the problems of keeping children alive are not real for children'.[5] With these words, I began to see the other side of my father which, earlier, had meant nothing to me. This was my reality: Despite troubling us with his paranoid behaviour as he aged, it was my father who had kept us alive, fed us and survived himself. It was he who had kept me alive throughout my mindless stints with the world, whether they were about education or a career or spirituality or material pursuits. I had been a failure through most of these, and it was he who had *fed* me. My mother too worked for twenty long years; she was our backbone, who never let us fall apart through moments of despair—and she never became a problem for herself or others. It was my father who fell victim to the brutality of society, after which he could not develop a vision for himself or his family.

My father had been defeated by the burden that family as an institution carries in India. Starting with his mother perceiving him as her possession, then having four children to feed within a span of eight years. It was not hard for me to imagine his inevitable decline in old age. I had seen many men in my basti being destroyed in the same way; they all felt alone towards the end of their lives. My father, drunk, often blabbered about his past, the life he had lived, and the strength they, as Mahar men, had. I think the reason we cling to the past is because we refuse to learn to accept the decay of our being in the present. In some people, this clinging turns into a wound that becomes septic over the years. Maybe it is also the reason for what we understand as 'madness'. So many Mahar men from my basti were iron-solid but melted by the end of their lives by loneliness, either quietly like ice, or like candle wax, burnt by fire.

As a Dalit man, I would like to believe that my father, from his childhood, had developed an instinct to break free. But somehow he had failed. This failure had a cost which we all paid over the years.

It is at this moment, when I am just beginning to sense the truth about my father's circumstances, that I realize that our freedom is correlated with the unfreedom of others. Perhaps it is only in his death that I will be completely free. Even the thought of it is frightful. But this fear is a part of my life now.

*

Surrounded by thoughts about the future and endless uncertainties about work and survival, I was finished reading *The General of the*

Dead Army. Then I began to read *My Name Is Why,* Lemn Sissay's memoir. Little did I know that this was going to be a book I would hold so close to my heart that its story and its triumph offered me the courage to keep going in life amidst all the social and emotional chaos I was dealing with at this time. I read it quickly, in two days. Then, I reread it several times; I marked a few lines here and there and stuck notes on several pages so I could go back again and fathom the depth those words offered me. Lemn's prose is unblemished and diligently true to the emotional complexity of himself when he was a child. The memoir ends at his eighteenth birthday. The book ends when a person normally begins his stints with life. While reading this book several times, I felt I was breaking free in my mind. I desperately wanted to write about it and tell the world that a book has the potential to change the way we look at life and also stands as a testimony of our own selves with different contexts and time and space. This is what I wrote for *Centre for Stories* about *My Name Is Why* and how I felt I had grown with it:

On 23 March 2020, nationwide lockdown was mindlessly declared in India. On 22 March 2020, I left Mumbai where I had been living for seven years for my studies: *the purpose*; but to escape the home: *the reason*. I hurriedly packed my bag and a few books leaving behind hundreds of books and memories of growing up. Among those few books, there was *My Name Is Why*, a memoir by Lemn Sissay. I was least aware of the impact it was going to leave on me, in me, strangely under the skin, profoundly arresting my way of thinking about the bleakness of my own life. *Home is the place*, I told myself, *I escaped once.* Now the pandemic was forcing me to face it once again. Reaching home on 23 March, I found the world shut. I had only two literary books with me. A novel, *The General of the*

Dead Army by Ismail Kadare. I read it quickly. I felt lonely once I was done with it. Now, it was the turn of *My Name Is Why*. I read it in two days. It left me feeling complete, courageous. I do not know why but I felt clear, about many things in my life now, after reading it. It is like an old friend has opened up his heart, his dejected world, and his story of overcoming the pain, before me.

Lemn writes with love and compassion, about cruelty. Remarkably overcoming the hate while revisiting his memories. I instantly connected to his story. I told myself, *I know what he is talking about, I know this cruelty*. In my case, this cruelty is social, more subtle, more normative, more disciplined.

For a dalit man to grow up in India, and possess an aspiration, a dream, is to struggle against the history of this country in which he is erased, and reduced to a redundant mind. His struggle is personal and at the same time inseparably social. He does not need to go to any institution to feel surveilled or abandoned. The caste-society is that system in which a dalit man is surveilled, hated, and abandoned from time to time. *My Name is Why* clarifies this so metaphorically, this struggle, this feeling of abandonment. *My Name is Why* is a struggle of a captive black man, in a white country, against his own memories and his longing for his *roots*. The very factor of *roots* in the life of a dalit man is crucial because his identity is destructively formed over the centuries during which, he is alienated from his roots, which are essentially located in the culture against caste society. He is an embodiment of the cruelty this nation carries as a social-system. I was thrilled by the sheer wisdom which Lemn had offered in it, despite all the pain. And he says something which solved the mystery of years for me, "Hurt people hurt people." Yes, caste hurts; caste *is* hurt. I am hurt, over the years, by institutions, by society, by individuals from dominant castes. *My Name Is Why* demands the need to rise above *hurt*. This one sentence helped me to see beyond my own hurt, to grow, to blossom in all my human potential.[6]

'Hurt people hurt people.' These words are engraved on my mind. They transported my imagination to the past of my father as well as Devika, wherein I began to make sense of a lot of things which earlier appeared impossible to understand. 'Hurt people hurt people' only when they seek revenge because they cannot see beyond it—the inability determined by their lack of efforts to imagine life in other possibilities. Although hurt is a genuine experience, revenge has never been its remedy. Forgiveness is. Love is. *Hurt people must heal people*: I began to imagine this as the purpose of my writing.

*

My grandmother died. It was May 2020. The life around us was still locked. My father expressed nothing, not grief or any sign of tears. He never cried. I had not seen him crying, ever. If liquor shops were open (which they were not because of the lockdown), he would have gotten drunk. Perhaps he was mourning inside his heart, silently. In any case, mourning could have helped him to move on and imagine life anew. But he did not. When we fail to come to terms with the truth or remain so stubborn, no matter how dejecting it is, we begin to live in a state of paranoia. I had not seen my grandmother showing any affection for my father, or maybe she did when I was not there. But from whatever I had seen, I can assert that she was someone who hardly made her children feel free and loved. I may be wrong, but I have no memory to support another view. Anyway, now she was dead. She was around ninety-four years old at the time of death. Ninety-four years is a long life. But what does her *long* life mean? For her children, her grandchildren? In her death, I searched for the meaning of us, all of us. Of her stories, I had nothing. I only have memories. I wrote my thoughts in an essay about memory, death and Dalits:

> Non-Dalits may find it unbelievable, but death for Dalits is metaphorical. An "Untouchable" never existed as a person worthy of respect from society or recognised as a mind. He was simply invisible, except when his labour was extracted, exploited and used for free. Thus, it was not very difficult for Dalits from a few generations ago to understand how it feels to remain invisible. This reality has not ceased to exist even today, although its forms vary. Not existing for others, not being recognised by others, is a condition of simply not being extant. It is in this sense that death is metaphorical for Dalits. . . . It is an abnormal condition, an ecology, to use a broad term, that has been constructed by brahmins and all other castes who follow them. . . .
>
> Suffice to say, that as long as the caste system will prevail, physical death for Dalits will always remain metaphorical. Their actual death lies in an inability to be in text, or transform into a text as a story, memory and history. But before death, there is life. And here, Dalit literature today proclaims their passionate existence, and passion for life.[7]

For us, the stories of our ancestors hardly have any documentation. To trace their history, we solely rely on our memories and oral tales. This is the truth that prevails, at least till my generation. But even if we have nothing, we have our memory, which I have always considered historical in the sense that when we write, it guides our imagination. Of my grandmother, I have no warm memories. Yet, hers is a story which may have lessons in the subject of unlearning.

So, not all is lost. I think, and I write. Thinking is reaching somewhere, perhaps to the roots. Perhaps there, I finally feel like I belong.

*

By July 2020, the state declared some relaxations in public activities, and people began to step out, the majority of them with the intention to newly start their lives, carrying terrible uncertainties in their mind about survival. The question of survival was haunting me as well. I had around Rs 50,000, saved over four years, in the publication's bank account, which was my only capital in the future to publish books. In my personal bank account, at the time of leaving Mumbai, I had around Rs 26,000, and over the period of five months, when life was almost shut in India, I began to run out of my savings. My parents were old now, and needed rest, but in spite of this, their intention to work if needed had not diminished at all. I insisted on them stopping work. The question of hunger and responsibility that I had been avoiding all my life had now become so real that it made my parents the centre of my life. I felt strangely responsible towards the people in my life, and this time, it became the source of my strength. My parents, who had survived on daily wages, worked in the informal sector in fields where there was no respect, had provided for me. They had never become an obstacle in my persuasions, which were often mindless and impulsive. I had tried my hand at many things and failed, and they were there to bear the brunt of it. For years, I had at times obnoxiously undermined the two most important things they have given me: freedom to do what I wanted without expecting anything in return and the means to live. Now it was my turn to keep them alive. To feed them. To be there for them when they needed me. It is what they did for their parents, and their parents for their parents in the past. This is how we as a community survived. This is our history. This is our legacy. No matter how insignificant it may appear as a story, it has my roots in it, and I feel I am incomplete without it. In search of my roots and my community's story, my own 'hurts' appeared trivial to me. They no longer remained a source of suffering or anxiety; they had already become lessons for me, and I jotted down their teachings. The question of earning my bread, to feed my parents and to survive suddenly took centre stage in my life. But I knew that I also had a dream—to write my story and reach the minds and hearts of people—and I needed to protect it. This was not a choice; this was the life I was committed to. Living, to survive and equally to tell your tale, is the biggest challenge to any writer in the world who knows in his guts that he could do nothing else in life except write. I had taken on this challenge thirteen years ago.

I had carried with me some books, published by Panther's Paw Publication, while leaving Mumbai. Now, I had nothing but them. These books were the only proof of the honest labour I had done in my life. Each book had consumed a part of my life. From these books, I had never imagined value in financial terms. Yet, I was well aware of the need to *sell* the books. As a publisher, I had mostly focused on publishing them but had not seriously thought about distributing them to all those who would be interested, with whom these books could converse and readers could enter the world of my people. This thought had not occurred to me, and I think it was because I had grown up among Dalit writers and readers who mostly gifted their books to each other and rarely bought from each other. I had seen Dalit writers pouring money from their own pockets, printing books and just sharing them among people without expecting anyone to buy them. It seems like a generous act, but these Dalit writers, who were otherwise talented in what they wrote, struggled financially. They simply did not value their writing in financial terms or conceive financial value in it. I realized that if I could not take care of my needs through my intellectual labour, then I would not survive too long in order to protect my dream. I drafted an appeal about 'sale of books' and posted it across a few social media platforms. In two days, I sold 127 books, worth Rs 35,000. It took me seven days to parcel them and make them ready for dispatch. It was one of the most rewarding moments of my life, because I saw my labour being recognized and helping me survive (at least for a couple of months). Because of this, I could take care of my parents, who were now dependent on me. Long ago, books had rescued me from moments of loneliness and depression. Now, they also became the source to fulfil my needs and maintain the dignity of my labour. Once upon a time, I was protected by books emotionally and intellectually; now, they brought food to my table. For a person, nothing is as liberating as selling his labour as per his needs while maintaining the dignity and value of his labour. This is the moment that changed my imagination to look at *life*. I began to understand: The path to my dream must pass through the dark and long tunnel of hunger.

*

A writer without critical readership is a bird without wings. I had seen brilliant writers among my people who remained wingless simply because this society and its systems remained prejudiced and cunning. For a Dalit man to dream to write and create readership across caste and class is an inconceivable challenge, and for me to have thought of this some thirteen years ago was a moment of horror. I knew that in the society I had grown up in, I was either invisibilized or mocked. And my biggest fear was living in this society but remaining invisible, thus *untouchable*. Ever since I had started reading Dr Ambedkar I found that society had long ago closed its door of dignified life to me. But then I thought that as a writer, it was my responsibility to create endless possibilities of a dignified life. So I took on the challenge. I knew that writing was going to be no less than a battle. Today, if you are reading this, then I know I fought my battle well, just like my ancestors who fought caste and survived, and today your reading these words is me living my dream.

Untouchability also means a state in which one ceases to exist for others as the embodiment of life. This reminds me of the words of Dr Ambedkar. He says, 'Ours is a battle, not for wealth or for power. It is a battle for freedom. It is a battle for the reclamation of human personality.'[8] These words were my map in the journey towards my dream. And I am here. When you close this book, I will wake up in your mind. Out there, I reclaim my place, I reclaim my human personality.

Acknowledgements

I acknowledge all the hurts that made this book possible. Hurts that I had borne so far and that have made me what I am today. Hurts, which have been a part of my life, and which only recently I have begun to see as more than hurts. I have begun to discover all the meanings they have contributed to my life. They have been crucial in my development as a writer. With love and privileges all around, anybody can survive. It is laborious and giant task to survive with hurts and to become a composer of them in stories and poetry. There is only one person that made me survive these hurts: Dr B.R. Ambedkar.

In the making of this book, I would like to express my gratitude towards Richa Burman (erstwhile with Penguin India), whose email almost two years ago, in the bleak time of the pandemic, came as a ray of hope. With it, I began to revise my life and went on to search for some meanings in the darkness that had shrouded my past: They are here in this book.

I would also like to thank my editor, Chirag Thakkar, who has escalated the process of this book and made it possible for this book to see the light of day.

These are **pseudonyms**: Sumedh, Abhay, Carol, Rajendra, Meghdoot, Saira, Jasmine, George, Abdul, Faisal, Saraswati, Alima, Devika, Prachi, Bharathi and Khushi.

Notes

LEARNING TO SEE

1. My father was alive when I began to write this book. He died on 1 August 2022. Some of my predictions about him turned out to be true. These predictions are much more painful than I had earlier thought.

2. 'Remembering Dalit Panthers on the Death Anniversary of their First Martyr', Ground Xero, 10 January 2019. Available at https://www.groundxero.in/2019/01/10/remembering-dalit-panthers-on-the-death-anniversary-of-their-first-martyr/.

3. Published in Chauffer section of Marathi daily *Loksatta*, on 30 October 1987.

4. Anand Teltumbde, 'On the Death of Bal Thackeray and the Grief of Athavale', Countercurrents.org, 5 December 2012. Available at https://www.countercurrents.org/teltumbde051212.htm.

5. Gopal Guru, 'Appropriating Ambedkar', *Economic and Political Weekly* 26, no. 27 (July 1991).

6. Yogesh Maitreya, *Flowers on the Grave of Caste* (Nagpur: Panther's Paw Publication, 2019).

MEN DON'T CRY?

1. B. R. Ambedkar, *Dr. Babasaheb Ambedkar Writing and Speeches (Vol. 2)* (Maharashtra: Bombay Education Department, 1982), 261. Available at https://www.mea.gov.in/Images/attach/amb/Volume_02.pdf.

KHAIRLANJI: KNOW MY PLACE

1. 'Khairlanji Massacre: A Collection of Reports', VJAS Press Release, Fact Finding Report. Available at https://www.sabrang.com/kherlanji/reports.pdf.
2. '"The Entire Village was Involved, Sir. Entire Village"—Bhaiyalal Bhotmange', Navayana, Blog. Available at https://navayana.org/blog/2017/01/22/the-entire-village-was-involved-sir-entire-village-bhaiyalal-bhotmange/?v=c86ee0d9d7ed.
3. Shone Satheesh, 'Payal Tadvi Suicide Case: The Death of a Doctor', *Mint*, 7 June 2019. Available at https://www.livemint.com/mint-lounge/features/payal-tadvi-suicide-case-the-death-of-a-doctor-1559891147950.html.
4. Anand Teltumbde, *Khairlanji: A Strange and Bitter Crop* (New Delhi: Navayana, 2008).
5. Ibid.
6. Ibid.
7. Ibid.
8. Ibid.
9. Ibid.
10. Ibid.
11. The translation into English is mine. Bhaiyalal was the lone survivor of the brutal Khairlanji massacre (2006). He later died of a heart attack, waiting for justice.

LEARNING TO READ

1. 'Temptation of a Poor Brahmin: *The Romantics* by Pankaj Mishra', Round Table India, 11 November 2014. Available at

https://www.roundtableindia.co.in/casteist-temptations-of-a-brahmin-the-romantics-by-pankaj-mishra-2/.

2.   Ibid.

3.   'Forty years after its controversial publication, "Baluta" proves that it transcends generations', Scroll.in, 23 September 2018. Available at https://scroll.in/article/895308/forty-years-after-its-controversial-publication-baluta-proves-that-it-transcends-generations.

4.   'Love in the Time of Baluta', *Economic and Political Weekly* 54, no. 24, 15 June 2019. Available at https://www.epw.in/journal/2019/24/postscript/love-time-baluta.html.

5.   Ibid.

I AM 'A PART APART'

1.   Yogesh Maitreya, 'Dalit Literature: On Memory or Death', *Indian Cultural Forum,* 13 May 2020. Available at https://indianculturalforum.in/2020/05/13/dalit-literature-on-memory-or-death/.

2.   Yogesh Maitreya, *Flowers on the Grave of Caste* (Nagpur: Panther's Paw Publication, 2019).

3.   Yogesh Maitreya, *The Bridge of Migration* (Mumbai: Panther's Paw Publication, 2016).

MUMBAI, ME AND DR AMBEDKAR

1.   Yogesh Maitreya, 'Jai Bhim to Ramabai Nagar, the Living Spirit of Resistance', Round Table India, 12 December 2013. Available at https://www.roundtableindia.co.in/jai-bhim-to-ramabai-nagar-the-living-spirit-of-resistance/.

2.   'The Ramabai Killings', Human Rights Watch, Reports. Available at https://www.hrw.org/reports/1999/india/India994-08.htm.

3.   Nikhil Inamdar, 'Chimamanda Ngozi Adichie's Dangerously Singular Story of Melania Trump', The Wire, 6 July 2016. Available at https://thewire.in/books/the-danger-of-a-single-story.

4.   Yogesh Maitreya, 'The Dalai Lama's Religion and Anti-Caste Buddhists', Round Table India, 12 February 2015. Available at https://www.roundtableindia.co.in/the-dalai-lama-s-religion-and-anti-caste-buddhists/.

5.   Yogesh Maitreya, 'Art and Ambedkarism: A Conversation with Sambhaji Bhagat', Round Table India, 11 January 2015. Available at https://www.roundtableindia.co.in/art-and-ambedkarism-a-conversation-with-sambhaji-bhagat/.

6.   'Remembering Dalit Panthers on the Death Anniversary of their First Martyr', Ground Xero, 10 January 2019. Available at https://www.groundxero.in/2019/01/10/remembering-dalit-panthers-on-the-death-anniversary-of-their-first-martyr/.

7.   B.R. Ambedkar, *Dr. Babasaheb Ambedkar Writing and Speeches (Vol. 17), Part 1* (Education Department, Government. of Maharashtra, 1979), 425.

LEARNING TO WRITE

1.   Jill Stauffer, *Ethical Loneliness: The Injustice of Not Being Heard* (New York: Columbia University Press, 2018).

AGAINST THE MADNESS OF MORALITY

1.   Loknath Yashwant, *Broken Man*, trans. K. Jamanadas and Yogesh Maitreya (Nagpur: Panther's Paw Publication, 2018).

2.   B.R. Ambedkar, *Dr. Babasaheb Ambedkar Writing and Speeches (Vol. 5)* (Education Department, Government of Maharashtra, 1979), 109.

3.   This poem was first published on my Facebook wall, and it has not yet appeared in any book.

4.   Viktor E. Frankl, *Man's Search for Meaning* (UK : Random House, 2008).

HURT AND HOLLOWNESS

1.   Jacques Attali, *Noise: The Political Economy of Music* (Minneapolis: University of Minnesota Press, 1985).

2. Kamal Dev Pall, *Days Will Come Back*, trans. Rajinder Azad (Mumbai: Panther's Paw Publication, 2019).

3. Viktor E. Frankl, *Man's Search for Meaning* (UK: Random House, 2008).

4. Namdeo Dhasal, *Currents of Blood* (New Delhi: Navayana,2010).

5. Sangeeta Mulay, *Savitribai Phule and I* (Nagpur: Panther's Paw Publication, 2019).

6. 'Nalgonda Honour Killing Trial Picks Up Momentum', *Deccan Chronicle*, 14 January 2022. Available at https://www.deccanchronicle.com/nation/crime/130122/nalgonda-honour-killing-trial-picks-up-momentum.html.

7. B.R. Ambedkar, *Dr. Babasaheb Ambedkar Writing and Speeches (Vol.1)* (Education Department, Government of Maharashtra, 1979).

8. B.R. Ambedkar, 'The Untouchables: Who Were They and Why They Became Untouchables?' in *Dr. Babasaheb Ambedkar Writing and Speeches (Vol. 7)* (Education Department, Government of Maharashtra, 1979).

BEGINNING FROM THE ROOTS

1. Hansda Sowvendra Shekhar, 'The Indian Publishing House that's Become a Movement', The Hindu, 14 March 2020. Available at https://www.thehindu.com/books/the-publishing-house-thats-become-a-movement/article61962851.ece.

2. James Baldwin, *Notes of a Native Son* (Boston: Bacon Press, 2012).

3. While I was an intern with Manuski in 2013, I went to a district called Parbhani, where we paid a visit to a village. In that village, Dalits (Mahar-Buddhists) confirmed this incident more than twice and narrated to us the whole episodes of their struggle to live a day-to-day existence after they were boycotted by the upper caste villagers.

4. James Baldwin, *Notes of a Native Son* (Boston: Bacon Press, 2012).

5. Ibid.

6. Yogesh Maitreya, 'Growing Up with a Book', Centre for Stories. Available at https://centreforstories.com/story/journal-yogesh-maitreya/.

7. Yogesh Maitreya, 'Dalit Literature: On Memory or Death', in *Singing, Thinking, Anti-Caste* (Nagpur: Panther's Paw Publication, 2021), 61.

8. B.R. Ambedkar, *Dr. Babasaheb Ambedkar Writing and Speeches (Vol. 17)* (Education Department, Government of Maharashtra, 1979).